I0393811

ABOUT THIS PUBLICATION

FOR SERVICE ASSISTANCE

Customer Service Department
1.704.898.0770

North Carolina General Statues is published by The Muliti-Media Group of Greater Charlotte in Charlotte, North Carolina. Copyright 2015 by the Multi-Media Group of Greater Charlotte. This book or parts thereof may not be reproduced in any form, stored in a retrieval system, or transmitted in any form by any means—electronic, mechanical, photocopy, recording or otherwise—without prior written permission of the publisher, except as provided by United States of America copyright law.

The records required by U.S. Code 2257(a) through (c) and the pertinent regulations 28 C.F.R. Cli. 1, Part 75 with respect to this publication and all materials associated with such records are maintained by The Multi-Media Group of Greater Charlotte, Publisher and available for review by Attorney General.

www.visionbooks.org

TID: 5038001
ISBN (10) digit: 1502746476
ISBN (13) digit: 978-1502746474

123-4-56789-01239-Paperback
123-4-56789-01239-Hardback

First Edition

090520140547

Printed in the United States of America

2015 EDITION

North Carolina Criminal Law

And Procedure-Pamphlet # 27

Printed In conjunction with the Administration of the Courts

North Carolina Criminal Law and Procedure
Pamphlet Reference Guide

11

13

14

Chapter 52

Powers and Liabilities of Married Persons.

§ 52-1. Property of married persons secured.

The real and personal property of any married person in this State, acquired before marriage or to which he or she may after marriage become in any manner entitled, shall be and remain the sole and separate estate and property of such married person and may be devised and conveyed by such married person subject to G.S. 50-20 and such other regulations and limitations as the General Assembly may prescribe. (Const., Art. X, s. 6; Rev., s. 2093; C.S., s. 2506; 1965, c. 878, s. 1; 1981, c. 815, s. 3; 2011-284, s. 52.)

§ 52-2. Capacity to contract.

Subject to the provisions of G.S. 52-10 or 52-10.1, G.S. 39-7 and other regulations and limitations now or hereafter prescribed by the General Assembly, every married person is authorized to contract and deal so as to affect his or her real and personal property in the same manner and with the same effect as if he or she were unmarried. (1871-2, c. 193, s. 17; Code, s. 1826; Rev., s. 2094; 1911, c. 109; C.S., s. 2507; 1945, c. 73, s. 16; 1965, c. 878, s. 1; 1977, c. 375, s. 13.)

§ 52-3. Married person may insure spouse's life.

Any married person in his or her own name, or in the name of a trustee with his assent, may cause to be insured for any definite time the life of his or her spouse, for his or her sole and separate use, and may dispose of the interest in the same by will. (Rev., s. 2099; C.S., s. 2512; 1965, c. 878, s. 1.)

§ 52-4. Earnings and damages.

The earnings of a married person by virtue of any contract for his or her personal service, and any damages for personal injuries, or other tort sustained by either, can be recovered by such person suing alone, and such earnings or recovery shall be his or her sole and separate property. (1913, c. 13, s. 1; C.S., s. 2513; 1965, c. 878, s. 1.)

§ 52-5. Torts between husband and wife.

A husband and wife have a cause of action against each other to recover damages sustained to their person or property as if they were unmarried. (1951, c. 263; 1965, c. 878, s. 1.)

§ 52-5.1. Tort actions between husband and wife arising out of acts occurring outside State.

A husband and wife shall have a cause of action against each other to recover damages for personal injury, property damage or wrongful death arising out of acts occurring outside of North Carolina, and such action may be brought in this State when both were domiciled in North Carolina at the time of such acts. (1967, c. 855.)

§ 52-6. Repealed by Session Laws 1977, c. 375, s. 1, effective January 1, 1978.

§ 52-7. Validation of certificates of notaries public as to contracts or conveyances between husband and wife.

Any contract between husband and wife coming within the provisions of G.S. 52-6, executed prior to the first day of January, 1955, acknowledged before a notary public and containing a certificate of the notary public of his conclusions and findings of fact that such conveyance is not unreasonable or injurious to the wife, is hereby in all respects validated and confirmed, to the same extent as though said certifying officer were one of the officers named in G.S. 52-6. (1955, c. 380; 1965, c. 878, s. 1.)

§ 52-8. Validation of contracts failing to comply with provisions of former § 52-6.

Any contract between husband and wife coming within the provisions of G.S. 52-6 executed between January 1, 1930, and January 1, 1978, which does not comply with the requirement of a private examination of the wife or with the requirements that there be findings that such a contract between a husband and wife is not unreasonable or injurious to the wife and which is in all other respects regular is hereby validated and confirmed to the same extent as if the

16

examination of the wife had been separate and apart from the husband. This section shall not affect pending litigation. (1957, c. 1178; 1959, c. 1306; 1965, c. 207; c. 878, s. 1; 1967, c. 1183, s. 1; 1971, c. 101; 1973, c. 1387, s. 1; 1975, c. 495, s. 1; 1977, c. 375, s. 15; 1981, c. 599, s. 16.)

§ 52-9. Effect of absolute divorce decree on certificate failing to comply with § 52-6.

Whenever it appears that, since the execution of a contract between a husband and wife in which the certificate of acknowledgment thereof fails to comply with the requirements of G.S. 52-6, a valid decree of absolute divorce between said husband and wife has been rendered, no action shall be maintained by her or anyone claiming under her for the recovery of the possession of, or to establish title to any interest in any property described in such contract unless such action is commenced within seven years after such decree of absolute divorce has become final or unless such action is commenced before January 1, 1978, whichever date is earlier. (1957, c. 1260; 1965, c. 878, s. 1; 1977, c. 375, s. 14.)

§ 52-10. Contracts between husband and wife generally; releases.

(a)   Contracts between husband and wife not inconsistent with public policy are valid, and any persons of full age about to be married and married persons may, with or without a valuable consideration, release and quitclaim such rights which they might respectively acquire or may have acquired by marriage in the property of each other; and such releases may be pleaded in bar of any action or proceeding for the recovery of the rights and estate so released. No contract or release between husband and wife made during their coverture shall be valid to affect or change any part of the real estate of either spouse, or the accruing income thereof for a longer time than three years next ensuing the making of such contract or release, unless it is in writing and is acknowledged by both parties before a certifying officer.

(a1)   A contract between a husband and wife made, with or without a valuable consideration, during a period of separation to waive, release, or establish rights and obligations to post separation support, alimony, or spousal support is valid and not inconsistent with public policy. A provision waiving, releasing, or establishing rights and obligations to post separation support, alimony, or spousal support shall remain valid following a period of reconciliation and subsequent separation, if the contract satisfies all of the following requirements:

17

(1)   The contract is in writing.

(2)   The provision waiving the rights or obligations is clearly stated in the contract.

(3)   The contract was acknowledged by both parties before a certifying officer.

A release made pursuant to this subsection may be pleaded in bar of any action or proceeding for the recovery of the rights released.

(b)   Such certifying officer shall be a notary public, or a justice, judge, magistrate, clerk, assistant clerk or deputy clerk of the General Court of Justice, or the equivalent or corresponding officers of the state, territory or foreign country where the acknowledgment is made. Such officer must not be a party to the contract.

(c)   This section shall not apply to any judgment of the superior court or other State court of competent jurisdiction, which, by reason of its being consented to by a husband and wife, or their attorneys, may be construed to constitute a contract or release between such husband and wife. (1871-2, c. 193, s. 28; Code, s. 1836; Rev., s. 2108; C.S., s. 2516; 1959, c. 879, s. 12; 1965, c. 878, s. 1; 1977, c. 375, s. 2; 2013-140, s. 1.)

§ 52-10.1. Separation agreements.

Any married couple is hereby authorized to execute a separation agreement not inconsistent with public policy which shall be legal, valid, and binding in all respects; provided, that the separation agreement must be in writing and acknowledged by both parties before a certifying officer as defined in G.S. 52-10(b). Such certifying officer must not be a party to the contract. This section shall not apply to any judgment of the superior court or other State court of competent jurisdiction, which, by reason of its being consented to by a husband and wife, or their attorneys, may be construed to constitute a separation agreement between such husband and wife. (1965, c. 803; 1977, c. 375, s. 3.)

§ 52-10.2. Resumption of marital relations defined.

18

"Resumption of marital relations" shall be defined as voluntary renewal of the husband and wife relationship, as shown by the totality of the circumstances. Isolated incidents of sexual intercourse between the parties shall not constitute resumption of marital relations. (1987, c. 664, s. 1.)

§ 52-11. Antenuptial contracts and torts.

The liability of a married person for any debts owing, or contracts made or damages incurred before marriage shall not be impaired or altered by such marriage. No person shall by marriage incur any liability for any debts owing, or contracts made, or for wrongs done by his or her spouse before the marriage. (1871-2, c. 193, ss. 13, 14; Code, ss. 1822, 1823; Rev., ss. 2101, 2106; C.S., s. 2517; 1965, c. 878, s. 1.)

§ 52-12. Postnuptial crimes and torts.

No married person shall be liable for damages accruing from any tort committed by his or her spouse, or for any costs or fines incurred in any criminal proceeding against such spouse. (1871-2, c. 193, s. 25; Code, s. 1833; Rev., s. 2105; C.S., s. 2518; 1921, c. 102; 1965, c. 878, s. 1.)

§ 52-13. Procedures in causes of action for alienation of affection and criminal conversation.

(a)   No act of the defendant shall give rise to a cause of action for alienation of affection or criminal conversation that occurs after the plaintiff and the plaintiff's spouse physically separate with the intent of either the plaintiff or plaintiff's spouse that the physical separation remain permanent.

(b)   An action for alienation of affection or criminal conversation shall not be commenced more than three years from the last act of the defendant giving rise to the cause of action.

(c)   A person may commence a cause of action for alienation of affection or criminal conversation against a natural person only. (2009-400, s. 1.)

Chapter 52A.

Uniform Reciprocal Enforcement of Support Act.

§§ 52A-1 through 52A-32: Repealed by Session Laws 1995, c. 538, s. 7(a).

Chapter 52B

Uniform Premarital Agreement Act.

§ 52B-1. Short title.

This Chapter may be cited as the "Uniform Premarital Agreement Act". (1987, c. 473, s. 1.)

§ 52B-2. Definitions.

As used in this Chapter:

(1)   "Premarital agreement" means an agreement between prospective spouses made in contemplation of marriage and to be effective upon marriage.

(2)   "Property" means an interest, present or future, legal or equitable, vested or contingent, in real or personal property, including income and earnings. (1987, c. 473, s. 1.)

§ 52B-3. Formalities.

A premarital agreement must be in writing and signed by both parties. It is enforceable without consideration. (1987, c. 473, s. 1.)

§ 52B-4. Content.

(a)   Parties to a premarital agreement may contract with respect to:

(1)   The rights and obligations of each of the parties in any of the property of either or both of them whenever and wherever acquired or located;

(2)   The right to buy, sell, use, transfer, exchange, abandon, lease, consume, expend, assign, create a security interest in, mortgage, encumber, dispose of, or otherwise manage and control property;

(3)   The disposition of property upon separation, marital dissolution, death, or the occurrence or nonoccurrence of any other event;

(4)   The modification or elimination of spousal support;

(5)   The making of a will, trust, or other arrangement to carry out the provisions of the agreement;

(6)   The ownership rights in and disposition of the death benefit from a life insurance policy;

(7)   The choice of law governing the construction of the agreement; and

(8)   Any other matter, including their personal rights and obligations, not in violation of public policy or a statute imposing a criminal penalty.

(b)   The right of a child to support may not be adversely affected by a premarital agreement. (1987, c. 473, s. 1.)

§ 52B-5. Effect of marriage.

A premarital agreement becomes effective upon marriage. (1987, c. 473, s. 1.)

§ 52B-6. Amendment, revocation.

After marriage, a premarital agreement may be amended or revoked only by a written agreement signed by the parties. The amended agreement or the revocation is enforceable without consideration. (1987, c. 473, s. 1.)

§ 52B-7. Enforcement.

(a)   A premarital agreement is not enforceable if the party against whom enforcement is sought proves that:

(1)   That party did not execute the agreement voluntarily; or

(2)   The agreement was unconscionable when it was executed and, before execution of the agreement, that party:

a.   Was not provided a fair and reasonable disclosure of the property or financial obligations of the other party;

b.   Did not voluntarily and expressly waive, in writing, any right to disclosure of the property or financial obligations of the other party beyond the disclosure provided; and

c.   Did not have, or reasonably could not have had, an adequate knowledge of the property or financial obligations of the other party.

(b)   If a provision of a premarital agreement modifies or eliminates spousal support and that modification or elimination causes one party to the agreement to be eligible for support under a program of public assistance at the time of separation or marital dissolution, a court, notwithstanding the terms of the agreement, may require the other party to provide support to the extent necessary to avoid that eligibility. Before the court orders support under this subsection, the court must find that the party for whom support is ordered is a dependent spouse, as defined by G.S. 50-16.1A, and that the requirements of G.S. 50-16.2A regarding postseparation support or G.S. 50-16.3A regarding alimony have been met.

(c)   An issue of unconscionability of a premarital agreement shall be decided by the court as a matter of law. (1987, c. 473, s. 1; 1995, c. 319, s. 11; 1997-456, s. 27.)

§ 52B-8. Enforcement: void marriage.

If a marriage is determined to be void, an agreement that would otherwise have been a premarital agreement is enforceable only to the extent necessary to avoid an inequitable result. (1987, c. 473, s. 1.)

§ 52B-9. Limitation of actions.

22

Any statute of limitations applicable to an action asserting a claim for relief under a premarital agreement is tolled during the marriage of the parties to the agreement. However, equitable defenses limiting the time for enforcement, including laches and estoppel, are available to either party. (1987, c. 473, s. 1.)

§ 52B-10. Application and construction.

The Uniform Premarital Agreement Act shall be applied and construed to effectuate its general purpose to make uniform among the states enacting it, the law on premarital agreements. (1987, c. 473, s. 1.)

§ 52B-11. Severability.

If any provision of this Chapter or its application to any person or circumstance is held invalid, the invalidity does not affect other provisions or applications of the Chapter which can be given effect without the invalid provision or application, and to this end the provisions of this act are severable. (1987, c. 473, s. 1.)

Chapter 52C.

Uniform Interstate Family Support Act.

Article 1.

General Provisions.

§ 52C-1-100. Short title.

This Chapter may be cited as the Uniform Interstate Family Support Act. (1995, c. 538, s. 7(c).)

§ 52C-1-101. Definitions.

As used in this Article, unless the context clearly requires otherwise, the term:

(1)   "Child" means an individual, whether over or under the age of majority, who is or is alleged to be owed a duty of support by the individual's parent or who is or is alleged to be the beneficiary of a support order directed to the parent.

(2)   "Child support order" means a support order for a child, including a child who has attained the age of majority under the law of the issuing state.

(3)   "Duty of support" means an obligation imposed or imposable by law to provide support for a child, spouse, or former spouse, including an unsatisfied obligation to provide support.

(4)   "Home state" means the state in which a child lived with a parent or a person acting as parent for at least six consecutive months immediately preceding the time of filing of a petition or comparable pleading for support and, if a child is less than six-months old, the state in which the child lived from birth with any of them. A period of temporary absence of any of them is counted as part of the six-month or other period.

(5)   "Income" includes earnings or other periodic entitlements to money from any source and any other property subject to withholding for support under the law of this State.

(6)   "Income-withholding order" means an order or other legal process directed to a payer of income to withhold support from the income of the obligor.

(7)   "Initiating state" means a state from which a proceeding is forwarded or in which a proceeding is filed for forwarding to a responding state under this Act or a law or procedure substantially similar to this Act, the Uniform Reciprocal Enforcement of Support Act, or the Revised Uniform Reciprocal Enforcement of Support Act.

(8)   "Initiating tribunal" means the authorized tribunal in an initiating state.

(9)   "Issuing state" means the state in which a tribunal issues a support order or renders a judgment determining parentage.

(10)   "Issuing tribunal" means the tribunal that issues a support order or renders a judgment determining parentage.

(11)   "Law" includes decisional and statutory law and rules and regulations having the force of law.

(12)   "Obligee" means:

a.   An individual to whom a duty of support is or is alleged to be owed or in whose favor a support order has been issued or a judgment determining parentage has been rendered;

b.   A state or political subdivision to which the rights under a duty of support or support order have been assigned or which has independent claims based on financial assistance provided to an individual obligee; or

c.   An individual seeking a judgment determining parentage of the individual's child.

(13)   "Obligor" means an individual, or the estate of a decedent:

a.   Who owes or is alleged to owe a duty of support;

b.   Who is alleged but has not been adjudicated to be a parent of a child; or

c.   Who is liable under a support order.

(14)   "Register" means to file a support order or judgment determining paternity in the appropriate location for the recording or filing of foreign judgments generally or foreign support orders specifically.

(15)   "Registering tribunal" means a tribunal in which a support order is registered.

(16)   "Responding state" means a state in which a proceeding is filed or to which a proceeding is forwarded for filing from an initiating state under this Act or a law or procedure substantially similar to this Act, the Uniform Reciprocal Enforcement of Support Act, or the Revised Uniform Reciprocal Enforcement of Support Act.

(17)   "Responding tribunal" means the authorized tribunal in a responding state.

(18)   "Spousal-support order" means a support order for a spouse or former spouse of the obligor.

(19)   "State" means a state of the United States, the District of Columbia, Puerto Rico, the United States Virgin Islands, or any territory or insular possession subject to the jurisdiction of the United States. The term includes:

a.   An Indian tribe; and

b.   A foreign jurisdiction that has enacted a law or established procedures for issuance and enforcement of support orders which are substantially similar to the procedures under this Act, the Uniform Reciprocal Enforcement of Support Act, or the Revised Uniform Reciprocal Enforcement of Support Act.

(20)   "Support enforcement agency" means a public official or agency authorized to seek:

a.   Enforcement of support orders or duties of support;

b.   Establishment or modification of child support;

c.   Determination of parentage; or

d.   To locate obligors or their assets.

(21)   "Support order" means a judgment, decree, or order, whether temporary, final, or subject to modification, for the benefit of a child, a spouse, or a former spouse, which provides for monetary support, health care, arrears, or reimbursement, and may include related costs and fees, interest, income withholding, attorneys' fees, and other relief.

(22)   "Tribunal" means a court, administrative agency, or quasi-judicial entity authorized to establish, enforce, or modify support orders or to determine paternity, except that, for matters heard in this State, tribunal means the General Court of Justice, District Court Division. (1995, c. 538, s. 7(c); 1997-433, s. 10; 1997-456, s. 27; 1998-17, s. 1.)

§ 52C-1-102. District court has jurisdiction under this Act.

The General Court of Justice, District Court Division is the court authorized to hear matters under this Act. (1995, c. 538, s. 7(c).)

§ 52C-1-103. Remedies.

Remedies provided by this Act are cumulative and do not affect the availability of remedies under other law. (1995, c. 538, s. 7(c).)

Article 2.

Jurisdiction.

Part 1. Extended Personal Jurisdiction.

§ 52C-2-201. Bases for jurisdiction over nonresident.

In a proceeding to establish, enforce, or modify a support order or to determine parentage, a tribunal of this State may exercise personal jurisdiction over a nonresident individual or the individual's guardian or conservator if:

(1)   The individual is personally served with a summons and complaint within this State;

(2)   The individual submits to the jurisdiction of this State by consent, by entering a general appearance, or by filing a responsive document having the effect of waiving any contest to personal jurisdiction;

(3)   The individual resided with the child in this State;

(4)   The individual resided in this State and provided prenatal expenses or support for the child;

(5)   The child resides in this State as a result of the acts or directives of the individual;

(6)   The individual engaged in sexual intercourse in this State and the child may have been conceived by that act of intercourse;

(7)   The individual asserted paternity in an affidavit which has been filed with the clerk of superior court; or

(8)   There is any other basis consistent with the constitutions of this State and the United States for the exercise of personal jurisdiction. (1995, c. 538, s. 7(c).)

§ 52C-2-202. Procedure when exercising jurisdiction over nonresident.

A court of this State exercising personal jurisdiction over a nonresident under G.S. 52C-2-201 may apply G.S. 52C-3-315 to receive evidence from another state, and G.S. 52C-3-317 to obtain discovery through a tribunal of another state. In all other respects, Articles 3 through 7 of this Chapter do not apply and the tribunal shall apply the procedural and substantive law of this State, including the rules on choice of law other than those established by this Chapter. (1995, c. 538, s. 7(c).)

Part 2. Proceedings Involving Two or More States.

§ 52C-2-203. Initiating and responding tribunal of state.

Under this Chapter, a tribunal of this State may serve as an initiating tribunal to forward proceedings to another state and as a responding tribunal for proceedings initiated in another state. (1995, c. 538, s. 7(c); 1997-433, s. 10.1; 1998-17, s. 1.)

§ 52C-2-204. Simultaneous proceedings in another state.

(a)   A tribunal of this State may exercise jurisdiction to establish a support order if the petition or comparable pleading is filed after a petition or comparable pleading is filed in another state only if:

(1)   The petition or comparable pleading in this State is filed before the expiration of the time allowed in the other state for filing a responsive pleading challenging the exercise of jurisdiction by the other state;

(2)   The contesting party timely challenges the exercise of jurisdiction in the other state; and

28

(3)   If relevant, this State is the home state of the child.

(b)   A tribunal of this State may not exercise jurisdiction to establish a support order if the petition or comparable pleading is filed before a petition or comparable pleading is filed in another state if:

(1)   The petition or comparable pleading in the other state is filed before the expiration of the time allowed in this State for filing a responsive pleading challenging the exercise of jurisdiction by this State;

(2)   The contesting party timely challenges the exercise of jurisdiction in this State; and

(3)   If relevant, the other state is the home state of the child. (1995, c. 538, s. 7(c).)

§ 52C-2-205. Continuing, exclusive jurisdiction.

(a)   A tribunal of this State issuing a support order consistent with the law of this State has continuing, exclusive jurisdiction over a child support order:

(1)   As long as this State remains the residence of the obligor, the individual obligee, or the child for whose benefit the support order is issued; or

(2)   Until all of the parties who are individuals have filed written consents with the tribunal of this State for a tribunal of another state to modify the order and assume continuing, exclusive jurisdiction.

(b)   A tribunal of this State issuing a child support order consistent with the law of this State may not exercise its continuing jurisdiction to modify the order if the order has been modified by a tribunal of another state pursuant to a law substantially similar to this Chapter.

(c)   If a child support order of this State is modified by a tribunal of another state pursuant to a law substantially similar to this Chapter, a tribunal of this State loses its continuing, exclusive jurisdiction with regard to prospective enforcement of the order issued in this State, and may only:

(1)   Enforce the order that was modified as to amounts accruing before the modification;

(2)   Enforce nonmodifiable aspects of that order; and

(3)   Provide other appropriate relief for violations of that order which occurred before the effective date of the modification.

(d)   A tribunal of this State shall recognize the continuing, exclusive jurisdiction of a tribunal of another state which has issued a child support order pursuant to a law substantially similar to this Chapter.

(e)   A temporary support order issued ex parte or pending resolution of a jurisdictional conflict does not create continuing, exclusive jurisdiction in the issuing tribunal.

(f)   A tribunal of this State issuing a support order consistent with the law of this State has continuing, exclusive jurisdiction over a spousal support order throughout the existence of the support obligation. A tribunal of this State may not modify a spousal support order issued by a tribunal of another state having continuing, exclusive jurisdiction over that order under the law of that state. (1995, c. 538, s. 7(c); 1997-433, s. 10.2; 1998-17, s. 1.)

§ 52C-2-206. Enforcement and modification of support order by tribunal having continuing jurisdiction.

(a)   A tribunal of this State may serve as an initiating tribunal to request a tribunal of another state to enforce or modify a support order issued in that state.

(b)   A tribunal of this State having continuing, exclusive jurisdiction over a support order may act as a responding tribunal to enforce or modify the order. If a party subject to the continuing, exclusive jurisdiction of the tribunal no longer resides in the issuing state, in subsequent proceedings the tribunal may apply G.S. 52C-3-315 to receive evidence from another state and G.S. 52C-3-317 to obtain discovery through a tribunal of another state.

(c)   A tribunal of this State which lacks continuing, exclusive jurisdiction over a spousal support order may not serve as a responding tribunal to modify a spousal support order of another state. (1995, c. 538, s. 7(c).)

Part 3. Reconciliation of Multiple Orders.

§ 52C-2-207. Recognition of controlling child support order.

(a)   If a proceeding is brought under this Chapter and only one tribunal has issued a child support order, the order of that tribunal controls and must be so recognized.

(b)   If a proceeding is brought under this Chapter, and two or more child support orders have been issued by tribunals of this State or another state with regard to the same obligor and child, a tribunal of this State shall apply the following rules in determining which order to recognize for purposes of continuing, exclusive jurisdiction:

(1)   If only one of the tribunals would have continuing, exclusive jurisdiction under this Chapter, the order of that tribunal controls and must be so recognized.

(2)   If more than one of the tribunals would have continuing, exclusive jurisdiction under this Chapter, an order issued by a tribunal in the current home state of the child controls and must be so recognized, but if an order has not been issued in the current home state of the child, the order most recently issued controls and must be so recognized.

(3)   If none of the tribunals would have continuing, exclusive jurisdiction under this Chapter, the tribunal of this State having jurisdiction over the parties shall issue a child support order, which controls and must be so recognized.

(c)   If two or more child support orders have been issued for the same obligor and child and if the obligor or the individual obligee resides in this State, a party may request a tribunal of this State to determine which order controls and must be so recognized under subsection (b) of this section. The request must be accompanied by a certified copy of every support order in effect. The requesting party shall give notice of the request to each party whose rights may be affected by a certified copy of every support order in the effect. The requesting party shall give notice of the request to each party whose rights may be affected by the determination.

(d)   The tribunal that issued the controlling order under subsection (a), (b), or (c) of this section is the tribunal that has continuing, exclusive jurisdiction under G.S. 52C-2-205.

(e)   A tribunal of this State which determines by order the identity of the controlling order under subdivision (b)(1) or (2) of this section or which issues a new controlling order under subdivision (b)(3) of this section shall state in that order the basis upon which the tribunal made its determination.

(f)   Within 30 days after issuance of an order determining the identity of the controlling order, the party obtaining the order shall file a certified copy of it with each tribunal that issued or registered an earlier order of child support. A party who obtains the order and fails to file a certified copy is subject to appropriate sanctions by a tribunal in which the issue of failure to file arises. The failure to file does not affect the validity or enforceability of the controlling order. (1995, c. 538, s. 7(c); 1997-433, s. 10.3(b); 1998-17, s. 1.)

§ 52C-2-208. Multiple child support orders for two or more obligees.

In responding to multiple registrations or petitions for enforcement of two or more child support orders in effect at the same time with regard to the same obligor and different individual obligees, at least one of which was issued by a tribunal of another state, a tribunal of this State shall enforce those orders in the same manner as if the multiple orders had been issued by a tribunal of this State. (1995, c. 538, s. 7(c).)

§ 52C-2-209. Credit for payments.

Amounts collected and credited for a particular period pursuant to a support order issued by a tribunal of another state must be credited against the amounts accruing or accrued for the same period under a support order issued by the tribunal of this State. (1995, c. 538, s. 7(c).)

Article 3.

Civil Provisions of General Application.

§ 52C-3-301. Proceedings under this Chapter.

(a)   Except as otherwise provided in this Chapter, this Article applies to all proceedings under this Chapter.

(b)   This Chapter provides for the following proceedings:

(1)   Establishment of an order for spousal support or child support pursuant to Article 4 of this Chapter;

(2)   Enforcement of a support order and income withholding order of another state without registration pursuant to Article 5 of this Chapter;

(3)   Registration of an order for spousal support or child support of another state or enforcement pursuant to Article 6 of this Chapter;

(4)   Modification of an order for child support or spousal support issued by a tribunal of this State pursuant to Article 2, Part 2 of this Chapter;

(5)   Registration of an order for child support of another state for modification pursuant to Article 6 of this Chapter;

(6)   Determination of paternity pursuant to Article 7 of this Chapter; and

(7)   Assertion of jurisdiction over nonresidents pursuant to Article 2, Part 1 of this Chapter.

(c)   An individual petitioner or a support enforcement agency may commence a proceeding authorized under this Chapter by filing a petition in an initiating tribunal for forwarding to a responding tribunal or by filing a petition or a comparable pleading directly in a tribunal of another state which has or can obtain personal jurisdiction over the respondent. (1995, c. 538, s. 7(c).)

§ 52C-3-302. Action by minor parent.

A minor parent, or a guardian or other legal representative of a minor parent, may maintain a proceeding on behalf of or for the benefit of the minor's child. (1995, c. 538, s. 7(c).)

§ 52C-3-303. Application of law of this State.

Except as otherwise provided by this Chapter, a responding tribunal of this State:

(1)   Shall apply the procedural and substantive law, including the rules on choice of law, generally applicable to similar proceedings originating in this State and may exercise all powers and provide all remedies available in those proceedings; and

(2)   Shall determine the duty of support and the amount payable in accordance with the law and support guidelines of this State. (1995, c. 538, s. 7(c).)

§ 52C-3-304. Duties of initiating tribunal.

(a)   Upon the filing of a petition authorized by this Chapter, an initiating tribunal of this State shall forward three copies of the petition and its accompanying documents:

(1)   To the responding tribunal or appropriate support enforcement agency in the responding state; or

(2)   If the identity of the responding tribunal is unknown, to the state information agency of the responding state with a request that they be forwarded to the appropriate tribunal and that receipt be acknowledged.

(b)   If a responding state has not enacted this act or a law or procedure substantially similar to this act, a tribunal of this State may issue a certificate or other document and make findings required by the law of the responding state. If the responding State is a foreign jurisdiction, the tribunal may specify the amount of support sought and provide other documents necessary to satisfy the requirements of the responding state. (1995, c. 538, s. 7(c); 1997-433, s. 10.4; 1998-17, s. 1.)

§ 52C-3-305. Duties and powers of responding tribunal.

(a)   When a responding tribunal of this State receives a petition or comparable pleading from an initiating tribunal or directly pursuant to G.S. 52C-3-301(c) it shall cause the petition or pleading to be filed and notify the petitioner where and when it was filed.

(b)   A responding tribunal of this State, to the extent otherwise authorized by law, may do one or more of the following:

34

(1)   Issue or enforce a support order, modify a child support order, or render a judgment to determine parentage;

(2)   Order an obligor to comply with a support order, specifying the amount and the manner of compliance;

(3)   Order income withholding;

(4)   Determine the amount of any arrears, and specify a method of payment;

(5)   Enforce orders by civil or criminal contempt, or both;

(6)   Set aside property for satisfaction of the support order;

(7)   Place liens and order execution on the obligor's property;

(8)   Order an obligor to keep the tribunal informed of the obligor's current residential address, telephone number, employer, address of employment, and telephone number at the place of employment;

(9)   Issue an order for arrest for an obligor who has failed after proper notice to appear at a hearing ordered by the tribunal and enter the order for arrest in any local and State computer systems for criminal warrants;

(10)   Order the obligor to seek appropriate employment by specified methods;

(11)   Award reasonable attorneys' fees and other fees and costs; and

(12)   Grant any other available remedy.

(c)   A responding tribunal of this State shall include in a support order issued under this Chapter, or in the documents accompanying the order, the calculations on which the support order is based.

(d)   A responding tribunal of this State may not condition the payment of a support order issued under this Chapter upon compliance by a party with provisions for visitation.

(e)   If a responding tribunal of this State issues an order under this Chapter, the tribunal shall send a copy of the order to the petitioner and the respondent and to the initiating tribunal, if any. (1995, c. 538, s. 7(c); 1997-433, s. 10.5; 1998-17, s. 1.)

§ 52C-3-306. Inappropriate tribunal.

If a petition or comparable pleading is received by an inappropriate tribunal of this State, it shall forward the pleading and accompanying documents to an appropriate tribunal in this State or another state and notify the petitioner where and when the pleading was sent. (1995, c. 538, s. 7(c); 1997-433, s. 10.6; 1998-17, s. 1.)

§ 52C-3-307. Duties of support enforcement agency.

(a)   A support enforcement agency of this State, upon request, shall provide services to a petitioner in a proceeding under this Chapter.

(b)   A support enforcement agency that is providing services to the petitioner as appropriate shall:

(1)   Take all steps necessary to enable an appropriate tribunal in this State or another state to obtain jurisdiction over the respondent;

(2)   Request an appropriate tribunal to set a date, time, and place for a hearing;

(3)   Make a reasonable effort to obtain all relevant information, including information as to income and property of the parties;

(4)   Within two days, exclusive of Saturdays, Sundays, and legal holidays, after receipt of a written notice from an initiating, responding, or registering tribunal, send a copy of the notice to the petitioner;

(5)   Within two days, exclusive of Saturdays, Sundays, and legal holidays, after receipt of a written communication from the respondent or the respondent's attorney, send a copy of the communication to the petitioner; and

(6)   Notify the petitioner if jurisdiction over the respondent cannot be obtained.

(c)   This Chapter does not create or negate a relationship of attorney and client or other fiduciary relationship between a support enforcement agency or the attorney for the agency and the individual being assisted by the agency. (1995, c. 538, s. 7(c); 1997-433, s. 10.7; 1998-17, s. 1.)

§ 52C-3-308. Representation of obligee.

It shall be the duty of the district attorney to represent the obligee in proceedings authorized by this Chapter unless alternative arrangements are made by the obligee. An obligee may employ private counsel to represent the obligee in proceedings authorized by this Chapter. (1995, c. 538, s. 7(c).)

§ 52C-3-309. Duties of State information agency.

(a)   The Department of Health and Human Services, Division of Social Services, is designated as the State information agency under this Chapter.

(b)   The State information agency shall:

(1)   Compile and maintain a current list, including addresses, of the tribunals in this State which have jurisdiction under this Chapter and any support enforcement agencies in this State and transmit a copy to the state information agency of every other state;

(2)   Maintain a register of tribunals and support enforcement agencies received from other states;

(3)   Forward to the appropriate tribunal in the place in this State in which the individual obligee or the obligor resides, or in which the obligor's property is believed to be located, all documents concerning a proceeding under this Chapter received from an initiating tribunal or the state information agency of the initiating state; and

(4)   Obtain information concerning the location of the obligor and the obligor's property within this State not exempt from execution, by such means as postal verification and federal or state locator services, examination of telephone directories, requests for the obligor's address from employers, and examination of governmental records, including, to the extent not prohibited by other law, those relating to real property, vital statistics, law enforcement,

taxation, motor vehicles, drivers licenses, and social security. (1995, c. 538, s. 7(c); 1997-443, s. 11A.118(a).)

§ 52C-3-310. Pleadings and accompanying documents.

(a)   A petitioner seeking to establish or modify a support order or to determine parentage in a proceeding under this Chapter must verify the petition. Unless otherwise ordered under G.S. 52C-3-311, the petition or accompanying documents must provide, so far as known, the name, residential address, and social security numbers of the obligor and the obligee, and the name, sex, residential address, social security number, and date of birth of each child for whom support is sought. The petition must be accompanied by a certified copy of any support order in effect. The petition may include any other information that may assist in locating or identifying the respondent.

(b)   The petition must specify the relief sought. The petition and accompanying documents must conform substantially with the requirements imposed by the forms mandated by federal law for use in cases filed by a support enforcement agency. (1995, c. 538, s. 7(c).)

§ 52C-3-311. Nondisclosure of information in exceptional circumstances.

Upon a finding, which may be made ex parte, that the health, safety, or liberty of a party or child would be unreasonably put at risk by the disclosure of identifying information, or if an existing order so provides, a tribunal shall order that the address of the child or party or other identifying information not be disclosed in a pleading or other document filed in a proceeding under this Chapter. (1995, c. 538, s. 7(c).)

§ 52C-3-312. Costs and fees.

(a)   The petitioner shall not be required to pay a filing fee or other costs.

(b)   If an obligee prevails, a responding tribunal may assess against an obligor filing fees, reasonable attorneys' fees, other costs, and necessary travel and other reasonable expenses incurred by the obligee and the obligee's witnesses. The tribunal may not assess fees, costs, or expenses against the obligee or the support enforcement agency of either the initiating or the responding state, except as provided by other law. Attorneys' fees may be taxed as costs, and may be ordered paid directly to the attorney, who may enforce the order in the attorney's own name. Payment of support owed to the obligee has priority over fees, costs, and expenses.

(c)   The tribunal shall order the payment of costs and reasonable attorneys' fees if it determines that a hearing was requested primarily for delay. In a proceeding under Article 6 of this Chapter, a hearing is presumed to have been requested primarily for delay if a registered support order is confirmed or enforced without change. (1995, c. 538, s. 7(c).)

§ 52C-3-313. Limited immunity of petitioner.

(a)   Participation by a petitioner in a proceeding before a responding tribunal, whether in person, by private attorney, or through services provided by the support enforcement agency, does not confer personal jurisdiction over the petitioner in another proceeding.

(b)   A petitioner is not amenable to service of civil process while physically present in this State to participate in a proceeding under this Chapter.

(c)   The immunity granted by this section does not extend to civil litigation based on acts unrelated to a proceeding under this Chapter committed by a party while present in this State to participate in the proceeding. (1995, c. 538, s. 7(c).)

§ 52C-3-314. Nonparentage as defense.

A party whose parentage of a child has been previously determined by or pursuant to law may not plead nonparentage as a defense to a proceeding under this Chapter. (1995, c. 538, s. 7(c).)

§ 52C-3-315. Special rules of evidence and procedure.

(a)   The physical presence of the petitioner in a responding tribunal of this State is not required for the establishment, enforcement, or modification of a support order or the rendition of a judgment determining parentage.

(b)   A verified petition, affidavit, document substantially complying with federally mandated forms, and a document incorporated by reference in any of them, not excluded under the hearsay rule if given in person, is admissible in evidence if given under oath by a party or witness residing in another state.

(c)   A copy of the record of child support payments certified as a true copy of the original by the custodian of the record may be forwarded to a responding tribunal. The copy is evidence of facts asserted in it and is admissible to show whether payments were made.

(d)   Copies of bills for testing for parentage, and for prenatal and postnatal health care of the mother and child, furnished to the adverse party at least 10 days before trial, are admissible in evidence to prove the amount of the charges billed and that the charges were reasonable, necessary, and customary.

(e)   Documentary evidence transmitted from another state to a tribunal of this State by telephone, telecopier, or other means that do not provide an original writing may not be excluded from evidence on an objection based on the means of transmission.

(f)   In a proceeding under this Chapter, a tribunal of this State may permit a party or witness residing in another state to be deposed or to testify by telephone, audiovisual means, or other electronic means at a designated tribunal or other location in that state. A tribunal of this State shall cooperate with tribunals of other states in designating an appropriate location for the deposition or testimony.

(g)   If a party called to testify at a civil hearing refuses to answer on the ground that the testimony may be self-incriminating, the trier of fact may draw an adverse inference from the refusal.

(h)   A privilege against disclosure of communication between spouses does not apply in a proceeding under this Chapter.

(i)   The defense of immunity based on the relationship of husband and wife or parent and child does not apply in a proceeding under this Chapter. (1995, c. 538, s. 7(c).)

§ 52C-3-316. Communications between tribunals.

A tribunal of this State may communicate with a tribunal of another state in writing, or by telephone or other means, to obtain information concerning the laws of that state, the legal effect of a judgment, decree, or order of that tribunal, and the status of a proceeding in the other state. A tribunal of this State may furnish similar information by similar means to a tribunal of another state. (1995, c. 538, s. 7(c).)

§ 52C-3-317. Assistance with discovery.

A tribunal of this State may request a tribunal of another state to assist in obtaining discovery, and upon request, may compel a person over whom it has jurisdiction to respond to a discovery order issued by a tribunal of another state. (1995, c. 538, s. 7(c).)

§ 52C-3-318. Receipt and disbursement of payments.

A support enforcement agency or tribunal of this State shall disburse promptly any amounts received pursuant to a support order, as directed by the order. The agency or tribunal shall furnish to a requesting party or tribunal of another state a certified statement by the custodian of the record of the amounts and dates of all payments received. (1995, c. 538, s. 7(c).)

Article 4.

Establishment of Support Order.

§ 52C-4-401. Petition to establish support order.

(a)   If a support order entitled to recognition under this Chapter has not been issued, a responding tribunal of this State may issue a support order if:

(1)   The individual seeking the order resides in another state; or

(2)   The support enforcement agency seeking the order is located in another state.

(b)   The tribunal may issue a temporary child support order if:

(1)   The respondent has signed a verified statement acknowledging parentage;

(2)   The respondent has been determined by or pursuant to law to be the parent; or

(3)   There is other clear and convincing evidence that the respondent is the child's parent.

(c)   Upon finding, after notice and opportunity to be heard, that an obligor owes a duty of support, the tribunal shall issue a support order directed to the obligor and may issue other orders pursuant to G.S. 52C-3-305. (1995, c. 538, s. 7(c).)

Article 5.

Enforcement of Order of Another State Without Registration.

§ 52C-5-501. Employer's receipt of income-withholding order of another state.

(a)   An income-withholding order issued in another state may be sent to the person or entity defined or identified as the obligor's employer under the income-withholding provisions of Chapter 50 or Chapter 110 of the General Statutes, as applicable, without first filing a petition or comparable pleading or registering the order with a tribunal of this State. In the event that an obligor is receiving unemployment compensation benefits from the Division of Employment Security (DES) in accordance with G.S. 96-17, an income-withholding order issued in another state may be sent to the DES without first filing a petition or comparable pleading or registering the order with a tribunal of this State. Upon receipt of the order, the employer or the DES shall:

(1)   Treat an income-withholding order issued in another state which appears regular on its face as if it had been issued by a tribunal of this State;

(2)   Immediately provide a copy of the order to the obligor; and

(3)   Distribute the funds as directed in the withholding order. The DES shall not withhold an amount to exceed twenty-five percent (25%) of the unemployment compensation benefits.

(b)   Repealed by Session Laws 1997-433, s. 10.8. (1995, c. 538, s. 7(c); 1997-433, s. 10.8; 1998-17, s. 1; 1999-293, s. 5; 2011-401, s. 3.3.)

§ 52C-5-502. Employer's compliance with income-withholding order of another state.

(a)   Upon receipt of an income-withholding order, the obligor's employer shall immediately provide a copy of the order to the obligor.

(b)   The employer shall treat an income-withholding order issued in another state which appears regular on its face as if it had been issued by a tribunal of this State.

(c)   Except as otherwise provided in subsection (d) of this section and G.S. 52C-5-503, the employer shall withhold and distribute the funds as directed in the income-withholding order by complying with terms of the order which specify:

(1)   The duration and amount of periodic payments of current child support, stated as a sum certain;

(2)   The person or agency designated to receive payments and the address to which the payments are to be forwarded;

(3)   Medical support, whether in the form of periodic cash payment, stated as a sum certain, or ordering the obligor to provide health insurance coverage for the child under a policy available through the obligor's employment;

(4)   The amount of periodic payments of fees and costs for a support enforcement agency, the issuing tribunal, and the obligee's attorney, stated as sums certain; and

(5)   The amount of periodic payments of arrearages and interest on arrearages, stated as sums certain.

(d)   An employer shall comply with the law of the state of the obligor's principal place of employment for withholding from income with respect to:

(1)   The employer's fee for processing an income-withholding order;

43

(2)   The maximum amount permitted to be withheld from the obligor's income; and

(3)   The times within which the employer must implement the income-withholding order and forward the child support payment. (1995, c. 538, s. 7(c); 1997-433, s. 10.8; 1998-17, s. 1.)

§ 52C-5-503. Compliance with multiple income-withholding orders.

If an obligor's employer receives multiple income-withholding orders with respect to the earnings of the same obligor, the employer satisfies the terms of the multiple orders if the employer complies with the law of the state of the obligor's principal place of employment to establish the priorities for withholding and allocating income withheld for multiple child support obligees. (1997-433, s. 10.8; 1998-17, s. 1.)

§ 52C-5-504. Immunity from civil liability.

An employer who complies with an income-withholding order issued in another state in accordance with this Article is not subject to civil liability to an individual or agency with regard to the employer's withholding of child support from the obligor's income. (1997-433, s. 10.8; 1998-17, s. 1.)

§ 52C-5-505. Penalties for noncompliance.

An employer who willfully fails to comply with an income-withholding order issued by another state and received for enforcement is subject to the same penalties that may be imposed for noncompliance with an order issued by a tribunal of this State. (1997-433, s. 10.8; 1998-17, s. 1.)

§ 52C-5-506. Contest by obligor.

(a)   An obligor may contest the validity or enforcement of an income-withholding order issued in another state and received directly by an employer in this State in the same manner as if the order had been issued by a tribunal of this State. G.S. 52C-6-604 applies to the contest.

44

(b)   The obligor shall give notice of the contest to:

(1)   A support enforcement agency providing services to the obligee;

(2)   Each employer that has directly received an income-withholding order; and

(3)   The person or agency designated to receive payments in the income-withholding order if no person or agency is designated, to the obligee. (1997-433, s. 10.8; 1998-17, s. 1.)

§ 52C-5-507. Administrative enforcement of orders.

(a)   A party seeking to enforce a support order or an income-withholding order, or both, issued by a tribunal of another state may send the documents required for registering the order to a support enforcement agency of this State.

(b)   Upon receipt of the documents, the support enforcement agency, without initially seeking to register the order, shall consider and, if appropriate, use any administrative procedure authorized by the law of this State to enforce a support order or an income-withholding order, or both. If the obligor does not contest administrative enforcement, the order need not be registered. If the obligor contests the validity or administrative enforcement of the order, the support enforcement agency shall register the order pursuant to this Chapter. (1997-433, s. 10.8; 1998-17, s. 1.)

Article 6.

Enforcement and Modification of Support Order After Registration.

Part 1. Registration and Enforcement of Support Order.

§ 52C-6-601. Registration of order for enforcement.

A support order or an income-withholding order issued by a tribunal of another state may be registered in this State for enforcement. (1995, c. 538, s. 7(c); 1997-433, s. 10.9; 1998-17, s. 1.)

§ 52C-6-602. Procedure to register order for enforcement.

(a)   A support order or income-withholding order of another state may be registered in this State by sending the following documents and information to the tribunal for the county in which the obligor resides in this State:

(1)   A letter of transmittal to the tribunal requesting registration and enforcement;

(2)   Two copies, including one certified copy, of all orders to be registered, including any modification of an order;

(3)   A sworn statement by the party seeking registration or a certified statement by the custodian of the records showing the amount of any arrearage;

(4)   The name of the obligor and, if known:

a.   The obligor's address and social security number;

b.   The name and address of the obligor's employer and another other source of income of the obligor; and

c.   A description and the location of property of the obligor in this State not exempt from execution; and

(5)   The name and address of the obligee and, if applicable, the agency or person to whom support payments are to be remitted.

(b)   On receipt of a request for registration, the registering tribunal shall cause the order to be filed as a foreign order, together with one copy of the documents and information, regardless of their form.

(c)   A petition or comparable pleading seeking a remedy that must be affirmatively sought under other law of this State may be filed at the same time as the request for registration or later. The pleading must specify the grounds for the remedy sought. (1995, c. 538, s. 7(c); 1997-456, s. 27.)

§ 52C-6-603. Effect of registration for enforcement.

(a)   A support order or income-withholding order issued in another state is registered when the order is filed in the registering tribunal of this State.

(b)   A registered order issued in another state is enforceable in the same manner and is subject to the same procedures as an order issued by a tribunal of this State.

(c)   Except as otherwise provided in this Article, a tribunal of this State shall recognize and enforce, but may not modify, a registered order if the issuing tribunal had jurisdiction. (1995, c. 538, s. 7(c).)

§ 52C-6-604. Choice of law.

(a)   The law of the issuing state governs the nature, extent, amount, and duration of current payments and other obligations of support and the payment of arrears under the order.

(b)   In a proceeding for arrears, the statute of limitations under the laws of this State or of the issuing state, whichever is longer, applies. (1995, c. 538, s. 7(c).)

Part 2. Contest of Validity of Enforcement.

§ 52C-6-605. Notice of registration of order.

(a)   When a support order or income-withholding order issued in another state is registered, the registering tribunal shall notify the nonregistering party. The notice must be accompanied by a copy of the registered order and the documents and relevant information accompanying the order.

(b)   The notice must inform the nonregistering party:

(1)   That a registered order is enforceable as of the date of registration in the same manner as an order issued by a tribunal of this State;

(2)   That a hearing to contest the validity or enforcement of the registered order must be requested within 20 days after notice;

47

(3)   That failure to contest the validity or enforcement of the registered order in a timely manner will result in confirmation of the order and enforcement of the order and the alleged arrears and precludes further contest of that order with respect to any matter that could have been asserted; and

(4)   Of the amount of any alleged arrears.

(c)   Upon registration of an income-withholding order for enforcement, the registering tribunal shall notify the obligor's employer pursuant to the income-withholding provisions of Chapter 50 or Chapter 110 of the General Statutes, as applicable. (1995, c. 538, s. 7(c); 1997-433, s. 10.10; 1998-17, s. 1.)

§ 52C-6-606. Procedure to contest validity or enforcement of registered order.

(a)   A nonregistering party seeking to contest the validity or enforcement of a registered order in this State shall request a hearing within 20 days after notice of the registration. The nonregistering party may seek to vacate the registration, to assert any defense to an allegation of noncompliance with the registered order, or to contest the remedies being sought or the amount of any alleged arrears pursuant to G.S. 52C-6-607.

(b)   If the nonregistering party fails to contest the validity or enforcement of the registered order in a timely manner, the order is confirmed by operation of law.

(c)   If a nonregistering party requests a hearing to contest the validity or enforcement of the registered order, the registering tribunal shall schedule the matter for hearing and give notice to the parties of the date, time, and place of the hearing. (1995, c. 538, s. 7(c); 1997-433, s. 10.11; 1998-17, s. 1.)

§ 52C-6-607. Contest of registration or enforcement.

(a)   A party contesting the validity or enforcement of a registered order or seeking to vacate the registration has the burden of proving one or more of the following defenses:

(1)   The issuing tribunal lacked personal jurisdiction over the contesting party;

48

(2)   The order was obtained by fraud;

(3)   The order has been vacated, suspended, or modified by a later order;

(4)   The issuing tribunal has stayed the order pending appeal;

(5)   There is a defense under the law of this State to the remedy sought;

(6)   Full or partial payment has been made; or

(7)   The statute of limitations under G.S. 52C-6-604 precludes enforcement of some or all of the arrears.

(b)   If a party presents evidence establishing a full or partial defense under subsection (a) of this section, a tribunal may stay enforcement of the registered order, continue the proceeding to permit production of additional relevant evidence, and issue other appropriate orders. An uncontested portion of the registered order may be enforced by all remedies available under the law of this State.

(c)   If the contesting party does not establish a defense under subsection (a) of this section to the validity or enforcement of the order, the registering tribunal shall issue an order confirming the order. (1995, c. 538, s. 7(c).)

§ 52C-6-608. Confirmed order.

Confirmation of a registered order, whether by operation of law or after notice and hearing, precludes further contest of the order with respect to any matter that could have been asserted at the time of registration. (1995, c. 538, s. 7(c).)

Part. 3. Registration and Modification of Child Support Order.

§ 52C-6-609. Procedure to register child support order of another state for modification.

A party or support enforcement agency seeking to modify, or to modify and enforce, a child support order issued in another state shall register that order in this State in the same manner provided in Part 1 of this Article if the order has not been registered. A petition for modification may be filed at the same time as a request for registration, or later. The pleading must specify the grounds for modification. (1995, c. 538, s. 7(c).)

§ 52C-6-610. Effect of registration for modification.

A tribunal of this State may enforce a child support order of another state registered for purposes of modification, in the same manner as if the order had been issued by a tribunal of this State, but the registered order may be modified only if the requirements of G.S. 52C-6-611 have been met. (1995, c. 538, s. 7(c).)

§ 52C-6-611. Modification of child support order of another state.

(a)   After a child support order issued in another state has been registered in this State, the responding tribunal of this State may modify that order only if G.S. 52C-6-613 does not apply and after notice and hearing it finds that:

(1)   The following requirements are met:

a.   The child, the individual obligee, and the obligor do not reside in the issuing state;

b.   A petitioner who is a nonresident of this State seeks modification; and

c.   The respondent is subject to the personal jurisdiction of the tribunal of this State; or

(2)   The child, or a party who is an individual, is subject to the personal jurisdiction of the tribunal of this State and all of the parties who are individuals have filed a written consent in the issuing tribunal for a tribunal of this State to modify the support order and assume continuing, exclusive jurisdiction over the order. However, if the issuing state is a foreign jurisdiction that has not enacted a law or established procedures substantially similar to the procedures under this act, the consent otherwise required of an individual residing in this State is not required for the tribunal to assume jurisdiction to modify the child support order.

(b)   Modification of a registered child support order is subject to the same requirements, procedures, and defenses that apply to the modification of an order issued by a tribunal of this State, and the order may be enforced and satisfied in the same manner.

(c)   A tribunal of this State may not modify any aspect of a child support order that may not be modified under the law of the issuing state. If two or more tribunals have issued child support orders for the same obligor and child, the order that controls and must be so recognized under G.S. 52C-2-207 establishes the aspects of the support order which are nonmodifiable.

(d)   On issuance of an order modifying a child support order issued in another state, a tribunal of this State becomes the tribunal of continuing, exclusive jurisdiction.

(e)   Repealed by Session Laws 1997-443, s. 10.12. (1995, c. 538, s. 7(c); 1997-433, s. 10.12; 1997-456, s. 27; 1998-17, s. 1.)

§ 52C-6-612. Recognition of order modified in another state.

A tribunal of this State shall recognize a modification of its earlier child support order by a tribunal of another state which assumed jurisdiction pursuant to a law substantially similar to this Chapter and, upon request, except as otherwise provided in this Chapter, shall:

(1)   Enforce the order that was modified only as to amounts accruing before the modification;

(2)   Enforce only nonmodifiable aspects of that order;

(3)   Provide other appropriate relief only for violations of that order which occurred before the effective date of the modification; and

(4)   Recognize the modifying order of the other state, upon registration, for the purpose of enforcement. (1995, c. 538, s. 7(c).)

§ 52C-6-613. Jurisdiction to modify child support order of another state when individual parties reside in this State.

(a)   If all of the parties who are individuals reside in this State and the child does not reside in the issuing state, a tribunal of this State has jurisdiction to

51

enforce and to modify the issuing state's child support order in a proceeding to register that order.

(b)   A tribunal of this State exercising jurisdiction under this section shall apply the provisions of Articles 1 and 2 of this Chapter, this Article, and the procedural and substantive law of this State to the proceeding for enforcement or modification. Articles 3, 4, 5, 7, and 8 of this Chapter do not apply. (1997-433, s. 10.13; 1998-17, s. 1.)

§ 52C-6-614. Notice to issuing tribunal of modification.

Within 30 days after issuance of a modified child support order, the party obtaining the modification shall file a certified copy of the order with the issuing tribunal that had continuing, exclusive jurisdiction over the earlier order, and in each tribunal in which the party knows the earlier order has been registered. A party who obtains the order and fails to file a certified copy is subject to appropriate sanctions by a tribunal in which the issue of failure to file arises. The failure to file does not affect the validity or enforceability of the modified order of the new tribunal having continuing, exclusive jurisdiction. (1997-433, s. 10.13; 1998-17, s. 1.)

Article 7.

Determination of Parentage.

§ 52C-7-701. Proceeding to determine parentage.

(a)   A tribunal of this State may serve as an initiating or responding tribunal in a proceeding brought under this Chapter or a law substantially similar to this Chapter, the Uniform Reciprocal Enforcement of Support Act, or the Revised Uniform Reciprocal Enforcement of Support Act to determine that the petitioner is a parent of a particular child or to determine that a respondent is a parent of that child.

(b)   In a proceeding to determine parentage, a responding tribunal of this State shall apply the procedural and substantive law of this State and the rules of this State on choice of law. (1995, c. 538, s. 7(c).)

Article 8.

Interstate Rendition.

§ 52C-8-801. Grounds for rendition.

(a)   For purposes of this Article, "governor" includes an individual performing the functions of governor or the executive authority of a state covered by this Chapter.

(b)   The Governor of this State may:

(1)   Demand that the governor of another state surrender an individual found in the other state who is charged criminally in this State with having failed to provide for the support of an obligee; or

(2)   On the demand by the governor of another state, surrender an individual found in this State who is charged criminally in the other state with having failed to provide for the support of an obligee.

(c)   A provision for extradition of individuals not inconsistent with this Chapter applies to the demand even if the individual whose surrender is demanded was not in the demanding state when the crime was allegedly committed and has not fled therefrom. (1995, c. 538, s. 7(c).)

§ 52C-8-802. Conditions of rendition.

(a)   Before making demand that the governor of another state surrender an individual charged criminally in this State with having failed to provide for the support of an obligee, the Governor of this State may require a prosecutor of this State to demonstrate that at least 60 days previously the obligee has initiated proceedings for support pursuant to this Chapter or that the proceeding would be of no avail.

(b)   If, under this Chapter or a law substantially similar to this Chapter, the Uniform Reciprocal Enforcement of Support Act, or the Revised Uniform Reciprocal Enforcement of Support Act, the governor of another state makes a demand that the Governor of this State surrender an individual charged criminally in that state with having failed to provide for the support of a child or other individual to whom a duty of support is owed, the governor may require a prosecutor to investigate the demand and report whether a proceeding for support has been initiated or would be effective. If it appears that a proceeding would be effective but has not been initiated, the governor may delay honoring the demand for a reasonable time to permit the initiation of a proceeding.

(c)   If a proceeding for support has been initiated and the individual whose rendition is demanded prevails, the governor may decline to honor the demand. If the petitioner prevails and the individual whose rendition is demanded is subject to a support order, the governor may decline to honor the demand if the individual is complying with the support order. (1995, c. 538, s. 7(c).)

Article 9.

Miscellaneous Provisions.

§ 52C-9-901. Uniformity of application and construction.

This Chapter shall be applied and construed to effectuate its general purpose to make uniform the law with respect to the subject of this Chapter among states enacting it. (1995, c. 538, s. 7(c).)

§ 52C-9-902. Severability clause.

If any provision of this Chapter or its application to any person or circumstance is held invalid, the invalidity does not affect other provisions or applications of this Chapter which can be given effect without the invalid provision or application, and to this end the provisions of this Chapter are severable. (1995, c. 538, s. 7(c).)

Chapter 53.

Regulation of Financial Services.

Article 1.

Definitions.

§ 53-1: Repealed by Session Laws 2012-56, s. 1, effective October 1, 2012.

Article 1A.

General Provisions.

§ 53-1.1. Banking definitions applicable to this Chapter.

Except as otherwise provided by law, the definitions contained in G.S. 53C-1-4 shall apply to terms used in this Chapter. (2012-56, s. 3.)

Article 2.

Creation.

§ 53-2: Repealed by Session Laws 2012-56, s. 1, effective October 1, 2012.

§ 53-3: Repealed by Session Laws 2012-56, s. 1, effective October 1, 2012.

§ 53-4: Repealed by Session Laws 2012-56, s. 1, effective October 1, 2012.

§ 53-5: Repealed by Session Laws 2012-56, s. 1, effective October 1, 2012.

§ 53-6: Repealed by Session Laws 2012-56, s. 1, effective October 1, 2012.

§ 53-7: Repealed by Session Laws 2012-56, s. 1, effective October 1, 2012.

§ 53-8: Repealed by Session Laws 2012-56, s. 1, effective October 1, 2012.

§ 53-9: Repealed by Session Laws 2012-56, s. 1, effective October 1, 2012.

§ 53-9.1: Repealed by Session Laws 2012-56, s. 1, effective October 1, 2012.

§ 53-10: Repealed by Session Laws 2012-56, s. 1, effective October 1, 2012.

§ 53-11: Repealed by Session Laws 2012-56, s. 1, effective October 1, 2012.

§ 53-12: Repealed by Session Laws 2012-56, s. 1, effective October 1, 2012.

§ 53-13: Repealed by Session Laws 2012-56, s. 1, effective October 1, 2012.

§ 53-14: Repealed by Session Laws 2012-56, s. 1, effective October 1, 2012.

§ 53-15. Repealed by Session Laws 1947, c. 696.

§ 53-16: Repealed by Session Laws 2012-56, s. 1, effective October 1, 2012.

§ 53-17: Repealed by Session Laws 2012-56, s. 1, effective October 1, 2012.

§ 53-17.1: Repealed by Session Laws 2012-56, s. 1, effective October 1, 2012.

§ 53-17.2: Repealed by Session Laws 2012-56, s. 1, effective October 1, 2012.

Article 3.

Dissolution and Liquidation.

§ 53-18: Repealed by Session Laws 2012-56, s. 1, effective October 1, 2012.

§ 53-19: Repealed by Session Laws 2012-56, s. 1, effective October 1, 2012.

§ 53-20: Repealed by Session Laws 2012-56, s. 1, effective October 1, 2012.

§ 53-21: Repealed by Session Laws 2012-56, s. 1, effective October 1, 2012.

§ 53-22: Repealed by Session Laws 2012-56, s. 1, effective October 1, 2012.

§ 53-23: Repealed by Session Laws 2012-56, s. 1, effective October 1, 2012.

§ 53-24: Repealed by Session Laws 2012-56, s. 1, effective October 1, 2012.

§ 53-25: Repealed by Session Laws 2012-56, s. 1, effective October 1, 2012.

§ 53-26: Repealed by Session Laws 2012-56, s. 1, effective October 1, 2012.

§ 53-27: Repealed by Session Laws 2012-56, s. 1, effective October 1, 2012.

§ 53-28: Repealed by Session Laws 2012-56, s. 1, effective October 1, 2012.

§ 53-29: Repealed by Session Laws 2012-56, s. 1, effective October 1, 2012.

§ 53-30: Repealed by Session Laws 2012-56, s. 1, effective October 1, 2012.

§ 53-31: Repealed by Session Laws 2012-56, s. 1, effective October 1, 2012.

§ 53-32: Repealed by Session Laws 2012-56, s. 1, effective October 1, 2012.

§ 53-33: Repealed by Session Laws 2012-56, s. 1, effective October 1, 2012.

§ 53-34: Repealed by Session Laws 2012-56, s. 1, effective October 1, 2012.

§ 53-35: Repealed by Session Laws 2012-56, s. 1, effective October 1, 2012.

§ 53-36: Repealed by Session Laws 2012-56, s. 1, effective October 1, 2012.

Article 4.

Reopening of Closed Banks.

§ 53-37: Repealed by Session Laws 2012-56, s. 1, effective October 1, 2012.

§ 53-38: Repealed by Session Laws 2012-56, s. 1, effective October 1, 2012.

Article 5.

Stockholders.

§ 53-39: Repealed by Session Laws 2012-56, s. 1, effective October 1, 2012.

§ 53-40: Repealed by Session Laws 2012-56, s. 1, effective October 1, 2012.

§ 53-41: Repealed by Session Laws 2012-56, s. 1, effective October 1, 2012.

§ 53-42: Repealed by Session Laws 2012-56, s. 1, effective October 1, 2012.

§ 53-42.1: Repealed by Session Laws 2012-56, s. 1, effective October 1, 2012.

Article 6.

Powers and Duties.

§ 53-43: Repealed by Session Laws 2012-56, s. 1, effective October 1, 2012.

§ 53-43.1: Repealed by Session Laws 2012-56, s. 1, effective October 1, 2012.

§ 53-43.2: Repealed by Session Laws 2012-56, s. 1, effective October 1, 2012.

§ 53-43.3: Repealed by Session Laws 2012-56, s. 1, effective October 1, 2012.

§ 53-43.4: Repealed by Session Laws 2012-56, s. 1, effective October 1, 2012.

§ 53-43.5: Repealed by Session Laws 2012-56, s. 1, effective October 1, 2012.

§ 53-43.6: Repealed by Session Laws 2012-56, s. 1, effective October 1, 2012.

§ 53-43.7: Repealed by Session Laws 2012-56, s. 1, effective October 1, 2012.

§ 53-44: Repealed by Session Laws 2012-56, s. 1, effective October 1, 2012.

§ 53-44.1: Repealed by Session Laws 2012-56, s. 1, effective October 1, 2012.

§ 53-44.2: Repealed by Session Laws 2012-56, s. 1, effective October 1, 2012.

§ 53-45: Repealed by Session Laws 2012-56, s. 1, effective October 1, 2012.

§ 53-46: Repealed by Session Laws 2012-56, s. 1, effective October 1, 2012.

§ 53-46.1: Repealed by Session Laws 2012-56, s. 1, effective October 1, 2012.

§ 53-47: Repealed by Session Laws 2012-56, s. 1, effective October 1, 2012.

§ 53-48: Repealed by Session Laws 2012-56, s. 1, effective October 1, 2012.

§ 53-49: Repealed by Session Laws 2012-56, s. 1, effective October 1, 2012.

§ 53-50: Repealed by Session Laws 2012-56, s. 1, effective October 1, 2012.

§ 53-51: Repealed by Session Laws 2012-56, s. 1, effective October 1, 2012.

§ 53-52. Repealed by Session Laws 1981, c. 599, s. 19, effective October 1, 1981.

§ 53-53. Repealed by Session Laws 1981, c. 599, s. 18, effective October 1, 1981.

§ 53-54: Repealed by Session Laws 2012-56, s. 1, effective October 1, 2012.

§ 53-55: Repealed by Session Laws 2012-56, s. 1, effective October 1, 2012.

§ 53-56: Repealed by Session Laws 2012-56, s. 1, effective October 1, 2012.

§§ 53-57 through 53-58. Repealed by Session Laws 1965, c. 700, s. 2.

§ 53-59: Repealed by Session Laws 1991, c. 677, s. 3.

§ 53-60: Repealed by Session Laws 2012-56, s. 1, effective October 1, 2012.

§ 53-61: Repealed by Session Laws 2012-56, s. 1, effective October 1, 2012.

§ 53-62: Repealed by Session Laws 2012-56, s. 1, effective October 1, 2012.

§ 53-63: Repealed by Session Laws 2012-56, s. 1, effective October 1, 2012.

§ 53-64: Repealed by Session Laws 2012-56, s. 1, effective October 1, 2012.

§ 53-65: Repealed by Session Laws 2012-56, s. 1, effective October 1, 2012.

§ 53-66. Repealed by Session Laws 1983, c. 214, s. 7, effective April 22, 1983.

§ 53-67: Repealed by Session Laws 2012-56, s. 1, effective October 1, 2012.

§ 53-68: Repealed by Session Laws 2012-56, s. 1, effective October 1, 2012.

§ 53-69. Repealed by Session Laws 1945, c. 635.

§ 53-70: Repealed by Session Laws 2012-56, s. 1, effective October 1, 2012.

§ 53-71: Repealed by Session Laws 2012-56, s. 1, effective October 1, 2012.

§ 53-72. Repealed by Session Laws 1971, c. 244, s. 3.

§ 53-73: Repealed by Session Laws 2012-56, s. 1, effective October 1, 2012.

§ 53-74. Repealed by Session Laws 1971, c. 244, s. 3.

§ 53-75: Repealed by Session Laws 2012-56, s. 1, effective October 1, 2012.

§ 53-76: Repealed by Session Laws 2012-56, s. 1, effective October 1, 2012.

§ 53-77: Repealed by Session Laws 2012-56, s. 1, effective October 1, 2012.

§ 53-77.1: Repealed by Session Laws 1989, c. 187, s. 9.

§ 53-77.1A: Repealed by Session Laws 2012-56, s. 1, effective October 1, 2012.

§ 53-77.2. Repealed by Session Laws 1971, c. 319, s. 2.

§ 53-77.2A: Repealed by Session Laws 1995 (Regular Session, 1996), c. 556, s. 1.

§ 53-77.3: Repealed by Session Laws 2012-56, s. 1, effective October 1, 2012.

Article 7.

Officers and Directors.

§ 53-78: Repealed by Session Laws 2012-56, s. 1, effective October 1, 2012.

§ 53-79: Repealed by Session Laws 2012-56, s. 1, effective October 1, 2012.

§ 53-80: Repealed by Session Laws 2012-56, s. 1, effective October 1, 2012.

§ 53-81: Repealed by Session Laws 2012-56, s. 1, effective October 1, 2012.

§ 53-82: Repealed by Session Laws 2012-56, s. 1, effective October 1, 2012.

§ 53-83: Repealed by Session Laws 2012-56, s. 1, effective October 1, 2012.

§ 53-84: Repealed by Session Laws 2012-56, s. 1, effective October 1, 2012.

§ 53-85: Repealed by Session Laws 2012-56, s. 1, effective October 1, 2012.

§ 53-86: Repealed by Session Laws 2012-56, s. 1, effective October 1, 2012.

§ 53-87: Repealed by Session Laws 2012-56, s. 1, effective October 1, 2012.

§ 53-87.1: Repealed by Session Laws 2012-56, s. 1, effective October 1, 2012.

§ 53-88: Repealed by Session Laws 2012-56, s. 1, effective October 1, 2012.

§ 53-89: Repealed by Session Laws 2012-56, s. 1, effective October 1, 2012.

§ 53-90: Repealed by Session Laws 2012-56, s. 1, effective October 1, 2012.

§ 53-91: Repealed by Session Laws 1995, c. 129, s. 17.

§ 53-91.1: Repealed by Session Laws 2012-56, s. 1, effective October 1, 2012.

§ 53-91.2: Repealed by Session Laws 2012-56, s. 1, effective October 1, 2012.

§ 53-91.3: Repealed by Session Laws 2012-56, s. 1, effective October 1, 2012.

Article 8.

Commissioner of Banks and State Banking Commission.

§ 53-92. (Repealed effective April 1, 2013) Appointment of Commissioner of Banks; State Banking Commission.

(a)   On or before April 1, 1983, and quadrennially thereafter, the Governor shall appoint a Commissioner of Banks subject to confirmation by the General Assembly by joint resolution. The name of the Commissioner of Banks shall be submitted to the General Assembly on or before February 1, of the year in which the term of his office begins. The term of office for the Commissioner of Banks shall be four years. In case of a vacancy in the office of Commissioner of Banks for any reason prior to the expiration of his term of office, the name of his successor shall be submitted by the Governor to the General Assembly, not later than four weeks after the vacancy arises. If a vacancy arises in the office when the General Assembly is not in session, the Commissioner of Banks shall be appointed by the Governor to serve on an interim basis pending confirmation by the General Assembly.

(b)   The State Banking Commission, which has heretofore been created, shall consist of the State Treasurer, who shall serve as an ex officio member thereof, 19 members appointed by the Governor, and two members appointed by the General Assembly under G.S. 120-121, one of whom shall be appointed upon the recommendation of the President Pro Tempore of the Senate and one of whom shall be appointed upon the recommendation of the Speaker of the House of Representatives. The Governor shall appoint five practical bankers, 11 persons selected primarily as representatives of the borrowing public, and two chief executive officers of State savings institutions. The person appointed by the General Assembly upon the recommendation of the President Pro Tempore of the Senate shall be a practical banker. The person appointed by the General Assembly upon the recommendation of the Speaker of the House shall be a person selected primarily as a representative of the borrowing public. The persons selected primarily as representatives of the borrowing public shall not be employees or directors of any financial institution nor shall they have any interest in any regulated financial institution other than as a result of being a depositor or borrower. Under this section, no person shall be considered to have an interest in a financial institution whose interest in any financial institution does not exceed one-half of one percent (1/2 of 1%) of the capital stock of that financial institution. These members of the Commission shall be selected so as to fully represent the consumer, industrial, manufacturing, professional, business and farming interests of the State. No person shall serve on the Commission for more than two complete consecutive terms. As the terms of office of the appointive members of the Commission expire, their successors shall be appointed by the person appointing them, for terms of four years each. Any vacancy occurring in the membership of the Commission shall be filled by the appropriate appointing officer for the unexpired term, except that vacancies among members appointed by the General Assembly shall be filled in accordance with G.S. 120-122. The appointed members of the Commission shall receive subsistence and travel expenses at the rates set forth in G.S. 120-

62

3.1. The subsistence and travel expenses shall be paid from the fees collected from the examination of banks as provided by law.

(c)   The Banking Commission shall meet at such time or times, and not less than once every three months, as the Commission shall, by resolution, prescribe, and the Commission may be convened in special session at the call of the Governor, or upon the request of the Commissioner of Banks. The State Treasurer shall be chairman of the said Commission.

No member of said Commission shall act in any matter affecting any bank in which he is financially interested, or with which he is in any manner connected. No member of said Commission shall divulge or make use of any information coming into his possession as a result of his service on such Commission, and shall not give out any information with reference to any facts coming into his possession by reason of his services on such Commission in connection with the condition of any State banking institution, unless such information shall be required of him at any hearing at which he is duly subpoenaed, or when required by order of a court of competent jurisdiction.

A quorum shall consist of a majority of the total membership of the Banking Commission. A majority vote of the members qualified with respect to a matter under review present at that meeting shall constitute valid action of the Banking Commission. The State Treasurer and all disqualified members who are present shall be counted to determine whether a quorum is present at a meeting.

The Commissioner of Banks shall act as the executive officer of the Banking Commission, but the Commission shall provide, by rules and regulations, for hearings before the Commission upon any matter or thing which may arise in connection with the banking laws of this State upon the request of any person interested therein, and review any action taken or done by the Commissioner of Banks.

(d)   The Banking Commission is hereby vested with full power and authority to supervise, direct and review the exercise by the Commissioner of Banks of all powers, duties, and functions now vested in or exercised by the Commissioner of Banks under the banking laws of this State. Upon an appeal to the Banking Commission by any party from an order entered by the Commissioner of Banks following an administrative hearing pursuant to Article 3A of Chapter 150B of the General Statutes, the chairman of the Commission may appoint an appellate review panel of not less than five members to review the record on appeal, hear oral arguments, and make a recommended decision to the Commission. Unless another time period for appeals is provided by this Chapter, any party to an order by the Commissioner of Banks may, within 20 days after the order and upon written notice to the Commissioner, appeal the Commissioner's order to the Banking Commission for review. The notice of appeal shall state the grounds for the appeal and set forth in numbered order the assignments of error for review by the Banking Commission. Failure to state the grounds for the appeal and assignments of error shall constitute grounds to dismiss the appeal. Failure to comply with the briefing schedule provided by the Banking Commission shall also constitute grounds to dismiss the appeal. Upon receipt of a notice of appeal, the Commissioner of Banks shall, within 30 days of the notice, certify to the Commission the record on appeal. Any party to a proceeding before the Banking Commission may, within 20 days after final order of the Commission, petition the Superior Court of Wake County for judicial review of a final determination of any question of law which may be involved. The petition for judicial review shall be entitled "(insert name) Petitioner v. State of North Carolina on Relation of the Banking Commission." A copy of the petition for judicial review shall be served upon the Commissioner of Banks pursuant to G.S. 150B-46. The petition shall be placed on the civil issue docket of the court and shall have precedence over other civil actions. Within 15 days of service of the petition for judicial review, the Commissioner shall certify the record to the Clerk of Superior Court of Wake County. The standard of review of a petition for judicial review of a final order of the Banking Commission shall be as provided in G.S. 150B-51(b). (1931, c. 243, s. 1; 1935, c. 266; 1939, c. 91, s. 1; 1949, c. 372; 1953, c. 1209, ss. 4, 6; 1961, c. 547, s. 2; 1967, c. 789, s. 16; 1969, c. 844, s. 6; c. 920; 1979, c. 478, s. 1; 1981, c. 884, s. 1; 1983, c. 328, ss. 1, 3; 1985, c. 318; 1989, c. 781, s. 41.1; 1995, c. 490, s. 9; 2001-193, s. 14; 2003-63, s. 2; 2006-203, s. 16; 2009-57, s. 1, 2012-56, s. 1.)

§ 53-92.1: Repealed by Session Laws 2012-56, s. 1, effective October 1, 2012.

§ 53-93: Repealed by Session Laws 2012-56, s. 1, effective October 1, 2012.

§ 53-93.1: Repealed by Session Laws 2012-56, s. 1, effective October 1, 2012.

§ 53-94: Repealed by Session Laws 2012-56, s. 1, effective October 1, 2012.

§ 53-95: Repealed by Session Laws 2012-56, s. 1, effective October 1, 2012.

§ 53-96: Repealed by Session Laws 2012-56, s. 1, effective October 1, 2012.

§ 53-96.1: Repealed by Session Laws 2012-56, s. 1, effective October 1, 2012.

§ 53-97. Repealed by Session Laws 1983, c. 328, s. 4, effective June 1, 1983.

§ 53-98: Repealed by Session Laws 2012-56, s. 1, effective October 1, 2012.

§ 53-99: Repealed by Session Laws 2012-56, s. 1, effective October 1, 2012.

§ 53-99.1: Repealed by Session Laws 2012-56, s. 1, effective October 1, 2012.

§ 53-100: Repealed by Session Laws 2012-56, s. 1, effective October 1, 2012.

§ 53-101: Repealed by Session Laws 2012-56, s. 1, effective October 1, 2012.

§ 53-102: Repealed by Session Laws 2012-56, s. 1, effective October 1, 2012.

§ 53-103. Repealed by Session Laws 1945, c. 743, s. 1.

§ 53-104: Repealed by Session Laws 2012-56, s. 1, effective October 1, 2012.

§ 53-104.1: Repealed by Session Laws 2012-56, s. 1, effective October 1, 2012.

§ 53-105: Repealed by Session Laws 2012-56, s. 1, effective October 1, 2012.

§ 53-106: Repealed by Session Laws 2012-56, s. 1, effective October 1, 2012.

§ 53-107: Repealed by Session Laws 2012-56, s. 1, effective October 1, 2012.

§ 53-107.1: Repealed by Session Laws 2012-56, s. 1, effective October 1, 2012.

§ 53-107.2: Repealed by Session Laws 2012-56, s. 1, effective October 1, 2012.

§ 53-108: Repealed by Session Laws 2012-56, s. 1, effective October 1, 2012.

§ 53-109: Repealed by Session Laws 2012-56, s. 1, effective October 1, 2012.

§ 53-110: Repealed by Session Laws 2012-56, s. 1, effective October 1, 2012.

§ 53-111: Repealed by Session Laws 2012-56, s. 1, effective October 1, 2012.

§ 53-112: Repealed by Session Laws 2012-56, s. 1, effective October 1, 2012.

§ 53-113: Repealed by Session Laws 2012-56, s. 1, effective October 1, 2012.

§ 53-114: Repealed by Session Laws 2012-56, s. 1, effective October 1, 2012.

§ 53-115: Repealed by Session Laws 2012-56, s. 1, effective October 1, 2012.

§ 53-116: Repealed by Session Laws 2012-56, s. 1, effective October 1, 2012.

Article 9.

Bank Examiners.

§ 53-117: Repealed by Session Laws 2012-56, s. 1, effective October 1, 2012.

§ 53-118: Repealed by Session Laws 2012-56, s. 1, effective October 1, 2012.

§ 53-119: Repealed by Session Laws 2012-56, s. 1, effective October 1, 2012.

§ 53-120: Repealed by Session Laws 2012-56, s. 1, effective October 1, 2012.

§ 53-121: Repealed by Session Laws 2012-56, s. 1, effective October 1, 2012.

§ 53-122: Repealed by Session Laws 2012-56, s. 1, effective October 1, 2012.

§ 53-123: Repealed by Session Laws 2012-56, s. 1, effective October 1, 2012.

Article 10.

Penalties.

§ 53-124: Repealed by Session Laws 2012-56, s. 1, effective October 1, 2012.

§ 53-125: Repealed by Session Laws 2012-56, s. 1, effective October 1, 2012.

§ 53-126: Repealed by Session Laws 2012-56, s. 1, effective October 1, 2012.

§ 53-127: Repealed by Session Laws 2012-56, s. 1, effective October 1, 2012.

§ 53-128: Repealed by Session Laws 2012-56, s. 1, effective October 1, 2012.

§ 53-129: Repealed by Session Laws 2012-56, s. 1, effective October 1, 2012.

§ 53-130: Repealed by Session Laws 2012-56, s. 1, effective October 1, 2012.

§ 53-131: Repealed by Session Laws 2012-56, s. 1, effective October 1, 2012.

§ 53-132: Repealed by Session Laws 2012-56, s. 1, effective October 1, 2012.

§ 53-133: Repealed by Session Laws 2012-56, s. 1, effective October 1, 2012.

§ 53-134: Repealed by Session Laws 2012-56, s. 1, effective October 1, 2012.

§ 53-135: Repealed by Session Laws 2012-56, s. 1, effective October 1, 2012.

Article 11.

Industrial Banks.

§ 53-136. Industrial bank defined.

The term "industrial bank," as used in this Article shall be construed to mean any corporation organized or authorized under this Article which is engaged in receiving, soliciting or accepting money or its equivalent on deposit and in lending money to be repaid in weekly, monthly, or other periodical installments or principal sums as a business: Provided, however, this definition shall not be construed to include building and loan associations, commercial banks, or credit unions. (1923, c. 225, s. 1; C.S., s. 225(a); 1945, c. 743, s. 1.)

§ 53-137. Manner of organization.

Any number of persons, not less than five, may organize an industrial bank by setting forth in a certificate of incorporation, under their hands and seals, the following:

(1)   The name of the industrial bank.

(2)   The location of its principal office in this State.

(3)   The nature of its business.

(4)   The amount of its authorized capital stock which shall be divided into shares of ten ($10.00), twenty ($20.00), twenty-five ($25.00), fifty ($50.00) or one hundred dollars ($100.00) each: Provided, fractional shares may be issued for the purpose of complying with the requirements of G.S. 53-88.

(5)   The names and post-office addresses of subscribers for stock, and the number of shares subscribed by each. The aggregate of such subscription shall be the amount of the capital with which the industrial bank will begin business.

(6)   Period, if any, limited for the duration of the industrial bank.

This section shall not apply to banks organized and doing business prior to the adoption of this section. (1923, c. 225, s. 2; C.S., s. 225(b); 1945, c. 743, s. 1.)

§ 53-138. Corporate title.

Every corporation incorporated or reorganized pursuant to the provisions of this Article shall be known as an industrial bank, and may use the word "bank" as part of its corporate title. (1923, c. 225, s. 3; C.S., s. 225(c).)

§ 53-139. Capital stock.

The amount of capital stock with which any industrial bank shall commence business shall not be less than fifty percent (50%) of that which would be required of a commercial bank under the provisions of G.S. 53-2. (1923, c. 225, s. 4; C.S., s. 225(d); 1967, c. 789, s. 18.)

§ 53-140. Sales of capital stock; accounting; fees.

The capital stock sold by any industrial bank in process of organization, or for an increase of the capital stock, shall be accounted for to the bank in the full amount paid for the same. No commission or fee shall be paid to any person, association, or corporation for selling such stock. The Commissioner of Banks shall refuse authority to commence business to any industrial bank where commissions or fees have been paid, or have been contracted to be paid by it, or by anyone in its behalf to any person, association, or corporation for securing subscriptions for or selling stock in such bank. (1923, c. 225, s. 5; C.S., s. 225(e); 1931, c. 243, s. 5.)

§ 53-141. Powers.

Industrial banks shall have perpetual duration and succession in their corporate name unless a limited period of duration is stated in their certificate of incorporation. They shall have the powers conferred by subdivisions (1), (2), and (3) of subsection (a) of G.S. 55-3-02, and subdivision (3) of G.S. 53-43, such additional powers as may be necessary or incidental for the carrying out of their corporate purposes, and in addition thereto the following powers:

(1)   To discount and negotiate promissory notes, drafts, bills of exchange and other evidences of indebtedness, and to loan money on real or personal security, and to purchase notes, bills of exchange, acceptances or other choses in action, and to take and receive interest or discounts subject to G.S. 53-43(1).

(2)   To make loans and charge and receive interest at rates not exceeding the rates of interest provided in G.S. 24-1.1 and G.S. 24-1.2.

(3)   To establish branch offices or places of business within the county in which its principal office is located, and elsewhere in the State, after having first obtained the written approval of the Commissioner of Banks, which approval may be given or withheld by the Commissioner of Banks in his discretion. The Commissioner of Banks, in exercising such discretion, shall take into account,

but not by way of limitation, such factors as the financial history and condition of the applicant bank, the adequacy of its capital structure, its future earnings prospects, and the general character of its management. Such approval shall not be given until he shall find

a.   That the establishment of such branch or limited service facility will meet the needs and promote the convenience of the community to be served by the bank, and

b.   That the probable volume of business and reasonable public demand in such community are sufficient to assure and maintain the solvency of said branch or limited service facility and of the existing bank or banks in said community.

Provided, that the Commissioner of Banks shall not authorize the establishment of any branch the paid-in capital of whose parent bank is not sufficient in amount to provide for capital in an amount equal to that required with respect to the establishment of branches of commercial banks under the provisions of G.S. 53-62. For the purposes of this paragraph, the provisions of G.S. 53-62 as to the meaning of the word "capital" shall be applicable.

A bank may discontinue a branch office upon resolution of its board of directors. Upon the adoption of such a resolution, the bank shall follow the procedures for closing a branch as set forth at G.S. 53-62(e). No branch shall be closed until approved by the Commissioner of Banks.

(4)   Subject to the approval of the Commissioner of Banks and on the authority of its board of directors, or a majority thereof, to enter into such contract, incur such obligations and generally to do and perform any and all such acts and things whatsoever as may be necessary or appropriate in order to take advantage of any and all memberships, loans, subscriptions, contracts, grants, rights or privileges, which may at any time be available or inure to banking institutions, or to their depositors, creditors, stockholders, conservators, receivers or liquidators, by virtue of those provisions of section eight of the Federal Banking Act of 1933 (section twelve B of the Federal Reserve Act as amended) which establish the Federal Deposit Insurance Corporation and provide for the insurance of deposits, or of any other provisions of that or any other act or resolution of Congress to aid, regulate or safeguard banking institutions and their depositors, including any amendments of the same or any substitutions therefor; also, to subscribe for and acquire any stock, debentures, bonds or other types of securities of the Federal Deposit Insurance Corporation

and to comply with the lawful regulations and requirements from time to time issued or made by such corporations.

(5)   To solicit, receive and accept money or its equivalent on deposit both in savings accounts and upon certificates of deposit.

(6)   Subject to the approval of the State Banking Commission, to solicit, receive and accept money or its equivalent on deposit subject to check; provided, however, no such approval shall be given unless and until such industrial bank meets the capital requirements of a commercial bank as set forth in G.S. 53-2.

(7)   To transact any lawful business in aid of the United States in time of war or engagement of the Armed Forces of the United States in hostile military operations. (1923, c. 225, s. 6; C.S., s. 225(f); 1925, c. 199, s. 1; 1931, c. 243, s. 5; 1935, c. 81, s. 2; 1939, c. 244, ss. 1, 2; 1943, c. 233; 1945, c. 283; 1949, c. 952, ss. 1, 2; 1959, c. 365; 1967, c. 789, s. 19; 1969, c. 1303, ss. 10-12; 1995, c. 129, s. 26; 1995 (Reg. Sess., 1996), c. 742, s. 20; 2011-183, s. 41.)

§ 53-142. Restriction on powers.

No industrial bank shall deposit any of its funds in any banking corporation unless such corporation has been designated as such depositary by a vote of a majority of the directors, or of the executive committee, exclusive of any director who is an officer, director, or trustee of the depositary so designated, present at any meeting duly called at which a quorum is in attendance, and approved by the Commissioner of Banks. (1923, c. 225, s. 7; C.S., s. 225(g); 1931, c. 243, s. 5; 1937, c. 220.)

§ 53-143. Investments; securities; loans; limitations.

The provisions of G.S. 53-46, 53-48 and 53-49, with reference to the limitations of investments in securities, limitations of loans and suspensions of investment and loan limitations, shall be applicable to industrial banks. (1923, c. 225, s. 8; C.S., s. 225(h); 1945, c. 127, s. 2.)

§ 53-144. Supervision and examination.

Every industrial bank now or hereafter transacting the business of an industrial bank as defined by this Article, whether as a separate business or in connection with any other business under the laws of and within this State, shall be subject to the provisions of this Article, and shall be under the supervision of the Commissioner of Banks. The Commissioner of Banks shall exercise control of and supervision over the industrial banks doing business under this Article, and it shall be his duty to execute and enforce, through the State bank examiners and such other agents as are now or may hereafter be created or appointed, all laws which are now or may hereafter be enacted relating to industrial banks as defined in this Article. For the more complete and thorough enforcement of the provisions of this Article, the State Banking Commission is hereby empowered to promulgate such rules, regulations, and instructions, not inconsistent with the provisions of this Article, as may, in its opinion, be necessary to carry out the provisions of the laws relating to industrial banks as in this Article defined, and as may be further necessary to insure such safe and conservative management of industrial banks under the supervision of the Commissioner of Banks as may provide adequate protection for the interest of creditors, stockholders, and the public, in their relations with such institutions. All industrial banks doing business under the provisions of this Article shall conduct their business in a manner consistent with all laws relating to industrial banks, and all rules, regulations and instructions that may be promulgated or issued by the State Banking Commission. (1923, c. 225, s. 11; C.S., s. 225(k); 1931, c. 243, s. 5; 1939, c. 91, s. 2.)

§ 53-145. Sections of general law applicable.

Sections 53-1, 53-3, 53-4, 53-5, 53-6, 53-7, 53-8, 53-9, 53-10, 53-11, 53-12, 53-13, 53-18, 53-20, 53-22, 53-23, 53-42, 53-42.1, 53-47, 53-50, 53-51, 53-54, 53-63, 53-64, 53-67, 53-68, 53-70, 53-71, 53-73, 53-78, 53-79, 53-80, 53-81, 53-82, 53-83, 53-85, 53-87, 53-88, 53-90, 53-91.2, 53-91.3, 53-105, 53-106, 53-107, 53-108, 53-109, 53-110, 53-111, 53-112, 53-117, 53-118, 53-119, 53-120, 53-121, 53-122, 53-123, 53-124, 53-125, 53-126, 53-128, 53-129, 53-132, 53-133, 53-134, relating to the supervision and examination of commercial banks, shall be construed to be applicable to industrial banks, insofar as they are not inconsistent with the provisions of this Article. Sections 53-19, 53-24, 53-37, 53-39, 53-40, 53-41, 53-44, 53-45, 53-61, 53-75, 53-76, 53-77, 53-86, 53-113, 53-114, 53-115, 53-116, 53-135, 53-146, and 53-148 through 53-158, relating to commercial banks, shall be construed to be applicable to industrial banks. (1923, c. 225, s. 13; C.S., s. 225(m); 1927, c. 141; 1939, c. 244, s. 3; 1945, c. 743, s. 1; 1981, c. 671, s. 14; 1995, c. 129, s. 27.)

Article 12.

Joint Deposits.

§ 53-146: Repealed by Session Laws 2012-56, s. 1, effective October 1, 2012.

§ 53-146.1: Repealed by Session Laws 2012-56, s. 1, effective October 1, 2012.

§ 53-146.2: Repealed by Session Laws 2011-236, s. 1, effective October 1, 2011.

§ 53-146.2A: Repealed by Session Laws 2012-56, s. 1, effective October 1, 2012.

§ 53-146.3: Repealed by Session Laws 2012-56, s. 1, effective October 1, 2012.

§ 53-147. Repealed by Session Laws 1943, c. 543.

Article 13.

Conservation of Bank Assets and Issuance of Preferred Stock.

§ 53-148: Repealed by Session Laws 2012-56, s. 1, effective October 1, 2012.

§ 53-149: Repealed by Session Laws 2012-56, s. 1, effective October 1, 2012.

§ 53-150: Repealed by Session Laws 2012-56, s. 1, effective October 1, 2012.

§ 53-151: Repealed by Session Laws 2012-56, s. 1, effective October 1, 2012.

§ 53-152: Repealed by Session Laws 2012-56, s. 1, effective October 1, 2012.

§ 53-153: Repealed by Session Laws 2012-56, s. 1, effective October 1, 2012.

§ 53-154: Repealed by Session Laws 2012-56, s. 1, effective October 1, 2012.

§ 53-155: Repealed by Session Laws 2012-56, s. 1, effective October 1, 2012.

§ 53-156: Repealed by Session Laws 2012-56, s. 1, effective October 1, 2012.

§ 53-157: Repealed by Session Laws 2012-56, s. 1, effective October 1, 2012.

§ 53-158: Repealed by Session Laws 2012-56, s. 1, effective October 1, 2012.

§ 53-158.1: Repealed by Session Laws 2012-56, s. 1, effective October 1, 2012.

§ 53-158.2: Reserved for future codification purposes.

§ 53-158.3: Reserved for future codification purposes.

§ 53-158.4: Reserved for future codification purposes.

§ 53-158.5: Reserved for future codification purposes.

§ 53-158.6: Reserved for future codification purposes.

§ 53-158.7: Reserved for future codification purposes.

§ 53-158.8: Reserved for future codification purposes.

§ 53-158.9: Reserved for future codification purposes.

Article 14.

Trust Institutions Acting in a Fiduciary Capacity.

Part 1. General Provisions.

§ 53-158.10. Definitions.

For purposes of this Article, the following definitions apply:

(1)   "Depository institution" has the same meaning as set forth in the Federal Deposit Insurance Act, 12 U.S.C. §§ 1811, et seq.

(2)   "Hazardous condition" has the same meaning as set forth in G.S. 53-301(a)(23).

(3)   "Trust institution" has the same meaning as set forth in G.S. 53-301(a)(52). (2011-339, s. 7.)

§ 53-159. Trust institution may act as fiduciary.

Any trust institution licensed by the Commissioner of Banks, where such powers or privileges are granted it in its charter, may be guardian, trustee, assignee, receiver, executor or administrator or act in another fiduciary capacity in this State without giving any bond; and the clerks of the superior courts, or other officers charged with the duty or clothed with the power of making such appointments, are authorized to appoint such trust institution to any such office. (1945, c. 743, s. 1; 2001-263, s. 3; 2011-339, s. 7.)

§ 53-159.1. Power of fiduciary or custodian to deposit securities in a clearing corporation.

Notwithstanding any other provision of law, any fiduciary holding securities in its fiduciary capacity, any trust institution holding securities in a fiduciary capacity or as a custodian or agent is authorized to deposit or arrange for the deposit of such securities with a securities intermediary as defined in G.S. 25-8-102. When such securities are so deposited, certificates representing securities of the same class of the same issuer may be merged and held in bulk in the name of the nominee of such securities intermediary with any other such securities deposited in such securities intermediary by any person regardless of the ownership of such securities, and certificates of small denomination may be merged into one or more certificates of larger denomination. The records of such fiduciary and the records of such trust institution acting as a fiduciary or as a custodian or managing agent shall at all times show the name of the party for whose account the securities are so deposited. Title to such securities may be transferred by bookkeeping entry on the books of such securities intermediary without physical delivery of certificates representing such securities. A trust institution so depositing securities pursuant to this section shall be subject to such rules as, in the case of State-chartered institutions, the State Banking Commission and, in the case of other institutions, their regulators may from time to time issue. A trust institution acting as custodian or agent for a fiduciary shall, on demand by the fiduciary, certify in writing to the fiduciary the securities so deposited by such trust institution in such securities intermediary for the account of such fiduciary. A fiduciary shall, on demand by any party to a judicial proceeding for the settlement of such fiduciary's account or on demand by the

75

attorney for such party, certify in writing to such party the securities deposited by such fiduciary in such securities intermediary for its account as such fiduciary. This section shall apply to any fiduciary holding securities in its fiduciary capacity, and to any trust institution holding securities as a fiduciary or as a custodian or managing agent acting on May 15, 1973, or who thereafter may act regardless of the date of the agreement, instrument or court order by which it is appointed and regardless of whether or not such fiduciary, custodian or agent owns capital stock of such securities intermediary. The fiduciary shall personally be liable for any loss to the trust resulting from an act of such nominee in connection with such securities so deposited. (1973, c. 497, s. 4; 1997-181, s. 26; 2001-263, s. 3; 2011-339, s. 7.)

§ 53-160. License to do business.

Before any such trust institution is authorized to act in any fiduciary capacity without bond, it must be licensed by the Commissioner of Banks of the State. For such license the licensee, for the purpose of defraying necessary expenses of the Commissioner of Banks and the Commissioner's agents, shall pay to the Commissioner of Banks an annual license fee of five hundred dollars ($500.00). (1945, c. 743, s. 1; 1967, c. 789, s. 20; 2001-263, s. 3; 2004-171, s. 5; 2011-339, s. 7.)

§ 53-161. Examination in connection with license as to solvency.

The Commissioner of Banks may, at the expense of the trust institution, make or cause to be made an examination of any trust institution, other than a federally chartered trust institution, that applies for or is licensed by the Commissioner of Banks. The Commissioner of Banks may refuse to issue a license to a trust institution that it finds to be in a hazardous condition. (1945, c. 743, s. 1; 2001-263, s. 3; 2011-339, s. 7.)

§ 53-162: Repealed by Session Laws 2011-339, s. 7, effective October 1, 2011.

§ 53-163. Clerk of superior court notified of license and revocation.

The Commissioner of Banks, upon granting license to any trust institution, shall immediately notify the clerk of the superior court of each county in the State that the trust institution has been licensed under this Article, and, whenever the

Commissioner of Banks is satisfied that any trust institution licensed by the Commissioner is in a hazardous condition, the Commissioner shall revoke the license granted to that trust institution and notify the clerk of the superior court of each county in the State of the revocation. (1945, c. 743, s. 1; 2001-263, s. 3; 2011-339, s. 7.)

§ 53-163.1. Funds held by a trust institution awaiting investment or distribution.

(a)   Funds held in a fiduciary capacity by a trust institution awaiting investment or distribution shall not be held uninvested or undistributed any longer than is reasonable for the proper management of the account. A trust institution has complied with this requirement if such funds awaiting investment or distribution in excess of one thousand dollars ($1,000) are invested or distributed within 30 days of receipt or accumulation thereof.

(b)   Funds held in a fiduciary capacity by a depository institution, awaiting investment or distribution may, unless prohibited by the instrument creating the fiduciary relationship, be deposited in the commercial or savings or other department of the depository institution, provided that it shall first set aside under control of the trust department as collateral security, the classes of securities listed in G.S. 159-30(c) as being eligible for the investment of funds by local governments and public authorities equal in market value of such deposited funds, or readily marketable commercial bonds having not less than a recognized "A" rating equal to one hundred and twenty-five percent (125%) of the funds so deposited.

The securities so deposited or securities substituted therefor as collateral in the trust department by the commercial or savings or other department (as well as the deposit of cash in the commercial or savings or other department by the trust department) shall be held pursuant to the provisions of G.S. 53-163.3.

If such funds are deposited in a depository institution insured under the provisions of the Federal Deposit Insurance Act, the above collateral security will be required only for that portion of uninvested balances of each trust which are not fully insured under the provisions of that act.

(c)   Funds held in a fiduciary capacity by a trust institution awaiting investment or distribution may, unless prohibited by the instrument creating the fiduciary relationship, be invested in short-term, trust-quality investment vehicles, through the medium of a collective investment fund or otherwise.

(d)   In addition to any other compensation to which it may be entitled under statutes governing the compensation of personal representatives, guardians, or other fiduciaries, or under any other authority, a trust institution shall be allowed to charge a fee for the temporary investment of funds held awaiting investment or distribution, which fee may be calculated upon the amount of such funds actually invested and upon the income produced thereby. The fee authorized by this subsection shall not exceed twelve percent (12%) of the income produced by such investment. A trust institution has complied with its duty to disclose fees and practices in connection with the investment of fiduciary funds awaiting investment or distribution if the trust institution's periodic account statements set forth the method of computing such fees. (1939, c. 197, s. 4; 1963, c. 243, ss. 1, 2; 1977, c. 502, s. 2; 1989, c. 443; 2004-139, s. 5; 2005-192, s. 1; 2011-339, s. 7; 2012-56, s. 9.)

§ 53-163.2. Investments in securities by trust institutions.

Unless the governing instrument, court order, or a statute specifically directs otherwise, a trust institution serving as trustee, guardian, agent, or in any other fiduciary capacity may invest in any security authorized by this Chapter even if such fiduciary or an affiliate thereof participates or has participated as a member of a syndicate underwriting such security, if:

(1)   The fiduciary does not purchase the security from itself or its affiliate; and

(2)   The fiduciary does not purchase the security from another syndicate member or an affiliate, pursuant to an implied or express agreement between the fiduciary or its affiliate and a selling member or its affiliate, to purchase all or part of each other's underwriting commitments. (1985, c. 549, s.1; 2005-192, s. 1; 2007-106, s. 51; 2011-339, s. 7.)

§ 53-163.3. Fiduciary funds awaiting investment.

A bank that is a trust institution may maintain separate departments and deposit in its commercial department to the credit of its trust department all uninvested fiduciary funds of cash and secure all such deposits in the name of the trust department, whether in consolidated deposits or for separate fiduciary accounts, by segregating and delivering to the trust department such securities as are required by G.S. 53-163.1 for such deposits. Such securities shall be held by the trust department as security for the full payment or repayment of all such deposits and shall be kept separate and apart from other assets of the trust department. Until all of the deposits shall have been accounted for to the trust department or to the individual fiduciary accounts, no creditor of the bank shall have any claim or right to such security. When fiduciary funds are deposited by the trust department in the commercial department of the bank, the deposit thereof shall not be deemed to constitute a use of such funds in the general business of the bank. To the extent and in the amount such deposits may be insured by the FDIC, the amount of security required for such deposits by this section may be reduced. The Banking Commission shall have power to make such rules as it may deem necessary for the enforcement of the provisions of this section. (2012-56, s. 10.)

§ 53-163.4: Reserved for future codification purposes.

Part 2. Uniform Common Trust Fund Act.

§ 53-163.5. Establishment of common trust funds.

(a)   Any trust institution duly authorized to act as a fiduciary in this State may establish and maintain one or more common trust funds for the collective investment of funds held in a fiduciary capacity by such trust institution hereafter referred to as the "maintaining institution." The maintaining institution may include for the purposes of collective investment in such common trust fund or funds established and maintained by it, funds held in a fiduciary capacity by any other trust institution duly authorized to act as a fiduciary with which it is affiliated, wherever located, which other trust institution is hereinafter referred to as the "participating institution."

(b)   For the purposes of this section, a maintaining institution shall be considered to be affiliated with a participating institution if it controls, is controlled by, or is under common control with the participating institution, as control is determined under the federal Bank Holding Company Act of 1956 or by rule, order, or declaratory ruling of the Commissioner of Banks.

(c)   Such common trust funds may include a fund composed solely of funds held under an agency agreement in which the trust institution assumes investment discretion and assumes fiduciary responsibility.

d)   Such trust institution may invest the funds held by it in any fiduciary capacity in one or more common trust funds, provided that (i) such investment is not prohibited by the instrument, judgment, decree or order creating such fiduciary relationship or amendment thereof, and (ii) the trust institution has no interest in the assets of the common trust fund other than as a fiduciary. (1939, c. 200, s. 1; 1973, c. 1276; 1977, c. 502, s. 2; 2005-192, s. 1; 2006-259, s. 13(q); 2011-339, s. 7.)

§ 53-163.6. Court accountings.

Unless ordered by a court of competent jurisdiction the trust institution operating such common trust fund or funds shall not be required to render a court accounting with regard to such fund or funds; but it may, by application to the superior court, secure approval of such an accounting on such conditions as the court may establish. This section shall not affect the duties of the trustees of the participating trusts under the common trust fund to render accounts of their several trusts. (1939, c. 200, s. 2; 1977, c. 502, s. 2; 2005-192, s. 1; 2011-339, s. 7.)

§ 53-163.7. Supervision by State Banking Commission.

All common trust funds established under the provisions of this Part shall be subject to the rules and regulations of the State Banking Commission. (1939, c. 200, s. 3; 1977, c. 502, s. 2; 2005-192, s. 1.)

§ 53-163.8. Uniformity of interpretation.

This Part shall be so interpreted and construed as to effectuate its general purpose to make uniform the law of those states which enact it. (1939, c. 200, s. 4; 1977, c. 502, s. 2; 2005-192, s. 1.)

§ 53-163.9. Short title.

This Part may be cited as the Uniform Common Trust Fund Act. (1939, c. 200, s. 5; 1977, c. 502, s. 2; 2005-192, s. 1.)

Article 15.

North Carolina Consumer Finance Act.

§ 53-164. Title.

This Article shall be known and may be cited as the North Carolina Consumer Finance Act. (1961, c. 1053, s. 1.)

§ 53-165. Definitions.

(a)   "Amount of the loan" shall mean the aggregate of the cash advance and the charges authorized by G.S. 53-173 and G.S. 53-176.

(b)   "Borrower" shall mean any person who borrows money from any licensee or who pays or obligates himself to pay any money or otherwise furnishes any valuable consideration to any licensee for any act of the licensee as a licensee.

(c)   "Cash advance" shall mean the amount of cash or its equivalent that the borrower actually receives or is paid out at his discretion or on his behalf.

(d)   "Commission" shall mean the State Banking Commission.

(e)   "Commissioner" shall mean the Commissioner of Banks.

(f)   "Deputy commissioner" shall mean the deputy commissioner of banks.

(g)   "License" shall mean the certificate issued by the Commissioner under the authority of this Article to conduct a consumer finance business.

(h)   "Licensee" shall mean a person to whom one or more licenses have been issued.

(i)   "Loanable assets" shall mean cash or bank deposits or installment loans made as a licensee pursuant to this Article or installment loans made as a licensee pursuant to the Article which this Article supersedes or such other loans payable on an installment basis as the Commissioner of Banks may approve, or any combination of two or more thereof.

(j)   "Person" shall include any person, firm, partnership, association or corporation. (1957, c. 1429, s. 1; 1961, c. 1053, s. 1; 2001-519, s. 1.)

§ 53-166. Scope of Article; evasions; penalties; loans in violation of Article void.

(a)   Scope. - No person shall engage in the business of lending in amounts of fifteen thousand dollars ($15,000) or less and contract for, exact, or receive, directly or indirectly, on or in connection with any such loan, any charges whether for interest, compensation, consideration, or expense, or any other purpose whatsoever, which in the aggregate are greater than permitted by Chapter 24 of the General Statutes, except as provided in and authorized by this Article, and without first having obtained a license from the Commissioner. The word "lending" as used in this section, shall include, but shall not be limited to, endorsing or otherwise securing loans or contracts for the repayment of loans.

(b)   Evasions. - The provisions of subsection (a) of this section apply to any person who seeks to avoid its application by any device, subterfuge, or pretense whatsoever. Devices, subterfuges, and pretenses include any transaction in which a cash rebate or other advance of funds is offered and all of the following apply:

(1)   The cash advance is made contemporaneously with the transaction or soon thereafter.

(2)   The amount of the cash advance is required to be repaid at a later date.

(3)   The selling or providing of any item, service, or commodity with the transaction is incidental to, or a pretext for, the advance of funds.

(c)   Penalties; Commissioner to Provide and Testify as to Facts in His Possession. - Any person not exempt from this Article, or any officer, agent, employee, or representative thereof, who fails to comply with or who otherwise violates any of the provisions of this Article, or any regulation of the Banking Commission adopted pursuant to this Article, shall be guilty of a Class 1 misdemeanor. Each violation shall be considered a separate offense. It is the duty of the Commissioner of Banks to provide the district attorney of the court having jurisdiction of any offense under this subsection with all facts and evidence in the Commissioner's actual or constructive possession, and to testify as to these facts upon the trial of any person for the offense.

82

(d)   Additional Penalties. - Any contract of loan, the making or collecting of which violates any provision of this Article, or regulation thereunder, except as a result of accidental or bona fide error of computation is void, and the licensee or any other party in violation shall not collect, receive, or retain any principal or charges whatsoever with respect to the loan. If an affiliate operating in the same office or subsidiary operating in the same office of a licensee makes a loan in violation of G.S. 53-180(i), the affiliate or subsidiary may recover only its principal on the loan. (1955, c. 1279; 1957, c. 1429, s. 8; 1961, c. 1053, s. 1; 1969, c. 1303, ss. 13, 14; 1973, c. 47, s. 2; c. 1042, s. 1; 1979, c. 33, s. 1; 1985, c. 154, ss. 6, 13; 1987, c. 444, s. 3; 1989, c. 17, ss. 1, 13; 1989 (Reg. Sess., 1990), c. 881, s. 1; 1993, c. 539, s. 425; 1994, Ex. Sess., c. 24, s. 14(c); 2006-243, s. 2; 2013-162, s. 1.)

§ 53-167. Expenses of supervision.

For the purpose of defraying necessary expenses of the Office of Commissioner of Banks for supervision, each licensee shall pay to the Commissioner an assessment not to exceed eighteen dollars ($18.00) per one hundred thousand dollars ($100,000) of assets, or fraction thereof, plus a fee of three hundred dollars ($300.00) per office; provided, however, a consumer finance licensee shall pay a minimum annual assessment of not less than five hundred dollars ($500.00). The assessment shall be determined on a consumer finance licensee's total assets as shown on its report of condition made to the Commissioner as of December 31 of each year, or the date most nearly approximating that date. If the Commissioner determines that the financial condition or manner of operation of a consumer finance licensee warrants further examination or an increased level of supervision, the licensee may be subject to assessment not to exceed the amount determined in accordance with the schedule set forth in this section. (1955, c. 1279; 1957, c. 1429, s. 1; 1961, c. 1053, s. 1; 2012-56, s. 11.)

§ 53-168. License required; showing of convenience, advantage and financial responsibility; investigation of applicants; hearings; existing businesses; contents of license; transfer; posting.

(a)   Necessity for License; Prerequisites to Issuance. - No person shall engage in or offer to engage in the business regulated by this Article unless and until a license has been issued by the Commissioner of Banks, and the

Commissioner shall not issue any such license unless and until the Commissioner finds:

(1)   That authorizing the applicant to engage in such business will promote the convenience and advantage of the community in which the applicant proposes to engage in business; and

(2)   That the financial responsibility, experience, character and general fitness of the applicant are such as to command the confidence of the public and to warrant the belief that the business will be operated lawfully and fairly, within the purposes of this Article; and

(3)   That the applicant has available for the operation of such business at the specified location loanable assets of at least fifty thousand dollars ($50,000).

(b)   Investigation of Applicants. - Upon the receipt of an application, the Commissioner shall investigate the facts. If the Commissioner determines from such preliminary investigation that the applicant does not satisfy the conditions set forth in subsection (a), the Commissioner shall so notify the applicant who shall then be entitled to an informal hearing thereon provided he so requests in writing within 30 days after the Commissioner has caused the above-referred to notification to be mailed to the applicant. In the event of a hearing, to be held in the offices of the Commissioner of Banks in Raleigh, the Commissioner shall reconsider the application and, after the hearing, issue a written order granting or denying such application. At the time of making such application, the applicant shall pay the Banking Department the sum of two hundred fifty dollars ($250.00) as a fee for investigating the application, which shall be retained irrespective of whether or not a license is granted the applicant.

(c)   Repealed by Session Laws 2001-519, s. 2.

(d)   Required Assets Available. - Each licensee shall continue at all times to have available for the operation of the business at the specified location loanable assets of at least fifty thousand dollars ($50,000). The requirements and standards of this subsection and subsection (a)(2) of this section shall be maintained throughout the period of the license and failure to maintain such requirements or standards shall be grounds for the revocation of a license under the provisions of G.S. 53-171 of this Article.

(e)   License, Posting, Continuing. - Each license shall state the address at which the business is to be conducted and shall state fully the name of the licensee, and if the licensee is a copartnership, or association, the names of the members thereof, and if a corporation, the date and place of its incorporation. Transfer or assignment of a license by one person to another by sale or otherwise is prohibited without the prior approval of the Commissioner. Each license shall be kept posted in the licensed place of business. Each license shall remain in full force and effect until surrendered, revoked, or suspended as hereinafter provided. (1961, c. 1053, s. 1; 1969, c. 1303, s. 15; 1973, c. 1042, s. 2; 1981, c. 671, s. 15; 1987, c. 827, s. 12; 2001-519, s. 2.)

§ 53-169. Application for license.

The application for license shall be made on a form prepared and furnished by the Commissioner of Banks and shall state:

(1)   The fact that the applicant desires to engage in business under this Article; and

(2)   Whether the applicant is an individual, partnership, association or corporation; and

(3)   The name and address of the person who will manage and be in immediate control of the business; and

(4)   The name and address of the owners and their percentage of equity in the company, except when the Commissioner does not deem it feasible to furnish such information because of the number of stockholders involved; and

(5)   When the applicant proposes to commence doing business; and

(6)   Such other information as the Commissioner of Banks deems necessary.

The statements made in such application shall be sworn to by the applicant or persons making application on the applicant's behalf. (1961, c. 1053, s. 1.)

§ 53-170. Locations; change of ownership or management.

(a)   Business Location. - A licensee may conduct and carry on his business only at such location or locations as may be approved by the Commissioner of

Banks, and no changes shall be made from one location to another without the approval of the Commissioner.

(b)   Additional Places of Business. - Not more than one place of business shall be maintained under the same license, but the Commissioner may issue more than one license to the same licensee upon compliance with all the provisions of this Article governing issuance of a single license.

(c)   Change of Location, Ownership or Management. - If any change occurs in the name and address of the licensee or of the president, secretary or agent of a corporation, or in the membership of any partnership under said sections, a true and full statement of such change, sworn to in the manner required by this Article in the case of the original application, shall forthwith be filed with the Commissioner. (1961, c. 1053, s. 1.)

§ 53-171. Revocation, suspension or surrender of license.

(a)   If the Commissioner shall find, after due notice and hearing, or opportunity for hearing, that any such licensee, or an officer, agent, employee, or representative thereof has violated any of the provisions of this Article, or has failed to comply with the rules, regulations, instructions or orders promulgated by the Commission pursuant to the powers and duties prescribed therein, or has failed or refused to make its reports to the Commissioner, or has failed to pay the fees for its examination and supervision, or has furnished false information to the Commissioner or the Commission, the Commissioner may issue an order revoking or suspending the right of such licensee and such officer, agent, employee or representative to do business in North Carolina as a licensee, and upon receipt of such an order from the Commissioner, the licensee shall immediately surrender his license to the Commissioner. Within five days after the entry of such an order the Commissioner shall place on file his findings of fact and mail or otherwise deliver a copy to the licensee. Any licensee who fails to make any loans during any period of 90 consecutive days after being licensed shall surrender his license to the Commissioner.

(b)   Any licensee may surrender any license by delivering it to the Commissioner with written notice of its surrender, but such surrender shall not affect his civil or criminal liability for acts committed prior thereto.

(c)   No revocation, suspension or surrender of any license shall impair or affect the obligation of any preexisting lawful contract between the licensee and any obligor.

(d)   The Commissioner, in his discretion, may reinstate suspended licenses or issue new licenses to a person whose license or licenses have been revoked, or surrendered if and when he determines no fact or condition exists which clearly would have justified the Commissioner in refusing originally to issue such license under this Article. (1955, c. 1279; 1961, c. 1053, s. 1.)

§ 53-172. Conduct of other business in same office.

(a)   No licensee shall conduct the business of making loans under this Article within any office, suite, room, or place of business in which any other business is solicited or transacted.

Installment paper dealers as defined in G.S. 105-83, the collection by a licensee of loans legally made in North Carolina or another state by another government regulated lender or lending agency, and the collection by a licensee of claims of, payments to, or payments for an insurance company licensed in North Carolina and arising in any way from a nonfiling or nonrecording insurance policy approved by the Commissioner of Insurance shall not be considered as being any other business within the meaning of this section.

(b)   Notwithstanding subsection (a) of this section, the Commissioner may authorize in writing the solicitation and transaction of other business in any office, suite, room, or place of business in which a licensee is conducting the business of making loans if the Commissioner determines that the other business would not be contrary to the best interests of the borrowing public.

(c)   The Commissioner may require, consistent with the provisions of 12 C.F.R. Part 226 (Regulation Z) of the federal Truth-In-Lending Act, the other business authorized under subsection (b) of this section to:

(1)   Disclose the cost of consumer credit of goods and services sold; and

(2)   Provide the purchaser with a reasonable cancellation period for goods and services purchased.

(d)   No licensee shall:

(1)   Make the purchase of goods and services sold under the authorization of subsection (b) of this section a condition of making a loan; or

(2)   Consider the borrower's decision to purchase, or not purchase, goods and services sold under the authorization of subsection (b) of this section a factor in its approval or denial of credit, or in its determination of the amount of or terms of credit for the borrower.

(e)   The licensee shall notify the borrower in writing that the purchase of the goods and services offered under the authorization under subsection (b) of this section is voluntary and that the borrower's decision whether or not to purchase the goods and services will not affect the licensee's decision to grant credit or the amount of or terms of the credit granted.

(f)   If, at any time, the Commissioner has reason to believe that the conduct of any other business authorized under this section is contrary to the best interests of the borrowing public, the Commissioner shall hold a hearing pursuant to Chapter 150B of the General Statutes to determine whether or not to revoke the authority to conduct that business. The Commissioner shall revoke the authority to conduct any other business if he or she finds that the conduct of any other business authorized under this section is contrary to the best interests of the borrowing public.

(g)   This section shall not be construed as authorizing the collection of any loans or charges in violation of the prohibitions contained in G.S. 53-190.

(h)   The books, records, and accounts relating to loans shall be kept in such manner as the Commissioner of Banks prescribes as to delineate clearly the loan business from any other business authorized by the Commissioner. (1961, c. 1053, s. 1; 1967, c. 769, s. 1; 1971, c. 1212; 1981, c. 464, s. 2; 1985, c. 154, ss. 7, 8, 9; 1987, c. 444, ss. 2, 3; 1989, c. 17, ss. 2, 13; 1991 (Reg. Sess., 1992), c. 765, s. 1; 2013-162, s. 2.)

§ 53-173. Computation of interest; application of payments; limitation on interest after judgment; limitation on interest after maturity of the loan.

(a),   (a1) Repealed by Session Laws 2013-162, s. 3, effective July 1, 2013.

(b)   Computation of Interest. - Interest on loans made pursuant to this section shall not be paid, deducted, or received in advance. Such interest shall not be compounded but interest on loans shall (i) be computed and paid only as a percentage of the unpaid principal balance or portion thereof and (ii) computed on the basis of the number of days actually elapsed; provided, however, if part or all of the consideration for a loan contract is the unpaid principal balance of a prior loan, then the principal amount payable under the loan contract may include any unpaid interest on the prior loan which have accrued within 90 days before the making of the new loan contract. For the purpose of computing interest, a day shall equal 1/365th of a year.

(b1)   Application of Payments. - Any payment made on a loan shall be applied first to late charges and other permissible charges under this Article, then to any accrued interest, and then to principal. Any portion or all of the principal balance may be prepaid at any time without penalty.

(c)   Limitation on Interest after Judgment. - If a money judgment is obtained against any party on any loan made under the provisions of this section neither the judgment nor the loan shall carry, from the date of the judgment, any interest in excess of eight percent (8%) per annum.

(d)   Limitation of Interest after Maturity of Loan. - After the maturity date of any loan contract made under the provisions of this section and until the loan contract is paid in full by cash, new loan, refinancing or otherwise, no charges other than interest at eight percent (8%) per annum shall be computed or collected from any party to the loan upon the unpaid principal balance of the loan.

(e)   Repealed by Session Laws 1989, c. 17, s. 3.

(f)   Repealed by Session Laws 2001-519, s. 3, effective January 1, 2002. (1961, c. 1053, s. 1; 1969, c. 1303, ss. 13, 17-22; 1973, c. 1042, s. 3; 1975, c. 110, s. 1; 1979, c. 33, s. 2; 1981, c. 561, ss. 1-3; 1983, c. 68, s. 1; c. 126, s. 13; 1989, c. 17, s. 3; 2001-519, s. 3; 2013-162, s. 3.)

§ 53-173.1: Repealed by Session Laws 1989, c. 17, s. 4.

§ 53-173.2. Repealed by Session Laws 1975, c. 110, s. 2.

§ 53-174: Repealed by Session Laws 1989, c. 17, s. 4.

§ 53-175. Fee for returned checks.

A licensee may collect the fee for returned checks to the extent permitted by G.S. 25-3-506. This section shall apply to any loan made by any licensee under this Article. (1961, c. 1053, s. 1; 1969, c. 1303, s. 23; 1981, c. 561, s. 4; 1983, c. 68, s. 1; c. 126, s. 12; 1989, c. 17, s. 5; 1995 (Reg. Sess., 1996), c. 742, s. 21.)

§ 53-176. Rates, maturities and amounts.

(a)   A licensee may make installment loans in aggregate amounts not exceeding fifteen thousand dollars ($15,000) and which shall not be repayable in fewer than 12 months or more than 96 months and which shall not be secured by deeds of trust or mortgages on real estate and which are repayable in substantially equal consecutive monthly payments and to charge and collect interest in connection therewith which shall not exceed the following actuarial rates:

(1)   With respect to a loan not exceeding ten thousand dollars ($10,000), thirty percent (30%) per annum on that part of the unpaid principal balance not exceeding four thousand dollars ($4,000), twenty-four percent (24%) per annum on that part of the unpaid principal balance exceeding four thousand dollars ($4,000) but not exceeding eight thousand dollars ($8,000), and eighteen percent (18%) per annum on that part of the remainder of the unpaid principal balance.

(2)   With respect to a loan exceeding ten thousand dollars ($10,000), eighteen percent (18%) per annum on the outstanding principal balance.

Interest shall be contracted for and collected at the single simple interest rate applied to the outstanding balance that would earn the same amount of interest as the above rates for payment according to schedule.

(b)   In addition to the interest permitted in this section, a licensee may assess at closing a fee for processing the loan as agreed upon by the parties, not to exceed twenty-five dollars ($25.00) for loans up to two thousand five hundred dollars ($2,500) and one percent (1%) of the cash advance for loans above two thousand five hundred dollars ($2,500), not to exceed a total fee of forty dollars ($40.00), provided that such charges may not be assessed more than twice in any 12-month period.

(c)   The provisions of G.S. 53-173(b), (b1), (c) and (d) and G.S. 53-180(b), (c), (d), (e), (f), (g), (h) and (i) shall apply to loans made pursuant to this section.

(d)   Repealed by Session Laws 2013-162, s. 4, effective July 1, 2013.

(e)   The due date of the first monthly payment shall not be more than 45 days following the disbursement of funds under any such installment loan. A borrower under this section may prepay all or any part of a loan made under this section without penalty. Except as otherwise provided for pursuant to G.S. 75-20(a), no more than twice in a 12-month period, a borrower may cancel a loan with the same licensee within three business days after disbursement of the loan proceeds without incurring or paying interest so long as the amount financed, minus any fees or charges, is returned to and received by the licensee within that time.

(f)   Repealed by Session Laws 2013-162, s. 4, effective July 1, 2013. (1961, c. 1053, s. 1; 1969, c. 1303, s. 12.1; 1981, c. 561, s. 7; 1983, c. 68, s. 1; c. 126, ss. 14, 15; 1989, c. 17, s. 6; 1995, c. 155, s. 1; 2001-519, s. 4; 2013-162, s. 4.)

§ 53-176.1: Repealed by Session Laws 1989, c. 17, s. 4.

§ 53-177. Fees.

(a)   Recording Fees. - The licensee may collect from the borrower the amount of any fees necessary to file or record its security interest with any public official or agency of a county or the State as may be required pursuant to Article 9 of Chapter 25 of the General Statutes or G.S. 20-58 et seq. Upon full disclosure to the borrower on how the fees will be applied, such fees may either (i) be paid by the licensee to such public official or agency of the county or State or (ii) in lieu of recording or filing, applied by the licensee to purchase nonfiling or nonrecording insurance on the instrument securing the loan; provided, however, the amount collected by the licensee from the borrower for the purchase of a nonfiling or nonrecording insurance policy shall be the premium amount for such insurance as fixed by the Commissioner of Insurance. Such premium shall be at least one dollar ($1.00) less than the cost of recording or filing a security interest. Provided further, a licensee shall not collect or permit to be collected any notary fee in connection with any loan made under this Article, nor may a licensee collect any fee from the borrower for the cost of releasing a security interest except such fee as actually paid to any public official or agency of the county or State for such purpose.

(b)   Late Fees. -

(1)   A licensee may charge a late payment fee for any payment which remains past due for 10 days or more after the due date.

(2)   No licensee may charge a late payment fee in an amount greater than fifteen dollars ($15.00) nor charge a late payment fee more than once with respect to a single late payment.

(3)   If a late payment fee has been once imposed with respect to a particular late payment, no such fee shall be imposed with respect to any future payment which would have been timely and sufficient but for the previous default.

(c)   Deferral Charges. - A licensee may, by agreement with the borrower, collect a deferral charge and defer the due date of all or part of one or more installments under an existing loan contract as permitted in the provisions of G.S. 25A-30.

(d)   Insurance Policy. - If a licensee, in lieu of recording, collects a fee to purchase a nonfiling or nonrecording insurance policy as authorized under subsection (a) of this section, to be valid, any claim arising from such policy shall only be used to compensate the licensee for damages arising from failure to record or file its security interest in accordance with Article 9 of Chapter 25 of the General Statutes. Following payment of such claim, the licensee shall do the following:

(1)   Properly credit the full claim amount posted to the balance of the loan effective the date the proceeds were received.

(2)   Close the loan account and cease collection efforts on any loan that was paid in full by a claim.

(3)   Provide the borrower written notice, unless otherwise prohibited by federal law, that (i) the claim has been partially paid or paid in full and (ii) to the extent the loan is subject to the insurance company's subrogation rights, instructions about direction of future payments.

(4)   Cancel of record or properly credit, as appropriate, any judgments against the borrower arising from the loan and, if the judgment has been paid in part, file a certificate of partial satisfaction.

(5)   Accurately report any account adjustments to any credit bureau used by the licensee. (1961, c. 1053, s. 1; 1989, c. 17, s. 7; 2000-169, s. 36; 2013-162, s. 5.)

§ 53-178. No further charges; no splitting contracts; certain contracts void.

No further or other charges or insurance commissions shall be directly or indirectly contracted for or received by any licensee except those specifically authorized by this Article or by the Commissioner under G.S. 53-172. No licensee shall divide into separate parts any contract made for the purpose of or with the effect of obtaining charges in excess of those authorized by this Article. All balances due to a licensee from any person as a borrower or as an endorser, guarantor or surety for any borrower or otherwise, or due from any husband or wife, jointly or severally, shall be considered a part of any loan being made by a licensee to such person for the purpose of computing interest or charges. (1961, c. 1053, s. 1; 1991 (Reg. Sess., 1992), c. 765, s. 2.)

§ 53-179. Multiple-office loan limitations.

A licensee shall not grant a loan in one office to any borrower who already has a loan in another office operated by the same entity or by an affiliate, parent, subsidiary or under the same ownership, management or control, whether partial or complete. This section shall apply to intrastate and interstate operations. A licensee shall take every reasonable precaution to prevent granting loans in violation of this section. Such loans granted inadvertently resulting in a total liability of three thousand dollars ($3,000) or less, shall be adjusted to the rates applicable under the Article to a single loan of equivalent amount, and when the total liability on such loans is in excess of three thousand dollars ($3,000), interest shall be adjusted to simple interest at eight percent (8%) per annum on the entire obligation. (1961, c. 1053, s. 1; 1969, c. 1303, s. 13; 1973, c. 1042, s. 6; 1981, c. 561, ss. 5, 6; 1983, c. 68, s. 1.)

§ 53-180. Limitations and prohibitions on practices and agreements.

(a)   Time and Payment Limitation. - Every loan contract shall provide for repayment of the amount loaned in substantially equal installments, either of principal or of principal and charges in the aggregate, at approximately equal periodic intervals of time. Nothing contained herein shall prevent a loan being

93

considered a new loan because the proceeds of the loan are used to pay an existing contract.

(b)   No Assignment of Earnings. - A licensee may not take an assignment of earnings of the borrower for payment or as security for payment of a loan. An assignment of earnings in violation of this section is unenforceable by the assignee of the earnings and is revocable by the borrower. A sale of unpaid earnings made in consideration of the payment of money to or for the account of the seller of the earnings is deemed to be a loan to the seller by an assignment of earnings.

(c)   Limitation on Default Provisions. - An agreement between a licensee and a borrower pursuant to a loan under this Article with respect to default by the borrower is enforceable only to the extent that (i) the borrower fails to make a payment as required by the agreement or fails to maintain contractually required insurance coverage or (ii) the prospect of payment, performance, or realization of collateral is significantly endangered or impaired, the burden of establishing the prospect of a significant endangerment or impairment being on the licensee.

(d)   Prohibitions on Discrimination. - No licensee shall deny any extension of credit or discriminate in the fixing of the amount, duration, application procedures or other terms or conditions of such extension of credit because of the race, color, religion, national origin, sex or marital status of the applicant or any other person connected with the transaction.

(e)   Limitation on Attorney's Fees. - With respect to a loan made pursuant to the provisions of G.S. 53-176, the agreement may not provide for payment by the borrower of attorney fees.

(f)   No Real Property as Security. - No licensee shall make any loan within this State which shall in any way be secured by real property.

(g)   Deceptive Acts or Practices. - No licensee shall engage in any unfair method of competition or unfair or deceptive trade practices in the conduct of making loans to borrowers pursuant to this Article or in collecting or attempting to collect any money alleged to be due and owing by a borrower.

(h)   Limitations on Home Loans. - No affiliate operating in the same office or subsidiary operating in the same office of a licensee shall make any home loan

94

as defined in G.S. 24-1.1A(e) in a principal amount of less than three thousand dollars ($3,000).

(i)   Limitation on Conditions to Making Loans. - A licensee or an affiliate operating in the same office or subsidiary operating in the same office of a licensee shall not make as a condition of any loan the refinancing of a borrower's home loan as defined in G.S. 24-1.1A(e) which is not currently in default.

(j)   No Solicitation of Deposits. - No licensee may directly or indirectly solicit from any borrower funds to be held on deposit in any bank; provided, however, a borrower may at his option, by way of a military allotment or other such program, designate a depository to receive and disburse funds for a designated purpose.

(k)   Loans made pursuant to this Article solicited using a facsimile or negotiable check shall be subject to the provisions of G.S. 75-20(a). (1961, c. 1053, s. 1; 1969, c. 1303, s. 24; 1973, c. 1042, s. 7; 1979, c. 33, s. 3; 1981, c. 464, s. 3; 1985, c. 154, ss. 10-12; 1987, c. 444, s. 3; 1989, c. 17, ss. 8, 13; 2001-519, s. 5; 2013-162, s. 6.)

§ 53-180.1. Military service members limitation.

(a)   Definition. - For purposes of this section, the term "military service member" means a member of the Armed Forces who is either (i) on active duty under a call or order that does not specify a period of 30 days or fewer or (ii) on active Guard and Reserve Duty, as that term is defined in 10 U.S.C. § 101(d)(6).

(b)   Verification; Requirements for Granting Loan. - Prior to making a loan under this Article, a licensee will confirm whether the borrower is a military service member and document this in the person's loan file. A licensee may not make a loan to a borrower who is a military service member with a rank of E4 or below ("covered member") unless the following requirements are met:

(1)   The licensee notifies the borrower's company-level commander or equivalent designee of the covered member before the loan is consummated. Notification may occur verbally, by electronic means, United States mail, or other equivalent methods of notification. The notification method and date shall be recorded in writing and included in the loan file along with the name of the company-level commander or equivalent designee communicated with and the

date of the communication with the company-level commander or equivalent designee.

(2)   The licensee shall deposit in the United States mail a copy of the federal Truth in Lending Act, 15 U.S.C. § 1601, et seq., disclosures and the complete contract for the loan addressed to the borrower's company-level commander or equivalent designee of the covered member within five business days of the consummation of the loan.

(3)   A covered member who has entered into a loan contract made pursuant to this Article may, within 30 days of entering into the loan contract, rescind the loan contract by returning to the licensee in cash or by certified bank check the amount advanced to or for the benefit of the covered member under the loan contract, and upon delivery of those funds to the licensee, the borrower shall have no further liability or obligations under the loan contract. Nothing in this provision shall be construed to restrict or eliminate any other penalties provided by State or federal law.

(4)   The licensee shall give the covered member a separate disclosure that includes the statements and information required under G.S. 53-181(a). The licensee shall include the name and address of the North Carolina Commissioner of Banks, the Consumer Protection Division of the North Carolina Department of Justice, and the Consumer Financial Protection Bureau. The licensee may include internal compliance information on the same disclosure.

(5)   Notwithstanding section 2 of Title 9 of the United States Code, 9 U.S.C. § 2, or any other federal or State law, rule, or regulation, no agreement to arbitrate any dispute involving the extension of consumer credit shall be enforceable against any covered member or dependent of such a member or any person who was a covered member or dependent of that member when the agreement was made.

(6)   A licensee shall take reasonable precaution to prevent making loans in violation of this section. In the event that a licensee does not take reasonable precautions to identify covered members prior to making a loan, such loans granted to covered members shall have the interest rate on the loan adjusted to eight percent (8%) per annum.

(c)   Penalties and Remedies. -

(1)   The remedies and rights provided under this section are in addition to and do not preclude any remedy otherwise available under law to the person claiming relief under this section, including any incidental, consequential, or punitive damages.

(2)   Any credit agreement, promissory note, or other contract prohibited under this section is null and void.

(3)   Nothing in this section may be construed to limit or otherwise affect the applicability of section 207 of the Servicemembers Civil Relief Act, 50 U.S.C. App. § 527.

(d)   Additional Restriction. - When a military servicemember has been deployed to a theater of combat, combat supporting role, an area where hostile fire and/or when Imminent Danger Pay is authorized to the servicemember, a licensee shall not contact the military servicemember or member's spouse by telephone or electronic mail for purposes of collecting on the loan upon receiving sufficient proof of the military servicemember's deployment. An official copy of the military service member's orders for deployment or written verification from the servicemember's commanding officer shall constitute sufficient proof. (2013-162, s. 7.)

§ 53-181. Statements and information to be furnished to borrowers; power of attorney or confession of judgment prohibited.

(a)   Contents of Statement Furnished to Borrower. - At the time a loan is made, the licensee shall deliver to the borrower, or if there be two or more borrowers, to one of them a copy of the loan contract, or a written statement, showing in clear and distinct terms:

(1)   The name and address of the licensee and one of the primary obligors on the loan;

(2)   The date of the loan contract;

(3)   Schedule of installments or descriptions thereof;

(4)   The cash advance;

(5)   The face amount of the note evidencing the loan;

(6)   The amount collected or paid for insurance, if any;

(7)   The amount collected or paid for filing or other fees allowed by this Article;

(8)   The collateral or security for the loan;

(9)   If the loan refinances a previous loan, the following relating to the refinanced loan: (i) the principal balance due; (ii) interest charged that is included in the new loan; and (iii) rebates on any credit insurance, listed separately.

(10)   In addition to any disclosures otherwise provided by law, a licensee soliciting loans using a facsimile or negotiable check shall provide the disclosures required by G.S. 75-20(a).

(b)   Schedule of Charges, etc., to Be Made Available; Copy Filed with Commissioner. - Each licensee doing business in North Carolina shall make readily available to the borrower at each place of business such full and accurate schedule of charges and insurance premiums, including refunds and rebates, on all classes of loans currently being made by such licensee, as the Commissioner shall prescribe, and a copy thereof shall be filed in the office of the Commissioner of Banks.

(c)   Power of Attorney or Confession of Judgment Prohibited. - No licensee shall take any confession of judgment or permit any borrower to execute a power of attorney in favor of any licensee or in favor of any third person to confess judgment or to appear for the borrower in any judicial proceeding and any such confession of judgment or power of attorney to confess judgment shall be absolutely void. (1955, c. 1279; 1961, c. 1053, s. 1; 1989, c. 17, s. 9; 2001-519, s. 6.)

§ 53-182. Payment of loans; receipts.

(a)   After each payment made on account of any loan, the licensee shall give to the person making such payment a signed, dated receipt showing the amount paid and the balance due on the loan. No receipt shall be required in the case of payments made by the borrower's check or money order, where the entire proceeds of the check or money order are applied to the loan. The use of a coupon book system shall be deemed in compliance with this section.

(b)   Upon payment of any loan in full, a licensee shall cancel and return to the borrower, within a reasonable length of time, originals or copies of any note, assignment, mortgage, deed of trust, or other instrument securing such loan, which no longer secures any indebtedness of the borrower to the licensee. (1955, c. 1279; 1961, c. 1053, s. 1; 2001-519, s. 7.)

§ 53-183. Advertising, broadcasting, etc., false or misleading statements.

No licensee subject to this Article shall advertise, display, distribute, telecast, or broadcast or cause or permit to be advertised, displayed, distributed, telecasted, or broadcasted, in any manner whatsoever, any false, misleading, or deceptive statement or representation with regard to the rates, terms, or conditions of loans. The Commissioner may require that charges or rates of charge, if stated by a licensee, be stated fully and clearly in such manner as he may deem necessary to prevent misunderstanding thereof by prospective borrowers. The Commissioner may permit or require licensees to refer in their advertising to the fact that their business is under State supervision, subject to conditions imposed by him to prevent an erroneous impression as to the scope or degree of protection provided by this Article. (1957, c. 1429, s. 3; 1961, c. 1053, s. 1.)

§ 53-184. Securing of information; records and reports; allocations of expense.

(a)   Each licensee shall maintain all books and records relating to loans made under this Article required by the Commissioner of Banks to be kept, and the Commissioner, his deputy, or duly authorized examiner or agent or employee is authorized and empowered to examine such records at any reasonable time. Such books and records may be maintained in the form of magnetic tape, magnetic disk, optical disk, or other form of computer, electronic or microfilm media available for examination on the basis of computer printed reproduction, video display or other medium acceptable to the Commissioner of Banks; provided, however, that such books and records so kept must be convertible into clearly legible tangible documents within a reasonable time. Any licensee having more than one licensed office may maintain such books and records at a location other than the licensed office location if such location is approved by the Commissioner; provided that, upon such requirements as may be imposed by the Commissioner of Banks, there shall be available to the borrower at each licensed location or such other location convenient to the borrower, as designated by the licensee, complete loan information; and provided further that such books and records of each licensed office shall be clearly segregated. When a licensee maintains its books and records outside of North Carolina, the licensee shall make them available for examination at the place where they are maintained and shall pay for all reasonable and necessary expenses incurred by the Commissioner in conducting such examination. Where the data processing for any licensee is performed by a person other than the licensee, the licensee shall provide to the Commissioner of Banks a copy of a binding agreement between the licensee and the data processor which allows the Commissioner of Banks, his deputy, or duly authorized examiner or agent or employee to examine that particular data processor's activities pertaining to the licensee to the same extent as if such services were being performed by the licensee on its own premises; and, notwithstanding the provisions of G.S. 53-167, when billed by the Commissioner of Banks, the licensee shall reimburse the Commissioner of Banks for all costs and expenses incurred by the Commissioner in such examination.

(b)   Each licensee shall file annually with the Commissioner of Banks on or before the thirty-first day of March for the 12 months' period ending the preceding December 31, reports on forms prescribed by the Commissioner. Reports shall disclose in detail and under appropriate headings the assets and liabilities of the licensee, the income, expense, gain, loss, and any other information as the Commissioner may require. Reports shall be verified by the oath or affirmation of the owner, manager, president, vice-president, cashier, secretary or treasurer of the licensee.

(c)   If a licensee conducts another business or is affiliated with other licensees under this Article, or if any other situation exists under which allocations of expense are necessary, the licensee or licensees shall make such allocation according to appropriate and reasonable accounting principles.

(d)   Repealed by Session Laws 1997-285, s. 3, effective January 1, 1998. (1955, c. 1279; 1957, c. 1429, s. 4; 1961, c. 1053, s. 1; 1981, c. 561, s. 8; 1983, c. 68, s. 1; 1989, c. 17, s. 10; 1997-285, ss. 2, 3; 2001-519, s. 8; 2012-56, s. 12.)

§ 53-185. Rules and regulations by Banking Commission and Commissioner.

The State Banking Commission is hereby authorized, empowered and directed to make all rules and regulations deemed by the Commission to be necessary in implementing this Article and in providing for the protection of the borrowing public and the efficient management of such licensees and to give all necessary

100

instructions to such licensees for the purpose of interpreting this Article; provided, the Commissioner is hereby authorized to make such rules and regulations and issue such orders as he deems necessary and desirable in implementing and carrying out the provisions of G.S. 53-184. And it shall be the duty of all such licensees, their officers, agents and employees, to comply fully with all such rules, regulations and instructions. When promulgated, any rule or regulation shall be forwarded by mail to each licensee at its licensed place of business at least 20 days prior to its effective date. (1955, c. 1279; 1961, c. 1053, s. 1.)

§ 53-186. Commissioner to issue subpoenas, conduct hearings, give publicity to investigations, etc.

The Commissioner of Banks shall have the power and duty to issue subpoenas including subpoenas duces tecum, and compel attendance of witnesses, administer oaths, conduct hearings and transcribe testimony in making the investigations and conducting the hearings provided for herein or in the other discharge of his duties, and to give such publicity to his investigations and findings as he may deem best for the public interest. (1957, c. 1429, s. 5; 1961, c. 1053, s. 1.)

§ 53-187. Injunctive powers; receivers.

Whenever the Commissioner has reasonable cause to believe that any person is violating or is threatening to violate any provision of this Article, he may in addition to all actions provided for in this Article, and without prejudice thereto, enter an order requiring such person to desist or to refrain from such violation; and an action may be brought in the name of the Commissioner on the relation of the State of North Carolina to enjoin such person from engaging in or continuing such violation or from doing any act or acts in furtherance thereof. In any such action an order or judgment may be entered awarding such preliminary or final injunction as may be deemed proper. In addition to all other means provided by law for the enforcement of a restraining order or injunction, the court in which such action is brought shall have power and jurisdiction to impound, and to appoint a receiver for the property and business of the defendant, including books, papers, documents and records pertaining thereto or so much thereof as the court may deem reasonably necessary to prevent violations of this Article through or by means of the use of said property and business. Such receiver, when appointed and qualified, shall have such powers and duties as to custody, collection, administration, winding up, and liquidation of such property and business as shall from time to time be conferred upon him by the court. (1957, c. 1429, s. 6; 1961, c. 1053, s. 1.)

§ 53-188. Review of regulations, order or act of Commission or Commissioner.

The Commission may review any rule, regulation, order or act of the Commissioner done pursuant to or with respect to the provisions of this Article. Any person aggrieved by any such rule, regulation, order or act may appeal, pursuant to G.S. 53C-2-6(b), to the Commission for review upon giving notice in writing within 20 days after such rule, regulation, order or act complained of is adopted, issued or done. Notwithstanding any other provision of law to the contrary, any aggrieved party to a decision of the Commission shall be entitled to petition for judicial review pursuant to G.S. 53C-2-6(b). (1957, c. 1429, s. 6; 1961, c. 1053, s. 1; 1973, c. 1331, s. 3; 1987, c. 827, s. 13; 1995, c. 129, s. 29; 2009-57, s. 2; 2012-56, s. 13.)

§ 53-189. Insurance.

(a)   Credit life, credit accident and health, credit unemployment, and credit property insurance may be written in accordance with the provisions of Article 57 of Chapter 58 of the General Statutes.

(b)   The premium or cost of credit life, credit accident and health, credit unemployment, or credit property insurance, when written by or through any lender or other creditor, its affiliate, associate or subsidiary shall not be deemed as interest or charges or consideration or an amount in excess of permitted charges in connection with the loan or credit transaction and any gain or advantage to any lender or other creditor, its affiliate, associate or subsidiary, arising out of the premium or commission or dividend from the sale or provision of such insurance shall not be deemed a violation of any other law, general or special, civil or criminal, of this State, or of any rule, regulation or order issued by any regulatory authority of this State. (1961, c. 1053, s. 1; 1969, c. 1303, s. 25; 1975, c. 660, s. 2; 1981, c. 759, s. 10; c. 876; 1987, c. 826, s. 10; 1993, c. 226, s. 14.)

§ 53-190. Loans made elsewhere.

(a)   No loan contract made outside this State in the amount or of the value of ten thousand dollars ($10,000) or less, for which greater consideration or charges than are authorized by G.S. 53-173 and G.S. 53-176 of this Article have been charged, contracted for, or received, shall be enforced in this State. Provided, the foregoing shall not apply to loan contracts in which all contractual activities, including solicitation, discussion, negotiation, offer, acceptance, signing of documents, and delivery and receipt of funds, occur entirely outside North Carolina.

(b)   If any lender or agent of a lender who makes loan contracts outside this State in the amount or of the value of ten thousand dollars ($10,000) or less, comes into this State to solicit or otherwise conduct activities in regard to such loan contracts, then such lender shall be subject to the requirements of this Article.

(c)   No lender licensed to do business under this Article may collect, or cause to be collected, any loan made by a lender in another state to a borrower, who was a legal resident of North Carolina at the time the loan was made. The purchase of a loan account shall not alter this prohibition. (1961, c. 1053, s. 1; 1967, c. 769, s. 2; 1969, c. 1303, s. 13; 1973, c. 1042, s. 8; 1979, c. 706, s. 2; 1989, c. 17, s. 11.)

§ 53-191. Businesses exempted.

Nothing in this Article shall be construed to apply to any person, firm or corporation doing business under the authority of any law of this State or of the United States relating to banks, trust companies, savings and loan associations, cooperative credit unions, agricultural credit corporations or associations organized under the laws of North Carolina, production credit associations organized under the act of Congress known as the Farm Credit Act of 1933, pawnbrokers lending or advancing money on specific articles of personal property, industrial banks, the business of negotiating loans on real estate as defined in G.S. 105-41, nor to installment paper dealers as defined in G.S. 105-83 other than persons, firms and corporations engaged in the business of accepting fees for endorsing or otherwise securing loans or contracts for repayment of loans. (1955, c. 1279; 1957, c. 1429, s. 8; 1961, c. 1053, s. 1; 1969, c. 1303, s. 26.)

Article 16.

Money Transmitters Act.

§§ 53-192 through 53-208: Repealed by Session Laws 2001-443, s. 1, effective November 1, 2001, and applicable to contracts entered into on or after that date.

Article 16A.

Money Transmitters Act.

§ 53-208.1. Citation of Article.

This Article shall be known and cited as the "Money Transmitters Act". (2001-443, s. 2.)

§ 53-208.2. Definitions.

(a)   Unless otherwise provided in this Article, or when the context clearly indicates that a different meaning is intended, the following definitions apply in this Article:

(1)   Applicant. - A person filing an application for a license under this Article.

(2)   Authorized delegate. - An entity designated by the licensee under the provisions of this Article to sell or issue payment instruments or stored value or engage in the business of transmitting money on behalf of a licensee.

(3)   Commissioner. - The Commissioner of Banks of the State of North Carolina.

(4)   Control. - Ownership of, or the power to vote, ten percent (10%) or more of the outstanding voting securities of a licensee or controlling person. For purposes of determining the percentage of a licensee controlled by any person, there shall be aggregated with the person's interest the interest of any other person controlled by the person or by any spouse, parent, or child of the person.

(5)   Controlling person. - Any person in control of a licensee.

104

(6)   Electronic instrument. - A card or other tangible object for the transmission or payment of money or monetary value which contains a microprocessor chip, magnetic strip, or other means for the storage of information that is prefunded and for which the value is decremented upon each use. The term does not include a card or other tangible object that is redeemable by the issuer in goods or services.

(7)   Executive officer. - The licensee's president, chair of the executive committee, senior officer responsible for the licensee's business, chief financial officer, and any other person who performs similar functions.

(8)   Key shareholder. - Any person, or group of persons acting in concert, who is the owner of ten percent (10%) or more of any voting class of an applicant's stock.

(9)   Licensee. - A person licensed under this Article.

(10)   Material litigation. - Any litigation that, according to generally accepted accounting principles, is deemed significant to an applicant's or licensee's financial health and would be required to be referenced in that entity's annual audited financial statements, report to shareholders, or similar documents.

(11)   Monetary transmission. - The term means either of the following:

a.   The sale or issuance of payment instruments or stored value.

b.   The act of engaging in the business of receiving money or monetary value for transmission within the United States or to locations abroad by any and all means, including payment instrument, wire, facsimile, or electronic transfer.

(12)   Monetary value. - A medium of exchange, whether or not redeemable in money.

(13)   Outstanding payment instrument. - Any payment instrument issued by the licensee which has been sold in the United States directly by the licensee or any payment instrument issued by the licensee which has been sold by an authorized delegate of the licensee in the United States, which has been reported to the licensee as having been sold and which has not yet been paid by or for the licensee.

(14)   Payment instrument. - Any electronic or written check, draft, money order, traveler's check, or other electronic or written instrument or order for the transmission or payment of money or monetary value, whether or not the instrument is negotiable. The term does not include a credit card voucher, letter of credit, or any other instrument that is redeemable by the issuer in goods or services.

(15)   Permissible investments. - One or more of the following:

a.   Cash.

b.   Certificates of deposit or other debt obligations of a financial institution, either domestic or foreign.

c.   Bills of exchange or time drafts drawn on and accepted by a commercial bank, otherwise known as bankers' acceptances, which are eligible for purchase by member banks of the Federal Reserve System.

d.   Any investment bearing a rating of one of the three highest grades as defined by a nationally recognized organization that rates securities.

e.   Investment securities that are obligations of the United States, its agencies, or instrumentalities or obligations that are guaranteed fully as to principal and interest of the United States or any obligations of any state, municipality, or any political subdivision thereof.

f.   Shares in a money market mutual fund, interest-bearing bills or notes or bonds, debentures, or preferred stock traded on any national securities exchange or on a national over-the-counter market, or mutual funds primarily composed of such securities or a fund composed of one or more permissible investments as set forth herein.

g.   Any demand borrowing agreement or agreements made to a corporation or a subsidiary of a corporation whose capital stock is listed on a national exchange.

h.   Receivables due to a licensee from its authorized delegates pursuant to a contract described in G.S. 53-208.19, which are not past due or doubtful of collection.

i.   Any other investments or security device approved by the Commissioner.

(16)   Person. - Any individual, partnership, association, joint-stock association, trust, or corporation.

(17)   Remit. - To do one or more of the following:

a.   Make direct payment of the funds to the licensee or its representatives authorized to receive those funds.

b.   Deposit the funds in a bank, credit union, or savings and loan association or other similar financial institution in an account specified by the licensee.

(18)   Stored value. - Monetary value that is evidenced by an electronic record. (2001-443, s. 2.)

§ 53-208.3. License required.

(a)   On or after October 1, 2001, no person except those exempt pursuant to G.S. 53-208.4 shall engage in the business of money transmission in this State without a license as provided in this Article.

(b)   A licensee may conduct its business in this State at one or more locations, directly or indirectly owned, or through one or more authorized delegates, or both, pursuant to the single license granted to the licensee.

(c)   For the purposes of this Article, a person is considered to be engaged in the business of money transmission in this State if that person makes available, from a location inside or outside of this State, an Internet website North Carolina citizens may access in order to enter into those transactions by electronic means. (2001-443, s. 2.)

§ 53-208.4. Exemptions.

(a)   This Article shall not apply to any of the following:

(1)   The United States or any department, agency, or instrumentality thereof.

(2)   The United States Postal Service.

(3)   The State or any political subdivisions thereof.

(4)   Banks, credit unions, savings and loan associations, savings banks, or mutual banks organized under the laws of any state or the United States.

(5)   A person registered as a securities broker-dealer under federal or state securities laws to the extent of its operation as a broker-dealer.

(6)   The provision of electronic transfer of government benefits for any federal, state, or county governmental agency as defined in Federal Reserve Board Regulation E, by a contractor for and on behalf of the United States or any department, agency, or instrumentality thereof, or any state or any political subdivisions thereof.

(b)   Authorized delegates of a licensee, acting within the scope of authority conferred by a written contract as described in G.S. 53-208.19 shall not be required to obtain a license pursuant to this Article. (2001-443, s. 2.)

§ 53-208.5. License qualifications.

(a)   Each licensee shall have at all times a net worth of not less than one hundred thousand dollars ($100,000) calculated in accordance with generally accepted accounting principles. Licensees engaging in money transmission at more than one location or through authorized delegates shall have an additional net worth of ten thousand dollars ($10,000) per location in this State, as applicable, to a maximum of five hundred thousand dollars ($500,000). Licensees with neither locations nor authorized delegates in this State shall have an additional net worth as established by the Commissioner in an amount not to exceed a maximum of five hundred thousand dollars ($500,000).

(b)   Every corporate applicant, at the time of filing of an application for license under this Article and at all times after a license is issued, shall be in good standing in the state of its incorporation and, if required by the North Carolina Business Corporations Act, Chapter 55 of the General Statutes, shall be registered or qualified to do business in this State. All noncorporate applicants shall, at the time of the filing of an application for a license under this Article and at all times after a license is issued, be registered or qualified to do business in the State as required by law. (2001-443, s. 2.)

108

§ 53-208.6. Permissible investments and statutory trust.

(a)   Each licensee under this Article shall possess at all times unencumbered permissible investments having an aggregate market value, calculated in accordance with generally accepted accounting principles, of not less than the aggregate face amount of all outstanding payment instruments and stored value obligations issued or sold. This requirement may be waived by the Commissioner if the dollar volume of a licensee's outstanding payment instruments and stored value do not exceed the bond or other security devices posted by the licensee pursuant to G.S. 53-208.8.

(b)   Permissible investments, even if commingled with other assets of the licensee, shall be deemed by operation of law to be held in trust for the benefit of the purchasers and holders of the licensee's outstanding payment instruments and stored value obligations in the event of the bankruptcy of the licensee. (2001-443, s. 2.)

§ 53-208.7. License application.

(a)   Each application for a license under this Article shall be made in writing, under oath, and in a form prescribed by the Commissioner. For all applicants, each application shall contain:

(1)   The exact name of the applicant, the applicant's principal address, any assumed or trade name used by the applicant in the conduct of its business, and the location of the applicant's business records.

(2)   The history of the applicant's material civil litigation for a 10-year period prior to the date of the application and a record of any criminal convictions.

(3)   A description of the activities conducted by the applicant and a history of operations.

(4)   A description of the business activities in which the applicant seeks to be engaged in the State.

(5)   A list identifying the applicant's proposed authorized delegates in the State, if any, at the time of the filing of the license application.

(6)   A sample authorized delegate contract, if applicable.

(7)   A sample form of payment instrument, if applicable, which bears the name and address or telephone number of the issuer clearly printed on the payment instrument.

(8)   The location or locations at which the applicant and its authorized delegates, if any, propose to conduct the licensed activities in the State.

(9)   The name and address of the clearing bank or banks on which the applicant's payment instruments will be drawn or through which the payment instruments will be payable.

(b)   If the applicant is a corporation, the applicant shall also provide:

(1)   The date of the applicant's incorporation and state of incorporation.

(2)   A certificate of good standing from the state in which the applicant was incorporated.

(3)   A certificate of authority from the Secretary of State to conduct business in this State, if required by the North Carolina Business Corporations Act, Chapter 55 of the General Statutes.

(4)   A description of the corporate structure of the applicant, including the identity of any parent or subsidiary of the applicant and the disclosure of whether any parent or subsidiary is publicly traded on any stock exchange.

(5)   The name, business and residence address, and employment history for the past five years of the applicant's executive officers and the officers or managers who will be in charge of the applicant's activities to be licensed pursuant to this Article.

(6)   The name, business and residence address, and employment history for the period five years prior to the date of the application of any key shareholder of the applicant.

(7)   The history of material civil litigation for a 10-year period prior to the date of the application and a record of any criminal conviction for every executive officer or key shareholder.

110

(8)   A copy of the applicant's most recent audited financial statement, including the balance sheet, statement of income or loss, statement of changes in shareholder equity, and statement of changes in financial position and, if available, the applicant's audited financial statements for the immediately preceding two-year period. However, if the applicant is a wholly owned subsidiary of another corporation, the applicant may submit either the parent corporation's consolidated audited financial statements for the current year and for the immediately preceding two-year period or the parent corporation's Form 10K reports filed with the United States Securities and Exchange Commission for the prior three years in lieu of the applicant's financial statements. If the applicant is a wholly owned subsidiary of a corporation having its principal place of business outside the United States, similar documentation filed with the parent corporation's non-United States regulator may be submitted to satisfy this provision.

(9)   Copies of all filings, if any, made by the applicant with the United States Securities and Exchange Commission, or with a similar regulator in a country other than the United States, within the year preceding the date of filing of the application.

(c)   If the applicant is not a corporation, the applicant shall also provide:

(1)   The name, business and residence address, personal financial statement, and employment history, for the past five years, of each principal of the applicant and the name, business and residence address, and employment history for the past five years of any other person or persons who will be in charge of the applicant's activities to be licensed pursuant to this Article.

(2)   The place and date of the applicant's registration or qualification to do business in this State.

(3)   The history of material civil litigation for a 10-year period prior to the date of the application and a record of any criminal conviction for each individual having an ownership interest in the applicant and each individual who exercises supervisory responsibility with respect to the applicant's activities.

(4)   Copies of the applicant's audited financial statements, including the balance sheet, statement of income or loss, and statement of changes in financial position, for the current year and, if available, for the immediately preceding two-year period.

The Commissioner is authorized, for good cause shown, to waive any requirements of this section with respect to any license application or to permit a license applicant to submit substituted information in its license application in lieu of the information required by this section. (2001-443, s. 2.)

§ 53-208.8. Surety bond.

(a)   Each application shall be accompanied by a surety bond acceptable to the Commissioner in the amount of one hundred fifty thousand dollars ($150,000). If the applicant proposes to engage in business under this Article at more than one location, through authorized delegates or otherwise, then the amount of the security bond will be increased by five thousand dollars ($5,000) per location, up to a maximum of two hundred fifty thousand dollars ($250,000). In the case of an applicant which engages in business under this Article, but has no locations or authorized delegates in this State, the amount of the security bond may be increased at the Commissioner's discretion to a maximum of two hundred fifty thousand dollars ($250,000). The surety bond shall be in a form satisfactory to the Commissioner and shall run to the State for the benefit of any claimants against the licensee to secure the faithful performance of the obligations of the licensee with respect to the receipt, handling, transmission, and payment of money or monetary value in connection with the sale and issuance of payment instruments, stored value, or transmission of money. The aggregate liability of the surety in no event shall exceed the principal sum of the bond. Claimants against the licensee may themselves bring suit directly on the security bond, or the Commissioner may bring suit on behalf of claimants, either in one action or in successive actions.

(b)   In lieu of a surety bond, the licensee may deposit with the Commissioner, or with any bank in this State designated by the licensee and approved by the Commissioner, to an aggregate amount, based upon principal amount or market value, whichever is lower, of not less than the amount of the surety bond or portion thereof, the following:

(1)   Unencumbered cash.

(2)   Unencumbered interest-bearing bonds.

(3)   Unencumbered notes.

(4)   Unencumbered debentures.

(5)   Unencumbered obligations of the United States or any agency or instrumentality thereof, or guaranteed by the United States.

(6)   Unencumbered obligations of this State or of any political subdivision of the State, or guaranteed by this State.

The securities or cash shall be deposited as aforesaid and held to secure the same obligations as would the surety bond, but the depositor shall be entitled to receive all interest and dividends thereon, shall have the right, with the approval of the Commissioner, to substitute other securities for those deposited, and shall be required to do so on written order of the Commissioner made for good cause shown.

(c)   The surety bond shall remain in effect until cancellation, which may occur only after 90 days' written notice to the Commissioner. Cancellation shall not affect any liability incurred or accrued during that period.

(d)   The surety bond shall remain in place for no longer than five years after the licensee ceases money transmission operations in the State. However, notwithstanding this provision, the Commissioner may permit the surety bond to be reduced or eliminated prior to that time to the extent that the amount of the licensee's outstanding payment instruments, stored value obligations, and money transmitted in this State is reduced.

(e)   The surety bond proceeds and any cash or other collateral posted as security by a licensee shall be deemed by operation of law to be held in trust for the benefit of the purchasers and holders of the licensee's outstanding payment instruments, stored value obligations, and money transmissions in the event of the bankruptcy of the licensee. (2001-443, s. 2.)

§ 53-208.9. Fees.

(a)   Investigation and License Fees. - Each application for a license shall be accompanied by a nonrefundable investigation fee of five hundred dollars ($500.00), together with the initial license fee of one thousand dollars ($1,000) plus ten dollars ($10.00) per location within this State at which a money transmission business is to be conducted by the applicant or an authorized delegate.

113

(b)   Annual License Fee. - On or before December 31 of each year, each licensee under this Article shall pay to the Commissioner a license fee in the amount of one thousand dollars ($1,000) plus ten dollars ($10.00) per location in this State at which the licensee or an authorized delegate is conducting a money transmitter business.

(c)   Location Fee. - Notwithstanding the number of locations within this State at which a licensee or authorized delegate conducts a money transmitter business, the per location fee provided in subsections (a) and (b) of this section shall not exceed five thousand dollars ($5,000) per licensee per year. The per year location fee shall be based on the number of locations set forth in the annual report required by G.S. 53-208.11. (2001-443, s. 2.)

§ 53-208.10. Issuance of license.

(a)   Upon the filing of a complete application, the Commissioner shall investigate the financial condition and responsibility, financial and business experience, and the character and general fitness of the applicant. The Commissioner may conduct an on-site investigation of the applicant, the reasonable cost of which shall be borne by the applicant. If the Commissioner finds that the applicant's business will be conducted honestly, fairly, and in a manner commanding the confidence and trust of the community and that the applicant has fulfilled the requirements imposed by this Article and has paid the required license fee, the Commissioner shall issue a license to the applicant authorizing the applicant to engage in the licensed activities in this State. If these requirements have not been met, the Commissioner shall deny the application in a written statement setting forth the reasons for the denial.

(b)   The Commissioner shall approve or deny every application for an original license within 120 days from the date a complete application is submitted, which period may be extended by the written consent of the applicant. The Commissioner shall notify the applicant of the date when the application is deemed complete. In the absence of approval or denial of the application, or consent to the extension of the 120-day period, the application is deemed approved and the Commissioner shall issue the license effective as of the first day after the 120-day or extended period has elapsed.

(c)   No license shall be denied except on 10 days' notice to the applicant. Any applicant aggrieved by a denial issued by the Commissioner under this section may at any time within five days from the date of receipt of written notice of the denial, contest the denial by serving a written demand for a hearing on the Commissioner. The serving of a written demand on the Commissioner shall automatically stay the denial until a ruling is issued. The Commissioner shall set a date for a hearing not later than 30 days after service of the response, unless a later date is set with the consent of the applicant. The hearing authorized by this subsection shall be an informal hearing. (2001-443, s. 2.)

§ 53-208.11. Renewal of license and annual report.

(a)   The annual license fee shall be accompanied by a report, in a form prescribed by the Commissioner, to be filed by the licensee on or before December 31 of each year. The licensee shall include all of the following in its annual renewal report:

(1)   A copy of its most recent audited consolidated annual financial statement, including balance sheet, statement of income or loss, statement of changes in shareholder's equity, and statement of changes in financial position, or, in the case of a licensee that is a wholly owned subsidiary of another corporation, the consolidated audited annual financial statement of the parent corporation may be filed in lieu of the licensee's audited financial statement.

(2)   For the most recent quarter for which data is available prior to the date of the filing of the renewal application, but in no event more than 120 days prior to the renewal date, the licensee shall provide the number of payment instruments sold by the licensee in the State, the dollar amount of those instruments, and the dollar amount of those instruments currently outstanding.

(3)   Any material changes to any of the information submitted by the licensee on its original application which have not previously been reported to the Commissioner on any other report required to be filed under this Article.

(4)   A list of the licensee's permissible investments.

(5)   A list of the locations within this State at which business regulated by this Article is being conducted by either the licensee or its authorized delegates, except for entities exempt under G.S. 53-208.4.

(b)   A licensee that has not filed a renewal report or paid its annual license fee by the renewal filing deadline and has not been granted an extension of time to do so by the Commissioner shall be notified by the Commission, in writing,

115

that a hearing will be scheduled at which time the licensee will be required to show cause why its license should not be suspended pending compliance with these requirements. (2001-443, s. 2.)

§ 53-208.12. Quarterly reports.

A licensee shall file for each calendar quarter, no later than 60 days after the quarter has ended, a report which contains the total number of authorized delegates in this State. In addition, a licensee shall promptly provide any additional information regarding any or all of its current and prior authorized delegates requested by the Commissioner. (2001-443, s. 2; 2004-171, s. 6.)

§ 53-208.13. Extraordinary reporting requirements.

(a)   Within 15 days of the occurrence of any one of the events listed below, a licensee shall file a written report with the Commissioner describing the event and its expected impact on the licensee's activities in the State:

(1)   The filing for bankruptcy or reorganization by the licensee.

(2)   The institution of revocation or suspension proceedings against the licensee by any State or governmental authority with regard to the licensee's money transmission activities.

(3)   Any felony indictment of the licensee or any of its key officers or directors related to money transmission activities.

(4)   Any felony conviction of the licensee or any of its key officers or directors related to money transmission activities.

(b)   A licensee shall update information contained in the original application filed with the Commissioner. If the information contained in the application is or becomes inaccurate in any material respect, the licensee shall file a corrected amendment as soon as practicable, but in no event later than 30 days after the effective date of the material changes. (2001-443, s. 2.)

§ 53-208.14. Changes in control of a license.

Within 15 days of a change or acquisition of control of a licensee, the licensee shall provide notice of the event to the Commissioner in writing and in a form prescribed by the Commissioner. The notice shall be accompanied by any information, data, and records required by the Commissioner. Notwithstanding the foregoing, the Commissioner may waive this notification requirement if, in the Commissioner's discretion, the change in control does not pose any risk to the interests of the public. (2001-443, s. 2.)

§ 53-208.15. Examinations.

(a)   The Commissioner may conduct an annual on-site examination of a licensee. Should the Commissioner conclude that an on-site examination of a licensee is necessary, the licensee shall pay all reasonably incurred costs of the examination. If the Commissioner determines, based on the licensee's financial statements and past history of operations in the State, that an on-site examination is unnecessary, then the on-site examination may be waived by the Commissioner. An on-site examination may be conducted in conjunction with examinations to be performed by representatives of agencies of another state or states. The Commissioner, in lieu of an on-site examination, may accept the examination report of an agency of another state, or a report prepared by an independent accounting firm, and reports so accepted are considered for all purposes as an official report of the Commissioner. The Commissioner may examine a licensee without prior notice if the Commissioner has a reasonable basis to believe that the licensee is not in compliance with this Article.

(b)   If the Commissioner has a reasonable basis to believe that the licensee or authorized delegate is not in compliance with this Article, the Commissioner may (i) request financial data from a licensee in addition to that required under G.S. 53-208.11, or (ii) conduct an on-site examination of any authorized delegate or of any location of a licensee within this State without prior notice to the authorized delegate or licensee. When the Commissioner examines an authorized delegate's operations, the authorized delegate shall pay all reasonably incurred costs of the examination. When the Commissioner examines a licensee's location within the State, the licensee shall pay all reasonably incurred costs of the examination. (2001-443, s. 2.)

§ 53-208.16. Maintenance of records and certificate of authority.

117

(a)   Each licensee shall make, keep, and preserve the following books, accounts, and other records for a period of three years:

(1)   A record or records of each payment instrument sold.

(2)   A general ledger containing all assets, liability, capital, income, and expense accounts, which general ledger shall be posted at least monthly.

(3)   Settlement sheets received from authorized delegates.

(4)   Bank statements and bank reconciliation records.

(5)   Records of outstanding payment instruments and stored value.

(6)   Records of each payment instrument paid within the three-year period.

(7)   A list of the names and addresses of all of the licensee's authorized delegates, if any.

(b)   Maintenance of the documents required by this section in a photographic, electronic, or other similar form shall constitute compliance with this section.

(c)   Records may be maintained at a location other than within this State so long as they are made accessible to the Commissioner on seven days' written notice. (2001-443, s. 2.)

§ 53-208.17. Confidentiality of data submitted to the Commissioner.

(a)   Notwithstanding any other provision of law, all information or reports obtained by the Commissioner from an applicant, licensee, or authorized delegate, whether obtained through reports, applications, examination, audits, investigation, or otherwise, including (i) all information contained in or related to examination, investigation, operating, or condition reports prepared by, on behalf of, or for the use of the Commissioner; and (ii) financial statements, balance sheets, or authorized delegate information are confidential and may not be disclosed by the Commissioner or any officer or employee of the Commissioner. The Commissioner, however, may provide for the release of information to representatives of State or federal agencies who state in writing under oath that they will maintain the confidentiality of the information if: (i) the licensee provides consent prior to the release; or (ii) the Commissioner finds that the release is reasonably necessary for the protection of the public or in the interests of justice.

(b)   Nothing in this section shall prohibit the Commissioner from releasing to the public a list of persons licensed under this Article or aggregated financial data on those licenses. (2001-443, s. 2.)

§ 53-208.18. Suspension or revocation of licenses.

After notice and hearing, the Commissioner may suspend or revoke a license issued under this Article if the Commissioner finds any of the following:

(1)   Any fact or condition exists that, if it had existed at the time when the licensee applied for its license, would have been grounds for denying the application.

(2)   The licensee's net worth becomes inadequate and the licensee, after 10 days' written notice from the Commissioner, fails to take such steps as the Commissioner deems necessary to remedy the deficiency.

(3)   The licensee knowingly violates any material provision of this Article or any rule or order validly adopted by the Commissioner under authority of this title.

(4)   The licensee is conducting its business in an unsafe or unsound manner.

(5)   The licensee is insolvent.

(6)   The licensee has suspended payment of its obligations, has made an assignment for the benefit of its creditors, or has admitted in writing its inability to pay its debts as they become due.

(7)   The licensee has applied for an adjudication for bankruptcy, reorganization, arrangement, or other relief under any bankruptcy.

(8)   The licensee refuses to permit the Commissioner to make any examination authorized by this Article.

(9)   The licensee willfully fails to make any report required by this Article. (2001-443, s. 2.)

§ 53-208.19. Authorized delegate contracts.

Licensees desiring to conduct licensed activities through authorized delegates in this State shall authorize each delegate to operate pursuant to an express written contract, which shall provide the following:

(1)   That the licensee appoints the person as its delegate with authority to engage in money transmission on behalf of the licensee.

(2)   That neither a licensee nor an authorized delegate may authorize subdelegates without the written consent of the Commissioner.

(3)   That licensees are subject to supervision and regulation by the Commissioner.

(4)   A licensee shall issue a certificate of authority for each location at which it conducts licensed activities in this State through authorized delegates. The certificate shall be posted in public view at each location and shall state as follows: "Money transmission on behalf of (licensee) is conducted at this location pursuant to the Money Transmitters Act." (2001-443, s. 2.)

§ 53-208.20. Authorized delegate conduct.

(a)   An authorized delegate shall not make any fraudulent or false statement or misrepresentation to a licensee or to the Commissioner.

(b)   All money transmission or sale or issuance of payment instrument activities conducted by authorized delegates shall be strictly in accordance with the licensee's written procedures provided to the authorized delegates.

(c)   An authorized delegate shall remit all money owing to the licensee in accordance with the terms of the contract between the licensee and the authorized delegate. The failure of an authorized delegate to remit all money owing to a licensee within the time presented shall result in liability of the authorized delegates to the licensee for three times the licensee's actual

120

damages. The Commissioner may set, by regulation, the maximum remittance time.

(d)   An authorized delegate is deemed to consent to the Commissioner's inspection, with or without prior notice to the licensee or authorized delegate, of the books and records of the authorized delegate of the licensee when the Commissioner has a reasonable basis to believe that the licensee or authorized delegate is not in compliance with this Article.

(e)   An authorized delegate is under a duty to act only as authorized under the contract with the licensee. An authorized delegate who exceeds its authority is subject to cancellation of its contract and further disciplinary action by the Commissioner.

(f)   All funds, less fees, received by an authorized delegate of a licensee from the sale or delivery of a payment instrument or stored value issued by a licensee or received by an authorized delegate for transmission shall constitute trust funds owned by and belonging to the licensee from the time the funds are received by the authorized delegate until the time when the funds or an equivalent amount are remitted by the authorized delegate to the licensee. If an authorized delegate commingles any funds with any other funds or property owned or controlled by the authorized delegate, all commingled proceeds and other property shall be impressed with a trust in favor of the licensee in an amount equal to the amount of the proceeds due the licensee.

(g)   An authorized delegate shall report to the licensee the theft or loss of payment instruments within 24 hours from the time it knew or should have known of the theft or loss.

(h)   An authorized delegate shall prominently post the certificate of authority specified in G.S. 53-208.19 at each location at which it conducts licensed activities in this State. (2001-443, s. 2.)

§ 53-208.21. Revocation or suspension of authorized delegates.

(a)   If, after notice and a hearing, the Commissioner finds that any authorized delegate of a licensee or any director, officer, employee, or controlling person of the authorized delegate: (i) has violated any provision of this Article or of any rule or regulation or order issued under this Article; (ii) has engaged or participated in any unsafe or unsound act with respect to the

121

business of selling or issuing payment instruments of the licensee or the business of money transmission; or (iii) has made or caused to be made in any application or report filed with the Commissioner or in any proceeding before the Commissioner, any statement which was at the time and in the circumstances under which it was made, false or misleading with respect to any material fact, or has omitted to state in any application or report any material fact which is required to be stated therein, the Commissioner may issue an order suspending or barring the authorized delegate from continuing to be or becoming an authorized delegate of any licensee during the period for which the order is in effect. Upon issuance of the order, the licensee shall terminate its relationship with the authorized delegate according to the terms of the order.

(b)   Any authorized delegate to whom an order is issued under this section may apply to the Commissioner to modify or rescind the order. The Commissioner shall not grant the application unless the Commissioner finds that (i) it is in the public interest to do so, and (ii) it is reasonable to believe that the person will comply with all applicable provisions of this Article and of any regulation and order issued under this Article if and when that person is permitted to resume being an authorized delegate of a licensee. The right of any authorized delegate to whom an order is issued under this section to petition for judicial review of the order shall not be affected by the failure of the person to apply to the Commissioner to modify or rescind the order. (2001-443, s. 2.)

§ 53-208.22. Licensee liability.

A licensee's responsibility to any person for a money transmission conducted on that person's behalf by the licensee or the licensee's authorized delegate shall be limited to the amount of money transmitted or the face amount of the payment instrument purchased. (2001-443, s. 2.)

§ 53-208.22A. Disclosures of transmissions.

(a)   At the time of a monetary transmission transaction to a location outside of the United States, the licensee shall provide a receipt to the customer. The receipt shall state clearly (i) the amount of funds presented for transmission and any fee charged by the licensee and (ii) a toll-free telephone number or a local number that a customer can access at no charge to receive information about a monetary transmission.

(b)   If the rate of exchange for a monetary transmission to be paid in the currency of another country is fixed by the licensee for a transaction at the time the monetary transmission is initiated, the receipt shall also state:

(1)   The rate of exchange for that transaction.

(2)   The amount to be paid in the foreign currency.

(3)   The period, if any, in which the payment shall be made in order to qualify for the fixed rate of exchange.

(c)   If the rate of exchange for a monetary transmission to be paid in the currency of another country is not fixed at the time the monetary transmission is initiated, the receipt shall also disclose that the rate of exchange for the transaction will be set at the time the recipient of the monetary transmission receives the funds in the foreign country.

(d)   The licensee shall provide the disclosures required by this section to the customer before completing the transaction if the customer requests the disclosures. (2005-104, s. 1.)

§ 53-208.23. Hearings; procedures.

Except as provided by G.S 53-208.10(c), hearings conducted pursuant to this Article shall proceed in accordance with Article 3A of Chapter 150B of the General Statutes. (2001-443, s. 2.)

§ 53-208.24. Civil penalties.

(a)   If, after notice and hearing, the Commissioner finds that a person has intentionally violated this Article or a rule adopted under this Article, the Commissioner may order the person to pay to the Commissioner a civil penalty in an amount specified by the Commissioner, not to exceed one thousand dollars ($1,000) for each violation or, in the case of a continuing violation, one thousand dollars ($1,000) for each day that the violation continues. No proceeding shall be initiated and no penalty shall be assessed pursuant to this section until after the person has been notified in writing of the nature of the violation and has been afforded a reasonable period of time, as set forth in the notice, to correct the violation and has failed to do so.

(b)   The Commissioner, in the exercise of the Commissioner's reasonable judgment, may compromise, settle, and collect civil penalties with any person for violations of any provision of this Article, or of any rule, regulation, or order issued or promulgated to this Article. (2001-443, s. 2.)

§ 53-208.25. Enforcement.

(a)   If it appears to the Commissioner that any person has committed or is about to commit a violation of any provision of this Article or of any rule or order of the Commissioner, the Commissioner may apply to the Wake County Superior Court for an order enjoining the person from violating or continuing to violate this Article or any rule, regulation, or order and for injunctive or such other relief as the nature of the case may require.

(b)   The Commissioner may enter into consent orders at any time with any person to resolve any matter arising under this Article. A consent order shall be signed by the person to whom it is issued or a duly authorized representative and shall indicate agreement to the terms contained therein. A consent order need not constitute an admission by any person that any provision of this Article, or any rule, regulation, or order promulgated or issued thereunder has been violated, nor need it constitute a finding by the Commissioner that the person has violated any provision of this Article or any rule, regulation, or order promulgated or issued thereunder.

(c)   Notwithstanding the issuance of a consent order, the Commissioner may seek civil or criminal penalties or compromise civil penalties concerning matters encompassed by the consent order, unless the consent order by its terms expressly precludes the Commissioner from so doing. (2001-443, s. 2.)

§ 53-208.26. Criminal penalties.

(a)   Any person who knowingly and willfully violates any provision of this Article for which a penalty is not specifically provided is guilty of a Class 1 misdemeanor.

(b)   Any person who knowingly and willfully makes a material, false statement in any document filed or required to be filed under this Article with the intent to deceive the recipient of the document is guilty of a Class 1 misdemeanor.

124

(c)   Any person who knowingly and willfully engages in the business of money transmission without a license as provided herein shall be guilty of a Class 1 misdemeanor. (2001-443, s. 2.)

§ 53-208.27. Rules.

(a)   The Banking Commission may adopt rules necessary to implement this Article.

(b)   The Banking Commission may review any rule, regulation, order, or act of the Commissioner done pursuant to or with respect to the provisions of this Article. Any person aggrieved by any such rule, regulation, order, or act may appeal, pursuant to G.S. 53C-2-6(b), to the Commission for review upon providing notice in writing within 20 days after any rule, regulation, order, or act complained of is adopted, issued, or done. Notwithstanding any other provision of law, any aggrieved party to a decision of the Banking Commission shall be entitled to petition for judicial review pursuant to G.S. 53C-2-6(b). (2001-443, s. 2; 2009-57, s. 3; 2012-56, s. 14.)

§ 53-208.28. Severability.

Should any provision, sentence, clause, section, or part of this Article for any reason be held unconstitutional, illegal, or invalid, such unconstitutionality, illegality, or invalidity shall not affect or impair any of the remaining provisions, sentences, clauses, sections, or part of this Article. (2001-443, s. 2.)

§ 53-208.29. Appointment of Secretary of State as agent for service of process.

(a)   Any licensee, authorized delegate, or other person who knowingly engages in business activities that are regulated under this Article, with or without filing an application, is deemed to have done both of the following:

(1)   Consented to the jurisdiction of the courts of this State for all actions arising under this Article; and

(2)   Appointed the Secretary of State as such person's agent for the purpose of accepting service of process in any action, suit, or proceeding that may arise under this Article.

(b)   Within three business days after service of process upon the Secretary of State, the Secretary shall transmit by certified mail copies of all lawful process accepted by the Secretary as an agent of that person at its last known address. Service of process shall be considered complete three business days after the Commissioner deposits copies of the documents in the United States mail. (2001-443, s. 2.)

§ 53-208.30. Transition.

Any person who holds in good standing a money transmitters license issued by the Commissioner of Banks on November 1, 2001 may continue to engage in such business subject to the renewal requirements of G.S. 53-208.11, and upon renewal, proof that the licensee meets the net worth requirements of G.S. 53-208.5(a), and the bonding or other security requirements of G.S. 53-208.8. (2001-443, s. 2.)

Article 17.

North Carolina Reciprocal Interstate Banking Act.

§ 53-209. Title.

This Article shall be known and may be cited as the North Carolina Reciprocal Interstate Banking Act. (1983 (Reg. Sess., 1984), c. 1113, s. 1; 1993, c. 175, s. 7; 1993 (Reg. Sess., 1994), c. 599, s. 1.)

§ 53-210. Definitions.

Notwithstanding any other section of this Chapter, for the purposes of this Article:

(1)   "Acquire" means:

a.   The merger or consolidation of one bank holding company with another bank holding company;

b.   The acquisition by a bank holding company of direct or indirect ownership or control of voting shares of another bank holding company or a

126

bank, if, after such acquisition, the bank holding company making the acquisition will directly or indirectly own or control more than five percent (5%) of any class of voting shares of the other bank holding company or the bank;

c.   The direct or indirect acquisition by a bank holding company of all or substantially all of the assets of another bank holding company or of a bank; or

d.   Any other action that would result in direct or indirect control by a bank holding company of another bank holding company or a bank.

(2)   "Bank" has the meaning set forth in Section 2(c) of the Bank Holding Company Act of 1956 as amended (12 U.S.C. 1841(c)).

(3)   "Banking office" means the principal office of a bank, any branch of a bank, any limited service facility of a bank or any other office at which a bank accepts deposits: Provided, however, that "banking office" shall not mean:

a.   Unmanned automatic teller machines, point of sale terminals or other similar unmanned electronic banking facilities at which deposits may be accepted;

b.   Offices located outside the United States; or

c.   Loan production offices, representative offices or other offices at which deposits are not accepted.

(4)   "Bank holding company" has the meaning set forth in Section 2(a)(1) of the Bank Holding Company Act of 1956 as amended (12 U.S.C. 1841(a)(1)).

(5)   "Commissioner" means the Commissioner of Banks of this State.

(6)   "Control" has the meaning set forth in Section 2(a)(2) of the Bank Holding Company Act of 1956 as amended (12 U.S.C. 1841(a)(2)).

(7)   "Deposits" means all demand, time, and savings deposits, without regard to the location of the depositor. For purposes of this Article, determination of deposits shall be made with reference to the most recent available regulatory reports of condition or similar reports made by or to state and federal regulatory authorities.

(8)   "North Carolina bank" means a bank that:

127

a.   Is organized under the laws of this State or of the United States; and

b.   Has banking offices located only in this State.

(9)   "North Carolina bank holding company" means a bank holding company:

a.   That has its principal place of business in this State; and

b.   Repealed by Session Laws 1993, c. 175, s. 8.

c.   That is not controlled by a bank holding company other than a North Carolina bank holding company.

(9a)   "Out-of-state bank holding company" means a bank holding company that has its principal place of business in a state other than North Carolina.

(10)   "Principal place of business" of a bank holding company means the state in which the total deposits held by the banking offices of the bank holding company's bank subsidiaries were the largest on July 1, 1966, or the date on which the company became a bank holding company, whichever is later.

(11)   through (13) Repealed by Session Laws 1993, c. 175, s. 8.

(14)   "State" means any state of the United States or the District of Columbia.

(15)   "Subsidiary" has the meaning set forth in Section 2(d) of the Bank Holding Company Act of 1956 as amended (12 U.S.C. 1841(d)). (1983 (Reg. Sess., 1984), c. 1113, s. 1; 1985 (Reg. Sess., 1986), c. 862; 1987 (Reg. Sess., 1988), c. 899; 1993, c. 175, ss. 1, 8; 1993 (Reg. Sess., 1994), c. 599, s. 1.)

§ 53-211. Acquisitions by out-of-state bank holding companies.

(a)   An out-of-state bank holding company that does not have a North Carolina bank subsidiary, other than a North Carolina bank subsidiary that was acquired in a transaction involving assistance by the Federal Deposit Insurance Corporation or in the regular course of securing or collecting a debt previously contracted in good faith, as provided in Section 3(a) of the Bank Holding Company Act of 1956 as amended (12 U.S.C. 1842(a)), may acquire a North Carolina bank holding company or a North Carolina bank with the approval of the Commissioner. The out-of-state bank holding company shall submit to the Commissioner an application for approval of such acquisition, which application shall be approved only if the Commissioner determines that the laws of the state in which the out-of-state bank holding company making the acquisition has its principal place of business permit North Carolina bank holding companies to acquire banks and bank holding companies in that state. Additionally, the Commissioner shall make the acquisition subject to any conditions, restrictions, requirements, or other limitations that would apply to the acquisition by a North Carolina bank holding company of a bank or bank holding company in the state where the out-of-state bank holding company making the acquisition has its principal place of business but that would not apply to the acquisition of a bank or bank holding company in such state by a bank holding company all of the subsidiaries of which are located in that state. The applicant shall submit an application fee of five thousand dollars ($5,000) plus two thousand dollars ($2,000) for each North Carolina bank or bank holding company being acquired.

(b)   An out-of-state bank holding company that has a North Carolina bank subsidiary (other than a North Carolina bank subsidiary that was acquired in a transaction involving assistance by the Federal Deposit Insurance Corporation or in the regular course of securing or collecting a debt previously contracted in good faith, as provided in Section 3(a) of the Bank Holding Company Act of 1956 as amended (12 U.S.C. 1842(a)), may acquire any North Carolina bank or North Carolina bank holding company with the approval of the Commissioner. The out-of-state bank holding company shall submit to the Commissioner an application for approval of such acquisition, which application shall be approved only if the Commissioner makes the acquisition subject to any conditions, restrictions, requirements or other limitations that would apply to the acquisition by a North Carolina bank holding company of a bank or bank holding company in the state where the out-of-state bank holding company making the acquisition has its principal place of business but that would not apply to the acquisition of a bank or bank holding company in such state by a bank holding company all the bank subsidiaries of which are located in that state.

(c)   The Commissioner shall rule on any application submitted under this section not later than 90 days following the date of submission of a complete application. If the Commissioner fails to rule on the application within the requisite 90-day period, the failure to rule shall be deemed a final decision of the Commissioner approving the application.

(d)   The Commissioner, within 30 days of receiving the complete application for acquisition, shall publish notice of the intent of an out-of-state bank holding company to acquire a North Carolina bank or North Carolina bank holding company under subsection (a) or (b) of this section. The notice shall be published in newspapers in the communities in which the principal offices of the North Carolina bank or North Carolina bank holding company and of the out-of-state bank holding company are located and, if there are no newspapers published in such communities, then in newspapers having a general circulation in such communities. Notwithstanding any other provision of this section, the application for acquisition shall not be approved until the requirement for publication has been met. (1983 (Reg. Sess., 1984), c. 1113, s. 1; 1987 (Reg. Sess., 1988), c. 898, ss. 1, 2; 1989, c. 9, s. 2, c. 471; 1993, c. 175, ss. 2, 9; 1993 (Reg. Sess., 1994), c. 599, ss. 1, 3.)

§ 53-212: Repealed by Session Laws 1993, c. 175, s. 10, as amended by Session Laws 1993 (Regular Session, 1994), c. 599, s. 1.

§ 53-212.1. Bank agent for deposit institution affiliate.

A bank may act as the agent of any depository institution affiliate in receiving deposits, renewing time deposits, closing loans, servicing loans, and receiving payments on loans and other obligations, without being deemed a branch of such affiliate, in accordance with Section 101(d) of the Reigle-Neal Interstate Banking and Branching Efficiency Act of 1994. An affiliate for the purposes of this section shall include (i) an affiliate as defined in Section 2(k) of the Bank Holding Company Act of 1956, as amended (12 U.S.C. § 1841(k)), and (ii) an affiliate as defined in Section 23A(b)(1) of the Federal Reserve Act, as amended (12 U.S.C. § 371c(b)(1)), but without regard to whether the bank or the affiliate is a member of the Federal Reserve System. (1995 (Reg. Sess., 1996), c. 557, s. 1; 1997-241, s. 2.1; 1997-456, s. 39.)

§ 53-213. Prohibitions.

(a)   Except as expressly permitted by this Article or by federal law, no out-of-state bank holding company shall acquire a North Carolina bank holding company or a North Carolina bank.

(b)   Repealed by Session Laws 1993, c. 175, s. 11. (1983 (Reg. Sess., 1984), c. 1113, s. 1; 1993, c. 175, s. 11; 1993 (Reg. Sess., 1994), c. 599, s. 1.)

§ 53-214. Applicable laws, rules and regulations.

(a)   Any North Carolina bank that is controlled by a bank holding company that is not a North Carolina bank holding company shall be subject to all laws of this State and all rules and regulations under such laws that are applicable to North Carolina banks that are controlled by North Carolina bank holding companies.

(b)   The State Banking Commission shall adopt rules to implement and effectuate the provisions of this Article. (1983 (Reg. Sess., 1984), c. 1113, s. 1; 1993, c. 175, s. 4; 1993 (Reg. Sess., 1994), c. 599, s. 2.)

§ 53-215. Appeal of Commissioner's decision.

Any aggrieved party in a proceeding under G.S. 53-211, 53C-10-102, or 53C-10-201 may, within 20 days after final decision of the Commissioner, appeal in writing any decision to the State Banking Commission. An appeal under this section shall be made pursuant to G.S. 53C-2-6. Notwithstanding any other provision of law, any aggrieved party to a decision of the State Banking Commission shall be entitled to petition for judicial review pursuant to G.S. 53C-2-6. (1983 (Reg. Sess., 1984), c. 1113, s. 1; 1985, c. 683, s. 3; 1993, c. 175, ss. 5, 12; 1993 (Reg. Sess., 1994), c. 599, s. 1; 2009-57, s. 4; 2012-56, s. 15.)

§ 53-216. Periodic reports; interstate agreements.

The Commissioner may from time to time require reports under oath in such scope and detail as he may reasonably determine of each out-of-state bank holding company subject to this Article for the purpose of assuring continuing compliance with the provisions of this Article.

The Commissioner may enter into cooperative agreements with other bank regulatory authorities for the periodic examination of any out-of-state bank holding company that has a North Carolina bank subsidiary and may accept reports of examination and other records from such authorities in lieu of conducting its own examinations. The Commissioner may enter into joint actions with other bank regulatory authorities having concurrent jurisdiction over any out-of-state bank holding company that has a North Carolina bank subsidiary or may take such actions independently to carry out its responsibilities under this Article and assure compliance with the provisions of this Article and the applicable banking laws of this State. (1983 (Reg. Sess., 1984), c. 1113, s. 1; 1993, c. 175, s. 13; 1993 (Reg. Sess., 1994), c. 599, s. 1.)

§ 53-217. Enforcement.

The Commissioner shall have the power to enforce the provisions of this Article through an action in any court of this State or any other state or in any court of the United States, as provided in G.S. 53C-8-12, for the purpose of obtaining an appropriate remedy for violation of any provision of this Article. (1983 (Reg. Sess., 1984), c. 1113, s. 1; 1993, c. 175, s. 14; 1993 (Reg. Sess., 1994), c. 599, s. 1; 2012-56, s. 16.)

§ 53-218. Nonseverability.

It is the purpose of this Article 17 to facilitate orderly development within North Carolina of banking organizations that have banking offices in more than one state. It is not the purpose of this Article to authorize acquisitions of North Carolina bank holding companies or North Carolina banks by bank holding companies that do not have their principal place of business in this State on any basis other than as expressly provided in this Article. Therefore, if any portion of this Article pertaining to the terms and conditions for and limitations upon acquisition of North Carolina bank holding companies and North Carolina banks by bank holding companies that do not have their principal place of business in this State is determined to be invalid for any reason by a final nonappealable order of any North Carolina or federal court of competent jurisdiction, then this entire Article shall be null and void in its entirety and shall be of no further force or effect from the effective date of such order: Provided, however, that any transaction that has been lawfully consummated pursuant to this Article prior to a determination of invalidity shall be unaffected by such determination. (1983 (Reg. Sess., 1984), c. 1113, s. 1; 1993, c. 175, s. 15; 1993 (Reg. Sess., 1994), c. 599, s. 1.)

Article 17A.

Interstate Branch Banking.

§§ 53-219 through 53-224.8: Repealed by Session Laws 1995, c. 322, s. 1.

Article 17B.

Interstate Branch Banking.

Part 1. Definitions.

§ 53-224.9. Definitions.

The following definitions apply in this Article:

(1)   "Acquisition of a branch" means the acquisition of a branch located in a host state without engaging in an "interstate merger transaction" as defined in Part 2 of this Article.

(2)   "Bank" has the meaning set forth in 12 U.S.C. § 1813(h); provided that the term "bank" shall not include any "foreign bank" as defined in 12 U.S.C. § 3101(7), except that such term shall include any foreign bank organized under the laws of a territory of the United States, Puerto Rico, Guam, American Samoa, or the Virgin Islands, the deposits of which are insured by the Federal Deposit Insurance Corporation.

(3)   "Bank holding company" has the meaning set forth in 12 U.S.C. § 1841(a)(1).

(4)   "Bank supervisory agency" means:

a.   The Office of the Comptroller of the Currency, the Federal Deposit Insurance Corporation, the Board of Governors of the Federal Reserve System, and any successor to these agencies; and

b.   Any agency of another state with primary responsibility for chartering and supervising banks.

(5)   "Branch" means a full service office of a bank through which it receives deposits, checks are paid, or loans are made, other than its principal office. Any of the functions or services authorized to be engaged in by a bank may be carried out in an authorized branch office.

(6)   "Commissioner" means the Commissioner of Banks for the State of North Carolina.

(7)   "Control" has the meaning set forth in 12 U.S.C. § 1841(a)(2).

(8)   "De novo branch" means a branch of a bank located in a host state which (i) is originally established by the bank as a branch and (ii) does not become a branch of the bank as a result of (A) the acquisition of another bank or a branch of another bank, or (B) the merger, consolidation, or conversion involving any such bank or branch.

(9)   "Home state" means:

a.   With respect to a national bank, the state in which the main office of the bank is located;

b.   With respect to a state bank, the state by which the bank is chartered;

c.   With respect to a foreign bank, the state determined to be the home state of such foreign bank under 12 U.S.C. § 103(c).

(10)   "Host state" means a state, other than the home state of a bank, in which the bank maintains, or seeks to establish and maintain a branch.

(11)   "Interstate merger transaction" means:

a.   The merger or consolidation of banks with different home states, and the conversion of branches of any bank involved in the merger or consolidation into branches of the resulting bank; or

b.   The purchase of all or substantially all of the assets, including all or substantially all of the branches, of a bank whose home state is different from the home state of the acquiring bank.

(12)   "North Carolina bank" means a bank whose home state is North Carolina.

(13)   "North Carolina State bank" means a bank chartered under the laws of North Carolina.

(14)   "Out-of-state bank" means a bank whose home state is a state other than North Carolina.

134

(15)   "Out-of-state state bank" means a bank chartered under the laws of any state other than North Carolina.

(16)   "Resulting bank" means a bank that has resulted from an interstate merger transaction under this Article.

(17)   "State" means any state of the United States, the District of Columbia, any territory of the United States, Puerto Rico, Guam, American Samoa, the Trust Territory of the Pacific Islands, the Virgin Islands, and the Northern Mariana Islands. (1995, c. 322, s. 2.)

Part 2. Interstate de novo Branching and Acquisition of Branches.

§ 53-224.10. Purpose.

It is the express intent of this Part to permit interstate branching under sections 102 and 103 of the Riegle-Neal Interstate Banking and Branching Efficiency Act of 1994, Public Law 103-328, in accordance with the provisions in this Part. (1995, c. 322, s. 2.)

§ 53-224.11. Interstate branching by North Carolina State banks.

(a)   With the prior approval of the Commissioner, any North Carolina State bank may establish and maintain a de novo branch or acquire a branch in a state other than North Carolina.

(b)   A North Carolina State bank desiring to establish and maintain a branch in another state under this section shall file an application on a form prescribed by the Commissioner. If the Commissioner finds that the applicant has the financial resources sufficient to undertake the proposed expansion without adversely affecting its safety or soundness and that the establishment of the proposed branch is in the public interest, the Commissioner may approve the application. In acting on the application, the Commissioner shall consider the views of the appropriate bank supervisory agencies. The applicant bank may establish the branch when it has received the written approval of the Commissioner. (1995, c. 322, s. 2; 2012-56, s. 17.)

§ 53-224.12. Interstate branching by de novo entry.

An out-of-state bank that does not have a branch in North Carolina and that meets the requirements of this Article may establish and maintain a de novo branch in this State. (1995, c. 322, s. 2.)

§ 53-224.13. Interstate branching through the acquisition of a branch.

An out-of-state bank that does not have a branch in North Carolina and that meets the requirements of this Article may establish and maintain a branch in this State through the acquisition of a branch. (1995, c. 322, s. 2.)

§ 53-224.14. Requirement of notice and other conditions.

(a)   An out-of-state bank desiring to establish and maintain a de novo branch or to acquire a branch in this State shall provide written notice of the proposed transaction to the Commissioner not later than the date on which the bank applies to the responsible federal bank supervisory agency for approval to establish or acquire the branch. The filing of such notice shall be accompanied by the filing fee prescribed by the Commissioner by regulation.

(b)   The out-of-state bank shall comply with the applicable requirements of Article 15 of Chapter 55 of the North Carolina General Statutes.

(c)   An out-of-state bank may establish and maintain a de novo branch or may establish and maintain a branch through acquisition of a branch if:

(1)   In the case of a de novo branch, the laws of the home state of the out-of-state bank permit North Carolina banks to establish and maintain de novo branches in that state under substantially the same terms and conditions as herein set forth; and

(2)   In the case of a branch established through the acquisition of a branch, the laws of the home state of the out-of-state bank permit North Carolina banks to establish and maintain branches in that state through the acquisition of branches under substantially the same terms and conditions as herein set forth. (1995, c. 322, s. 2; 1997-54, s. 1; 1999-72, s. 3.)

§ 53-224.15. Conditions for approval.

In the case of notice under G.S. 53-224.14 by an out-of-state state bank, the notice shall be subject to approval by the Commissioner, which approval shall be effective only if:

(1)   The bank confirms in writing to the Commissioner that as long as it maintains a branch in North Carolina, it will comply with all applicable laws of this State.

(2)   The Commissioner, acting within 60 days after receiving notice of an application under G.S. 53-224.14, certifies to the responsible federal bank supervisory agency that the requirements of this Part have been met by the bank. (1995, c. 322, s. 2.)

§ 53-224.16. Powers.

(a)   An out-of-state state bank which establishes and maintains one or more branches in North Carolina under this Article may conduct any activities at such branch or branches that are authorized under the laws of this State for North Carolina State banks, except to the extent such activities may be prohibited by other laws, regulations, or orders applicable to the out-of-state state bank.

(b)   A North Carolina State bank may conduct any activities at a branch outside of North Carolina that are permissible for a bank chartered by the host state where the branch is located, except to the extent such activities are expressly prohibited by the laws of this State or by any regulation or order of the Commissioner applicable to the North Carolina State bank. (1995, c. 322, s. 2.)

Part 3. Interstate Bank Mergers.

§ 53-224.17. Purpose.

It is the express intent of this Part to permit interstate branching by merger under section 102 of the Riegle-Neal Interstate Banking and Branching Efficiency Act of 1994, Public Law 103-328, in accordance with the provisions of this Part. (1995, c. 322, s. 2.)

137

§ 53-224.18. Authority of State banks to establish interstate branches by merger.

With the prior approval of the Commissioner, a North Carolina State bank may establish, maintain, and operate one or more branches in a state other than North Carolina pursuant to an interstate merger transaction in which the North Carolina State bank is the resulting bank. Not later than the date on which the required application for the interstate merger transaction is filed with the responsible federal bank supervisory agency, the applicant North Carolina State bank shall file an application on a form prescribed by the Commissioner. The applicant shall also comply with the applicable provisions of Part 2 of Article 7 of Chapter 53C of the General Statutes. If the Commissioner finds that (i) the proposed transaction will not be detrimental to the safety and soundness of the applicant or the resulting bank, (ii) any new officers and directors of the resulting bank are qualified by character, experience, and financial responsibility to direct and manage the resulting bank, and (iii) the proposed merger is consistent with the convenience and needs of the communities to be served by the resulting bank in this State and is otherwise in the public interest, it shall approve the interstate merger transaction and the operation of branches outside of North Carolina by the North Carolina State bank. Such an interstate merger transaction may be consummated only after the applicant has received the Commissioner's written approval. (1995, c. 322, s. 2; 2012-56, s. 18.)

§ 53-224.19. Interstate merger transactions and branching permitted.

One or more North Carolina banks may enter into an interstate merger transaction with one or more out-of-state banks under this Article, and an out-of-state bank resulting from such an interstate merger transaction may maintain and operate the branches in North Carolina of a merged North Carolina bank provided that the conditions and filing requirements of this Article are met. (1995, c. 322, s. 2.)

§ 53-224.20. Notice and filing requirements.

Any out-of-state bank that will be the resulting bank pursuant to an interstate merger transaction involving a North Carolina bank shall notify the Commissioner of the proposed merger not later than the date on which it files an application for an interstate merger transaction with the responsible federal bank supervisory agency, and shall submit a copy of that application to the

138

Commissioner and pay the filing fee required by the Commissioner. All banks which are parties to such interstate merger transaction involving a North Carolina State bank shall comply with Part 2 of Article 7 of Chapter 53C of the General Statutes and with other applicable state and federal laws. Any out-of-state bank which shall be the resulting bank in such an interstate merger transaction shall comply with Article 15 of Chapter 55 of the North Carolina General Statutes. (1995, c. 322, s. 2; 2012-56, s. 19.)

§ 53-224.21. Conditions for interstate merger prior to June 1, 1997.

An interstate merger transaction prior to June 1, 1997, involving a North Carolina bank shall not be consummated, and any out-of-state bank resulting from such a merger shall not operate any branch in North Carolina, unless the laws of the home state of each out-of-state bank involved in the interstate merger transaction permit North Carolina banks under substantially the same terms and conditions as are set forth in Part 3 to acquire banks and establish and maintain branches in that state by means of interstate merger transactions. (1995, c. 322, s. 2; 1995 (Reg. Sess., 1996), c. 742, s. 22.)

§ 53-224.22. Powers.

(a)   An out-of-state state bank which establishes and maintains one or more branches in North Carolina under this Article may conduct any activities at such branch or branches that are authorized under the laws of this State for North Carolina State banks, except to the extent such activities may be prohibited by other laws, regulations, or orders applicable to the out-of-state state bank.

(b)   A North Carolina State bank may conduct any activities at a branch outside of North Carolina that are permissible for a bank chartered by the host state where the branch is located, except to the extent such activities are expressly prohibited by the laws of this State or by any regulation or order of the Commissioner applicable to the North Carolina State bank. (1995, c. 322, s. 2.)

Part 4. Supervisory Authority.

§ 53-224.23. Applicability of supervisory authority.

The supervisory powers and other provisions set forth in G.S. 53-224.24 through G.S. 53-224.31 shall apply to Parts 2 and 3 of this Article. (1995, c. 322, s. 2.)

§ 53-224.24. Examinations; periodic reports; cooperative agreements; assessment of fees.

(a)   The Commissioner may make such examinations of any branch of an out-of-state state bank established under this Article and located in this State as the Commissioner may deem necessary to determine whether the branch is operating in compliance with the laws of this State and to ensure that the branch is being operated in a safe and sound manner. The provisions of Article 8 of Chapter 53C of the General Statutes apply to such examinations.

(b)   The Commissioner may require periodic reports regarding any branch in North Carolina of an out-of-state bank to the extent that comparable reports are required from North Carolina State banks. Such reports shall be filed under oath with such frequency and in such scope and detail as may be appropriate for the purpose of assuring continuing compliance with the provisions of this Article.

(c)   The Commissioner may enter into cooperative, coordinating, and information-sharing agreements with any other bank supervisory agencies or any organization affiliated with or representing one or more bank supervisory agencies with respect to the periodic examination or other supervision of any branch in North Carolina of an out-of-state state bank, or any branch of a North Carolina State bank in a host state, and the Commissioner may accept such parties' reports of examination and reports of investigation in lieu of conducting an additional examination or investigation. The Commissioner may enter into joint examinations or joint enforcement actions with other bank supervisory agencies having concurrent jurisdiction over any branch in North Carolina of an out-of-state state bank or any branch of a North Carolina State bank in any host state; provided, however, that the Commissioner may at any time take such actions independently if the Commissioner deems such actions to be necessary or appropriate to carry out the Commissioner's responsibilities under this Article and to ensure compliance with the laws of this State.

(d)   Each out-of-state state bank that maintains one or more branches in this State may be assessed and, if assessed, shall pay supervisory and examination fees in accordance with the laws of this State and regulations of the Commissioner. Such fees may be shared with other bank supervisory agencies or any organization affiliated with or representing one or more bank supervisory agencies in accordance with agreements between such parties and the Commissioner. (1995, c. 322, s. 2; 2012-56, s. 20.)

§ 53-224.25. Enforcement.

If the Commissioner determines that a branch maintained by an out-of-state state bank in this State is being operated in violation of any provision of the laws of this State, or that such branch is being operated in an unsafe and unsound manner, the Commissioner shall have the authority to take all such enforcement actions as the Commissioner would be empowered to take if the branch were a North Carolina State bank. (1995, c. 322, s. 2.)

§ 53-224.26. Rules.

The Commissioner, subject to review and approval of the North Carolina State Banking Commission, may adopt rules needed to implement this Article. Chapter 150B of the General Statutes governs the adoption of rules by the Commissioner. (1995, c. 322, s. 2.)

§ 53-224.27. Additional branches.

An out-of-state bank that has a branch in North Carolina may establish and acquire additional branches in this State to the same extent as a North Carolina State bank or to the same extent otherwise permitted by federal law. (1995, c. 322, s. 2.)

§ 53-224.28. Notice of subsequent merger or other change in control.

An out-of-state bank that maintains a branch in this State established pursuant to this Article shall give 30 days' prior written notice to the Commissioner of any merger, consolidation, or other transaction that would cause a change of control with respect to such out-of-state bank or any bank holding company that controls such bank, with the result that an application would be required to be filed pursuant to the federal Change in Bank Control Act of 1978, as amended, 12 U.S.C. § 1817(j) or the federal Bank Holding Company Act of 1956, as

141

amended, 12 U.S.C. § 1841 et seq., or any successor statutes thereto. (1995, c. 322, s. 2.)

§ 53-224.29. Branch closings.

An out-of-state state bank that is subject to an order or written agreement revoking its authority to establish or maintain a branch in North Carolina and any North Carolina State bank that is subject to an order or written agreement revoking its authority to establish or maintain a branch in another state shall wind up the business of that branch in an orderly manner that protects the depositors, customers, and creditors of the branch and that complies with all North Carolina laws and all other applicable laws regarding the closing of the branch. (1995, c. 322, s. 2.)

§ 53-224.30. Appeal of Commissioner's decision.

Any aggrieved party in a proceeding under this Article may, within 20 days after final decision of the Commissioner, appeal, in writing, such decision to the North Carolina State Banking Commission. An appeal under this section shall be made pursuant to G.S. 53C-2-6. Notwithstanding any other provision of law, any aggrieved party to a decision of the Commission shall be entitled to petition for judicial review pursuant to G.S. 53C-2-6. (1995, c. 322, s. 2; 2009-57, s. 5; 2012-56, s. 21.)

§ 53-224.31. Severability.

If any provision of this Article or the application of such provision is found invalid as to any bank, branch, bank holding company, person, or circumstances, or shall otherwise be deemed superseded by federal law, the remaining provisions of this Article shall not be affected and shall remain valid and in effect as to any bank, branch, bank holding company, person, or circumstance. (1995, c. 322, s. 2.)

Article 18.

Bank Holding Company Act of 1984.

§ 53-225. Title and scope.

(a)   This Article shall be known and may be cited as the North Carolina Bank Holding Company Act of 1984.

(b), (c) Repealed by Session Laws 1985, c. 683, s. 1.

(d)   Except for the provisions of G.S. 53-227.1, nothing in this Article shall be deemed to apply to the registration, examination or supervision of banks or trust companies. (1983 (Reg. Sess., 1984), c. 1113, s. 1; 1985, c. 683, s. 1.)

§ 53-226. Definitions.

For the purposes of this Article:

(1)   "Bank" means any insured bank as the term is defined in Section 3(h) of the Federal Deposit Insurance Act (12 U.S.C. Section 1813(h)), or any institution eligible to become an insured bank as the term is defined therein, which, in either event:

a.   Accepts deposits that the depositor has a legal right to withdraw on demand; and

b.   Engages in the business of making commercial loans.

(2)   "Bank holding company" means any company which has control over any bank.

(3)   "Commissioner" means the Commissioner of Banks of this State.

(4)   "Company" means a corporation, joint stock company, business trust, partnership, voting trust, association, and any similar organized group of persons, whether incorporated or not, and whether or not organized under the laws of this State or any other state or any territory or possession of the United States or under the laws of the foreign country, territory, colony or possession thereof, other than a corporation all the capital of which is owned by the United States or a corporation which is chartered by the Congress of the United States; "company" includes subsidiary and parent companies.

(5)   "Control" means that:

143

a.   Any company directly or indirectly or acting through one or more persons owns, controls, or has power to vote twenty-five per centum (25%) or more of the voting securities of the bank;

b.   The company controls in any manner the election of a majority of the directors, managers or trustees of the bank or company; or

c.   The Commissioner determines, after notice and opportunity for hearing, that the company directly or indirectly exercises a controlling influence over the management or policies of the bank or company.

(6)   "Subsidiary", with respect to a bank holding company, means:

a.   Any company twenty-five per centum (25%) or more of whose voting shares (excluding shares owned by the United States or by any company wholly owned by the United States) is held by it with power to vote;

b.   Any company the election of a majority of whose directors is controlled in any manner by a bank holding company; or

c.   Any company with respect to the management or policies of which a bank holding company has the power, directly or indirectly, to exercise control, as determined by the Commissioner.

(7)   For the purposes of any proceeding under subdivisions (5)c. and (6)c. of this section, there is a presumption that any company which directly or indirectly owns, controls, or has power to vote less than five percent (5%) of any class of voting securities of a given bank or company does not have control over that bank or company. (1983 (Reg. Sess., 1984), c. 1113, s. 1.)

§ 53-227. Registration of bank holding companies.

Every bank holding company, not later than July 1, 1985, or within 180 days after becoming a bank holding company controlling a North Carolina federally or State-chartered bank or banks, or within 180 days after acquiring control, directly or indirectly, over a nonbank subsidiary or subsidiaries having offices located in this State shall register with the Commissioner on forms supplied by the Commissioner. (1983 (Reg. Sess., 1984), c. 1113, s. 1; 1989, c. 10.)

144

§ 53-227.1. Criteria for certain bank holding company acquisitions.

(a)   In addition to the criteria set forth in G.S. 53-211(a) and (b) to be used by the Commissioner in reviewing applications for acquisitions of North Carolina banks and bank holding companies, the Commissioner shall:

(1)   Apply the criteria which would be applied to a North Carolina bank holding company making an acquisition in another state by the regulatory authorities of the State in which the applicant has its principal place of business, as defined by G.S. 53-210(10); and

(2)   Shall approve that application only if the Commissioner finds it meets those additional criteria.

(b)   In the event that the state in which the applicant has its principal place of business has no criteria other than the criteria similar to those set forth in G.S. 53-211(a) and (b), the Commissioner shall approve that application only if he determines that:

(1)   The proposed acquisition would be not detrimental to the safety and soundness of the applicant or of the North Carolina bank or bank holding company which applicant seeks to control or whose stock is to be acquired; and

(2)   The applicant, its directors and officers, if applicable, and any proposed new directors and officers of the North Carolina bank or bank holding company which applicant seeks to control or whose stock is to be acquired, are qualified by character, experience and financial responsibility to control and operate a North Carolina bank. (1985, c. 683, s. 2.)

§ 53-228. Cease and desist.

Upon a finding that any action of a bank holding company or nonbank subsidiary subject to this Article may be in violation of any North Carolina banking law, the Commissioner, after a reasonable notice to the bank holding company or its nonbank subsidiary and an opportunity for it to be heard, shall have the authority to order it to cease and desist from such action. If the bank holding company or nonbank subsidiary fails to appeal such decision in accordance with G.S. 53-231 hereof and continues to engage in such action in violation of the Commissioner's order to cease and desist such action, it shall be subject to a penalty of one thousand dollars ($1,000), to be recovered with costs by the

Commissioner in any court of competent jurisdiction in a civil action prosecuted by the Commissioner. The penalty provision of this section shall be in addition to and not in lieu of any other provision of law applicable to a bank holding company's or its nonbank subsidiary's failure to comply with an order of the Commissioner.

The clear proceeds of penalties provided for in this section shall be remitted to the Civil Penalty and Forfeiture Fund in accordance with G.S. 115C-457.2. (1983 (Reg. Sess., 1984), c. 1113, s. 1; 1998-215, s. 32.)

§ 53-229: Repealed by Session Laws 1995, c. 129, s. 31.

§ 53-230. Rules.

The Banking Commission may adopt such reasonable rules as may be necessary to effectuate the purposes of this Article. (1983 (Reg. Sess., 1984), c. 1113, s. 1; 1995, c. 129, s. 32.)

§ 53-231. Appeal of Commissioner's decision.

Any aggrieved party in a proceeding under this Article may, within 20 days after final decision of the Commissioner, appeal such decision in writing to the Banking Commission. An appeal under this section shall be made pursuant to G.S. 53-92(d). Notwithstanding any other provision of law, any aggrieved party to a decision of the Banking Commission shall be entitled to petition for judicial review pursuant to G.S. 53-92(d). (1983 (Reg. Sess., 1984), c. 1113, s. 1; 1995, c. 129, s. 33; 2009-57, s. 6.)

§ 53-232. Fees.

Each bank holding company subject to this act shall pay the following fees:

(1)   An initial registration fee of $1,000.

(2)   An annual registration fee of $750.00.

(3)   A fee of $50.00 for the issuance of any certified copies of documents plus $1.00 per page over a number of pages specified by the Commissioner. (1983 (Reg. Sess., 1984), c. 1113, s. 1.)

Article 18A.

North Carolina International Banking Act.

§ 53-232.1. Title and scope.

(a)   This act shall be known and cited as the North Carolina International Banking Act.

(b)   This Article is intended to set forth the terms and conditions under which an international banking corporation may enter and do business in North Carolina. (1991, c. 679, s. 1.)

§ 53-232.2. Definitions.

(a)   The following definitions apply in this Article:

(1)   Commissioner. - The North Carolina Commissioner of Banks.

(2)   Federal international bank institution. - A branch, agency, or representative office of an international banking corporation established and operating under the federal International Banking Act of 1978, 12 U.S.C. §§ 3101 et seq., as amended, and its regulations.

(3)   Foreign country. - A country other than the United States, but including a territory or possession of the United States.

(4)   International bank agency. - A business or any part of a banking business conducted in this State or through an office located in this State, other than a federal international bank institution, which exercises powers as set forth in G.S. 53-232.9(f) on behalf of an international banking corporation.

(5)   International bank branch. - A business or any part of a banking business conducted in this State or through an office located in this State, other

than a federal international bank institution, which exercises powers as set forth in G.S. 53-232.9(e) on behalf of an international banking corporation.

(6)   International banking corporation. - A banking corporation organized and licensed under the laws of a foreign country or a political subdivision of a foreign country.

(7)   International representative office. - A business location of a representative of an international banking corporation, other than a federal international bank institution, established to act in a liaison capacity with existing and potential customers of the international banking corporation and to generate new loans and other activities for the international banking corporation that is operating outside the State.

(b)   Legal and financial terms used in this Article refer to equivalent terms used by the country in which the international banking corporation is organized. (1991, c. 679, s. 1.)

§ 53-232.3. Authority to establish and operate federal international bank institutions, international bank branches, international bank agencies, and international representative offices.

(a)   An international banking corporation with a home state other than North Carolina may establish and operate, directly or indirectly, a federal international bank institution in this State in accordance with applicable federal law.

(b)   An international banking corporation with no home state may establish and operate, directly or indirectly, a federal international bank institution in this State in accordance with applicable federal law.

(c)   An international banking corporation with a home state other than North Carolina may establish and operate, directly or indirectly, an international bank branch, an international bank agency, or an international representative office in accordance with this Article and applicable federal law.

(d)   An international banking corporation with no home state may establish and operate, directly or indirectly, an international bank branch, an international bank agency, or an international representative office in accordance with this Article and applicable federal law.

148

(e)   For the purposes of this section, the home state of an international banking corporation that has branches, agencies, subsidiary commercial lending companies, or subsidiary banks, or any combination of branches, agencies, subsidiary commercial lending companies, or subsidiary banks in more than one state is whichever of the states is so elected by the international banking corporation. If the international banking corporation does not elect a home state, the Board of Governors of the Federal Reserve System or the Commissioner, as applicable, shall elect the home state. (1991, c. 679, s. 1.)

§ 53-232.4. Application of this Chapter.

(a)   International banking corporations, other than federal international bank institutions, are subject to Articles 1 through 14 and Articles 17 and 18 of this Chapter, except where it appears, from the context or otherwise, that a provision is clearly applicable only to banks or trust companies organized under the laws of this State or the United States. An international banking corporation has no greater right under, or by virtue of, this Article than is granted to banks organized under the laws of this State.

(b)   Nothing in this Article is construed as granting any authority, directly or indirectly, for a domestic bank or domestic bank holding company, the operations of which are conducted principally outside this State, to operate a branch in this State or to acquire, directly or indirectly, any voting shares of, or interest in, or all or substantially all of the assets of a bank in this State. (1991, c. 679, s. 1.)

§ 53-232.5. Application of the North Carolina Business Corporation Act.

Notwithstanding the definition of the term "foreign corporation" in G.S. 55-1-40(10), Article 15 of Chapter 55, relating to foreign corporations, where it is not inconsistent with Chapter 53, shall apply to all international banking corporations doing business in this State. (1991, c. 679, s. 1.)

§ 53-232.6. Requirements for carrying on banking business.

(a)   No international banking corporation, other than a federal international bank institution, shall transact a banking business or maintain in this State any office for carrying on a banking business or any part of a banking business unless the corporation:

(1)   Is authorized by its Articles to carry on a banking business and has complied with the laws of the country under which it is chartered;

(2)   Has furnished to the Commissioner any proof as to the nature and character of its business and as to its financial condition as the Commissioner may require;

(3)   Has filed with the Commissioner:

a.   A duly executed instrument in writing, by its terms of indefinite duration and irrevocable, appointing the Commissioner its true and lawful attorney upon whom all process in any action against it may be served with the same force and effect as if it were a domestic corporation and had been lawfully served with process within the State;

b.   A written certificate of designation, which may be changed from time to time thereafter by the filing of a new certificate of designation, specifying the name and address of the officer, agent, or other person to whom the Commissioner shall forward the process; and

c.   A certified copy of that information required to be supplied by foreign corporations to the Secretary of State by Article 15 of Chapter 55 of the General Statutes.

(4)   Has paid to the Commissioner the fee established by regulation to defray the cost of investigation and supervision; and

(5)   Has received a license duly issued to it by the Commissioner.

(b)   The Commissioner shall not issue a license to an international banking corporation unless it is chartered in a foreign country that permits banks chartered in the United States or any of its states to establish similar facilities in that country. (1991, c. 679. s. 1.)

§ 53-232.7. Actions against international banking corporations.

150

(a)   A resident of this State may maintain an action against an international banking corporation doing business in this State for any cause of action. For purposes of this subsection, the term "resident of this State" includes any individual domiciled in this State, or any corporation, partnership, or trust formed under the laws of this State.

(b)   An international banking corporation or a nonresident of this State may maintain an action against an international banking corporation doing business in this State in the following cases only:

(1)   Where the action is brought to recover damages for the breach of a contract made or to be performed within this State or relating to property situated within this State at the time of the making of the contract;

(2)   Where the subject matter of the litigation is situated within this State;

(3)   Where the cause of action arose within this State, except where the object of the action is to affect the title of real property situated outside this State; or

(4)   Where the action is based on a liability for acts done within this State by an international banking corporation or its international bank agency, international bank branch, or international representative office.

(c)   The limitations contained in subsection (b) of this section do not apply to a corporation formed and existing under the laws of the United States and that maintains an office in this State. (1991, c. 679, s. 1.)

§ 53-232.8. Application for license.

(a)   Every international banking corporation, before being licensed by the Commissioner to transact a banking business in this State as an international bank branch or as an international bank agency or before maintaining in this State any office to carry on a banking business or any part of a banking business, shall subscribe and acknowledge and submit to the Commissioner, at the Commissioner's office, a separate application, in duplicate, which shall state:

(1)   The name of the international banking corporation;

151

(2)   The location by street and post office address and county where its business is to be transacted in this State and the name of the person who is in charge of the business and affairs of the office;

(3)   The location where its initial registered office will be located in this State;

(4)   The amount of its capital actually paid in and the amount subscribed for and unpaid; and

(5)   The actual value of the assets of the international banking corporation, which must be at least fifty million dollars ($50,000,000) in excess of its liabilities, and a complete and detailed statement of its financial condition as of a date within 60 days before the date of the application; except that the Commissioner may, when necessary or expedient, accept the statement of financial condition as of a date within 120 days before the date of the application.

(b)   When the application is submitted to the Commissioner, the corporation shall also submit a duly authenticated copy of its Articles of Incorporation, or equivalent corporate document, and an authenticated copy of its bylaws, or an equivalent of the bylaws that is satisfactory to the Commissioner, and pay an investigation and supervision fee to be established by regulation. The international banking corporation shall also submit to the Commissioner a certificate issued by the banking or supervisory authority of the country in which the international banking corporation is organized and licensed stating that the international banking corporation is duly organized and licensed and lawfully existing in good standing, and is empowered to conduct a general banking business.

(c)   The Commissioner may approve or disapprove the application, but the Commissioner shall not approve the application unless, in the Commissioner's opinion, the applicant meets every requirement of this Article and any other applicable provision of this Chapter and any regulations adopted under this Chapter. The Commissioner may specify any conditions as the Commissioner deems appropriate, considering the public interest, the need to maintain a sound and competitive banking system, and the preservation of an environment conducive to the conduct of an international banking business in this State.

(d)   An international banking corporation may operate more than one international bank branch in this State, each at a different place of business, provided each branch office is separately licensed to transact a banking

152

business or any part of a banking business under this Article. An international banking corporation may operate more than one international bank agency in this State, each at a different place of business, provided each agency office is separately licensed to transact a banking business or any part of a banking business under this Article.

(e) Notwithstanding subsection (d) of this section, no international banking corporation licensed to maintain one or more international bank branches in this State shall be licensed to maintain an international bank agency in this State except upon termination of the operation of its international bank branches under G.S. 53-232.13(b), and no international banking corporation licensed to maintain one or more international bank agencies in this State shall be licensed to maintain an international bank branch in this State except upon the termination of the operation of its international bank agencies under G.S. 53-232.13(b). (1991, c. 679, s. 1.)

§ 53-232.9. Effect, renewal, and revocation of licenses; permissible activities.

(a) When the Commissioner has issued a license to an international banking corporation, it may engage in the business authorized by this Article at, and only at, the office specified in the license for a period not exceeding one year from the date of the license or until the license is surrendered or revoked. No license is transferable or assignable. Every license shall be, at all times, conspicuously displayed in the place of business specified in the license.

(b) The international banking corporation may renew the license annually upon application to the Commissioner upon forms to be supplied by the Commissioner for that purpose. The application for renewal shall be submitted to the Commissioner no later than 60 days before the expiration of the license. The license may be renewed by the Commissioner upon a determination, with or without examination, that the international banking corporation is in a safe and satisfactory condition, that it has complied with applicable requirements of law, and that the renewal of the license is proper and has been duly authorized by proper corporate action. Each application for renewal of an international banking corporation license shall be accompanied by an annual renewal fee to be determined by the Commissioner by regulation.

(c) The Commissioner may revoke the license, with or without examination, upon a determination that the international banking corporation does not meet the criteria established by subsection (b) of this section for renewal of licenses.

153

(d)   If the Commissioner refuses to renew the license and, as a result, the license is revoked, all the rights and privileges of the international banking corporation to transact the business for which it was licensed shall immediately cease, and the license shall be surrendered to the Commissioner within 24 hours after written notice of the decision has been mailed by the Commissioner to the registered office of the international banking corporation set forth in its application, as amended, or has been personally delivered to any officer, director, employee, or agent of the international banking corporation who is physically present in this State.

(e)   An international banking corporation licensed under this Article to carry on business in this State as an international bank branch may conduct a general banking business, including the right to receive deposits and exercise fiduciary powers, through its international bank branch in the same manner as banks existing under the laws of this State and under applicable federal law.

(f)   An international banking corporation licensed under this Article to carry on business in this State as an international bank agency may conduct a general banking business through its international bank agency in the same manner as banks existing under the laws of this State, except that no international banking corporation shall, through its bank agency, exercise fiduciary powers or receive deposits, but may maintain for the account of others credit balances incidental to or arising out of the exercise of its lawful powers. (1991, c. 679, s. 1.)

§ 53-232.10. Securities, etc., to be held in this State.

(a)   An international banking corporation licensed under this Article shall hold, at its office in this State, currency, bonds, notes, debentures, drafts, bills of exchange, or other evidence of indebtedness or other obligations payable in the United States or in United States funds or, with the prior approval of the Commissioner, in funds freely convertible into United States funds in an amount that is not less than one hundred eight percent (108%) of the aggregate amount of liabilities of the international banking corporation payable at or through its office in this State or as a result of the operations of the international bank branch or international bank agency, including acceptances, but excluding:

(1)   Accrued expenses; and

(2)   Amounts due and other liabilities to other offices, agencies, or branches of and wholly owned, except for a nominal number of directors' shares, subsidiaries of the international banking corporation.

(b)   For the purpose of this Article, the Commissioner shall value marketable securities at principal amount or market value, whichever is lower, and may determine the value of any nonmarketable bond, note, debenture, draft, bill of exchange, or other evidence of indebtedness or of any other obligation held by or owed to the international banking corporation in this State. In determining the amount of assets for the purpose of computing the above ratio of assets, the Commissioner may exclude any particular assets, but may give credit, subject to any rules adopted by the Commissioner, to deposits and credit balances with unaffiliated banking institutions outside this State if the deposits or credit balances are payable in United States funds or in currencies freely convertible into United States funds. In no case shall credit given for the deposits and credit balances exceed in aggregate amounts any percentage, but not less than eight percent (8%), as the Commissioner may from time to time prescribe, of the aggregate amount of liabilities of the international banking corporations.

(c)   If, by reason of the existence or the potential occurrence of unusual or extraordinary circumstances, the Commissioner considers it necessary or desirable for the maintenance of a sound financial condition, for the protection of creditors and the public interest, and to maintain public confidence in the business of the international bank agency of the international banking corporation, the Commissioner may reduce the credit to be given as provided in this section for deposits and credit balances with unaffiliated banking institutions outside this State and may require the assets to be held in this State under this Article with any bank or trust company existing under the laws of this State that the international banking corporation designates and the Commissioner approves.

(d)   An international bank branch and international bank agency shall file any reports with the Commissioner as the Commissioner may require in order to determine compliance by the international bank branch or international bank agency with this section. (1991, c. 679, s. 1.)

§ 53-232.11. Financial certification; restrictions on investments, loans, and acceptances.

155

(a)   Before opening an office in this State, and annually thereafter so long as a bank office is maintained in this State, an international banking corporation licensed under this Article shall certify to the Commissioner the amount of its paid-in capital, its surplus, and its undivided profits, each expressed in the currency of the country of its incorporation. The dollar equivalent of this amount, as determined by the Commissioner, is considered to be the amount of its capital, surplus, and undivided profits.

(b)   Purchases and discounts of bills of exchange, bonds, debentures, and other obligations and extensions of credit and acceptances by an international bank agency within this State are subject to the same limitations as to amount in relation to capital, surplus, and undivided profits as are applicable to banks organized under the laws of this State. With the prior approval of the Commissioner, the capital notes and capital debentures of the international banking corporation may be treated as capital in computing the limitations. (1991, c. 679, s. 1.)

§ 53-232.12. Reports.

(a)   An international banking corporation licensed under this Article shall, at the times and in the form prescribed by the Commissioner, make written reports in the English language to the Commissioner, under the oath of one of its officers, managers, or agents transacting business in this State, showing the amount of its assets and liabilities and containing any other matters required by the Commissioner. If an international banking corporation fails to make a report, as directed by the Commissioner, or if a report contains a false statement knowingly made, this is grounds for revocation of the license of the international banking corporation.

(b)   Repealed by Session Laws 2012-56, s. 22, effective October 1, 2012. (1991, c. 679, s. 1; 2012-56, s. 22.)

§ 53-232.13. Dissolution.

(a)   When an international banking corporation licensed to maintain an international bank branch or an international bank agency in this State is dissolved or its authority or existence is otherwise terminated or canceled in the jurisdiction of its incorporation, a certificate of the official responsible for records of banking corporations of the jurisdiction of incorporation of the international banking corporation attesting to the occurrence of this event or a certified copy of an order or decree of a court of the jurisdiction directing the dissolution of the international banking corporation or the termination of its existence or the cancellation of its authority shall be delivered to the Commissioner. The filing of the certificate, order, or decree has the same effect as the revocation of the international banking corporation's license as provided in G.S. 53-232.9(d).

(b)   An international banking corporation that proposes to terminate the operation in this State of an international bank branch, an international bank agency, or an international representative office in this State shall comply with any procedures as the Commissioner may prescribe by rule to insure an orderly cessation of business in a manner that is not harmful to the public interest and shall surrender its license to the Commissioner or shall surrender its right to maintain an office in this State, as applicable.

(c)   The Commissioner shall continue as agent of the international banking corporation upon whom process against it may be served in any action based upon any liability or obligation incurred by the international banking corporation within this State before the filing of the certificate, order, or decree; and the Commissioner shall promptly cause a copy of the process to be mailed by registered or certified mail, return receipt requested, to the international banking corporation at the post office address specified for this purpose on file with the Commissioner's office. (1991, c. 679, s. 1.)

§ 53-232.14. International representative offices.

(a)   An international banking corporation that does not transact a banking business or any part of a banking business in or through an office in this State, but maintains an office in this State for other purposes is considered to have an international representative office in this State.

(b)   An international representative office located in this State shall register with the Commissioner annually on forms prescribed by the Commissioner. The registration shall be filed before January 31 of each year, shall be accompanied by a registration fee prescribed by regulation, and shall list the name of the local representative, the street address of the office, and the nature of the business to be transacted in or through the office.

(c)   The Commissioner may review the operations of an international representative office annually or at any greater frequency as is necessary to assure that the office does not transact a banking business.

(d)   An international banking corporation desiring to convert its existing registered international representative office to a licensed international bank branch or licensed international bank agency shall submit to the Commissioner the application required by G.S. 53-232.8, and is required to meet the minimum criteria for licensing of an international bank branch or licensed international bank agency under this Article.

(e)   An international representative office may act in a liaison capacity with existing and potential customers of an international banking corporation and in undertaking these activities may, through its employees or agents, without limitation, solicit loans, assemble credit information, make proprietary inspections and appraisals, complete loan applications and other preliminary paperwork in preparation for making a loan, but may not solicit or accept deposits. No international representative office shall conduct any banking business or part of a banking business in this State. (1991, c. 679, s. 1.)

§ 53-232.15. Rules.

The Banking Commission may adopt rules necessary to implement this Article. (1991, c. 679, s. 1.)

§ 53-232.16. Cease and desist.

Upon a finding that any action of an international banking corporation or its international banking agency, international banking branch, or international representative office subject to this Article may be in violation of any North Carolina banking law, the Commissioner, after a reasonable notice to the international banking corporation, international bank agency, international bank branch, or international representative office and an opportunity for it to be heard, may order it to cease and desist from the action. If the international banking corporation, international bank agency, international bank branch, or international representative office fails to appeal the decision in accordance with G.S. 53-232.17 and continues to engage in the action in violation of the Commissioner's order to cease and desist the action, it is subject to a penalty of one thousand dollars ($1,000), to be recovered with costs by the Commissioner

158

in any court of competent jurisdiction in a civil action prosecuted by the Commissioner. This penalty is in addition to and not in lieu of any other law applicable to the failure of an international banking corporation, international bank agency, international bank branch, or international representative office to comply with an order of the Commissioner.

The clear proceeds of penalties provided for in this section shall be remitted to the Civil Penalty and Forfeiture Fund in accordance with G.S. 115C-457.2. (1991, c. 679, s. 1; 1998-215, s. 33.)

§ 53-232.17. Appeal of Commissioner's decision.

Any aggrieved party in a proceeding under this Article may, within 20 days after final decision of the Commissioner, appeal such decision in writing to the Banking Commission. An appeal under this section shall be made pursuant to G.S. 53C-2-6. Notwithstanding any other provision of law, any aggrieved party to a decision of the Banking Commission shall be entitled to petition for judicial review pursuant to G.S. 53C-2-6. (1991, c. 679, s. 1; 1995, c. 129, s. 34; 2009-57, s. 7; 2012-56, s. 23.)

Article 19.

Registration of Mortgage Bankers and Brokers: Repealed.

§§ 53-233 through 53-243: Repealed by Session Laws 2001-393, s. 1, effective July 1, 2002.

Article 19A.

Mortgage Lending Act.

§ 53-243.01: Repealed by Session Laws 2009-374, s. 1, effective July 31, 2009, and applicable to all applications for licensure as a mortgage loan originator, mortgage lender, mortgage broker, or mortgage servicer filed on or after that date.

§ 53-243.02: Repealed by Session Laws 2009-374, s. 1, effective July 31, 2009, and applicable to all applications for licensure as a mortgage loan originator, mortgage lender, mortgage broker, or mortgage servicer filed on or after that date.

§ 53-243.03: Repealed by Session Laws 2009-374, s. 1, effective July 31, 2009, and applicable to all applications for licensure as a mortgage loan originator, mortgage lender, mortgage broker, or mortgage servicer filed on or after that date.

§ 53-243.04: Repealed by Session Laws 2009-374, s. 1, effective July 31, 2009, and applicable to all applications for licensure as a mortgage loan originator, mortgage lender, mortgage broker, or mortgage servicer filed on or after that date.

§ 53-243.05: Repealed by Session Laws 2009-374, s. 1, effective July 31, 2009, and applicable to all applications for licensure as a mortgage loan originator, mortgage lender, mortgage broker, or mortgage servicer filed on or after that date.

§ 53-243.05A: Repealed by Session Laws 2009-374, s. 1, effective July 31, 2009, and applicable to all applications for licensure as a mortgage loan originator, mortgage lender, mortgage broker, or mortgage servicer filed on or after that date.

§ 53-243.06: Repealed by Session Laws 2009-374, s. 1, effective July 31, 2009, and applicable to all applications for licensure as a mortgage loan originator, mortgage lender, mortgage broker, or mortgage servicer filed on or after that date.

§ 53-243.07: Repealed by Session Laws 2009-374, s. 1, effective July 31, 2009, and applicable to all applications for licensure as a mortgage loan originator, mortgage lender, mortgage broker, or mortgage servicer filed on or after that date.

§ 53-243.08: Repealed by Session Laws 2009-374, s. 1, effective July 31, 2009, and applicable to all applications for licensure as a mortgage loan originator, mortgage lender, mortgage broker, or mortgage servicer filed on or after that date.

§ 53-243.09: Repealed by Session Laws 2009-374, s. 1, effective July 31, 2009, and applicable to all applications for licensure as a mortgage loan originator, mortgage lender, mortgage broker, or mortgage servicer filed on or after that date.

§ 53-243.10: Repealed by Session Laws 2009-374, s. 1, effective July 31, 2009, and applicable to all applications for licensure as a mortgage loan originator, mortgage lender, mortgage broker, or mortgage servicer filed on or after that date.

§ 53-243.11: Repealed by Session Laws 2009-374, s. 1, effective July 31, 2009, and applicable to all applications for licensure as a mortgage loan originator, mortgage lender, mortgage broker, or mortgage servicer filed on or after that date.

§ 53-243.12: Repealed by Session Laws 2009-374, s. 1, effective July 31, 2009, and applicable to all applications for licensure as a mortgage loan originator, mortgage lender, mortgage broker, or mortgage servicer filed on or after that date.

§ 53-243.13: Repealed by Session Laws 2009-374, s. 1, effective July 31, 2009, and applicable to all applications for licensure as a mortgage loan originator, mortgage lender, mortgage broker, or mortgage servicer filed on or after that date.

§ 53-243.14: Repealed by Session Laws 2009-374, s. 1, effective July 31, 2009, and applicable to all applications for licensure as a mortgage loan originator, mortgage lender, mortgage broker, or mortgage servicer filed on or after that date.

§ 53-243.15: Repealed by Session Laws 2009-374, s. 1, effective July 31, 2009, and applicable to all applications for licensure as a mortgage loan originator, mortgage lender, mortgage broker, or mortgage servicer filed on or after that date.

§ 53-243.16: Repealed by Session Laws 2009-374, s. 1, effective July 31, 2009, and applicable to all applications for licensure as a mortgage loan originator, mortgage lender, mortgage broker, or mortgage servicer filed on or after that date.

§ 53-243.17: Repealed by Session Laws 2009-374, s. 1, effective July 31, 2009, and applicable to all applications for licensure as a mortgage loan originator, mortgage lender, mortgage broker, or mortgage servicer filed on or after that date.

§ 53-243.18: Repealed by Session Laws 2009-374, s. 1, effective July 31, 2009, and applicable to all applications for licensure as a mortgage loan originator, mortgage lender, mortgage broker, or mortgage servicer filed on or after that date.

§ 53-244. Reserved for future codification purposes.

Article 19B.

The Secure and Fair Enforcement Mortgage Licensing Act.

§ 53-244.010. Title.

This act may be cited as the "North Carolina Secure and Fair Enforcement (S.A.F.E.) Mortgage Licensing Act." (2009-374, s. 2.)

§ 53-244.020. Purpose and construction.

(a)   Purpose. - A primary purpose of this Article is to protect consumers seeking mortgage loans and to ensure that the mortgage lending industry

162

operates without unfair, deceptive, and fraudulent practices on the part of mortgage loan originators. Therefore, the General Assembly establishes within this Article an effective system of supervision and enforcement of the mortgage lending industry by giving the Commissioner of Banks broad administrative authority to administer, interpret, and enforce this Article and adopt rules implementing this Article in order to carry out the intentions of the General Assembly.

(b)   Construction. - It is the intent of the General Assembly that provisions of this Article be liberally construed to effect the purposes stated or clearly encompassed by the Article. (2009-374, s. 2.)

§ 53-244.030. Definitions.

For purposes of the Article, the following definitions apply:

(1)   "Affiliate" means any company that controls, is controlled by, or is under common control with another company, as set forth in the Bank Holding Company Act of 1956 (12 U.S.C. § 1841, et seq.), as amended from time to time.

(2)   "Audited Statement of Financial Condition" means a statement of financial condition prepared in accordance with generally accepted accounting principles and certified by a certified public accountant as fairly and accurately reflecting financial condition of the licensee as of the date specified in the statement.

(2a)   "Banking Commission" means the North Carolina Banking Commission. For the purpose of complying with this Article by credit unions, Banking Commission means the North Carolina Credit Union Commission.

(3)   "Branch manager" means the individual who is assigned to, is in charge of, and is responsible for the business operations of a branch office of a mortgage broker or mortgage lender.

(4)   "Branch office" means an office of a mortgage broker or mortgage lender that is separate and distinct from the mortgage broker's or lender's principal office and from which its employees engage in the mortgage business. A branch office shall not be located at an individual's home or residence.

(5)   "Certified Statement of Financial Condition" means a statement of financial condition prepared in accordance with generally accepted accounting principles and certified by the preparer or licensee as fairly and accurately reflecting the financial condition of the licensee as of the date specified in the statement.

(6)   "Commissioner" means the North Carolina Commissioner of Banks and the Commissioner's designees. For the purpose of compliance with this Article by credit unions, Commissioner means the Administrator of the Credit Union Division of the Department of Commerce.

(7)   "Control" means the power, directly or indirectly, to direct the management or policies of a company, whether through ownership of securities, by contract, or otherwise. Any person that (i) is a director, general partner, or executive officer; (ii) directly or indirectly has the right to vote ten percent (10%) or more of a class of voting security or has the power to sell or direct the sale of ten percent (10%) or more of a class of voting securities; (iii) in the case of a limited liability company, is a managing member; or (iv) in the case of a partnership, has the right to receive upon dissolution, or has contributed, ten percent (10%) or more of the capital, is presumed to control the company.

(8)   "Depository institution" has the same meaning as in section 3 of the Federal Deposit Insurance Act and includes any credit union whose share and deposit accounts are insured by the National Credit Union Administration under the Federal Credit Union Act.

(9)   "Dwelling" means a residential structure that contains one to four units, whether or not that structure is attached to real property. The term includes an individual condominium unit, cooperative unit, manufactured home, mobile home, or trailer if it is used as a residence.

(10)   "Employee" means an individual who has an employment relationship with a mortgage broker, mortgage lender, or mortgage servicer and who is treated as a common law employee for purposes of compliance with the federal income tax laws and whose income is reported on IRS Form W-2.

(11)   "Engaging in the mortgage business" means:

a.   For compensation or gain, or in the expectation of compensation or gain, either directly or indirectly, to accept or offer to accept an application for a residential mortgage loan from prospective borrowers, solicit or offer to solicit a

164

residential mortgage loan from prospective borrowers, negotiate the terms or conditions of a residential mortgage loan with prospective borrowers, issue residential mortgage loan commitments or interest rate guarantee agreements to prospective borrowers, or engage in tablefunding of residential mortgage loans, whether any such acts are done through contact by telephone, by electronic means, by mail, or in person with the borrowers or prospective borrowers.

b.	To make or fund, or offer to make or fund, or advance funds on residential mortgage loans for compensation or gain, or in the expectation of compensation or gain.

c.	To engage, whether for compensation or gain from another or on one's own behalf, in the business of receiving any scheduled periodic payments from a borrower pursuant to the terms of any residential mortgage loan, including amounts for escrow accounts, and making the payments of principal and interest and such other payments with respect to the amounts received from the borrower as may be required pursuant to the terms of the residential mortgage loan, the residential mortgage loan servicing documents, or servicing contract, or otherwise to meet the definition of the term "servicer" in 12 U.S.C. § 2605(i)(2) with respect to residential mortgage loans.

(11a)	"Exclusive mortgage broker" means an individual who acts as a mortgage broker exclusively for a single mortgage lender or mortgage broker licensee or a single exempt mortgage lender and who is licensed pursuant to G.S. 53-244.050(b)(3). Unless otherwise indicated, an exclusive mortgage broker shall be subject to the requirements of a mortgage broker under this Article.

(12)	"Federal banking agencies" means the Board of Governors of the Federal Reserve System, the Office of the Comptroller of the Currency, the Office of Thrift Supervision, the National Credit Union Administration, and the Federal Deposit Insurance Corporation.

(13)	"Immediate family member" means a spouse, child, sibling, parent, grandparent, or grandchild, or the spouse of an immediate family member. This term includes stepparents, stepchildren, stepsiblings, and adoptive relationships.

(14)	"Individual" means a natural person.

165

(15)   "Licensee" means a mortgage loan originator, transitional mortgage loan originator, mortgage broker, mortgage lender, or mortgage servicer or other person who is licensed pursuant to this Article.

(16)   "Loan processor or underwriter" means an individual who performs clerical or support duties as an employee at the direction of and subject to the supervision and instruction of a person licensed or exempt from licensing under this Article. Clerical or support duties may include, subsequent to the receipt of an application:

a.   The receipt, collection, distribution, and analysis of information common for the processing or underwriting of a residential mortgage loan; and

b.   Communicating with a consumer to obtain the information necessary for the processing or underwriting of a loan, to the extent that such communication does not include offering or negotiating loan rates or terms or counseling consumers about residential mortgage loan rates or terms.

Any person who represents to the public, through advertising or other means of communication, or provides information, including the use of business cards, stationery, brochures, signs, rate lists, or other promotional items, that the individual can or will perform any of the activities of a mortgage loan originator shall not be deemed to be a loan processor or underwriter under this definition.

(17)   "Loss mitigation specialist" means an employee of a mortgage servicer authorized to (i) collect or receive payments, including payments of principal, interest, escrow amounts, and other amounts due on existing residential mortgage loans due and owing to the licensed lender or servicer when the borrower is in default or in reasonably foreseeable likelihood of default, (ii) work with the borrower to collect data, and (iii) make decisions necessary to modify, either temporarily or permanently, certain terms of those residential mortgage loans or to otherwise finalize collection through the foreclosure process. Such decisions shall include any change in the principal amount of the debt, the rate of annual interest charged, the term of the loan, the waiver of any fees or charges, including late charges, the deferral of payments, or any other similar matter.

(18)   "Make a residential mortgage loan" means to advance funds, to offer to advance funds, to make a commitment to advance funds to a borrower under a mortgage loan, or to fund a residential mortgage loan.

166

(19)   "Mortgage broker" means a person engaged in the mortgage business as defined in sub-subdivision a. of subdivision (11) of this section.

(20)   "Mortgage lender" means a person engaged in the mortgage business as defined in sub-subdivision b. of subdivision (11) of this section. However, the definition does not include a person who acts as a mortgage lender only in a tablefunding transaction.

(21)   "Mortgage loan originator" means:

a.   An individual who for compensation or gain or in the expectation of compensation or gain, whether through contact by telephone, by electronic means, by mail, or in person with prospective borrowers, either:

1.   Takes a residential mortgage loan application or offers or negotiates terms of a residential mortgage loan,

2.   Accepts or offers to accept applications for mortgage loans,

3.   Solicits or offers to solicit a mortgage loan,

4.   Negotiates the terms or conditions of a mortgage loan, or

5.   Issues mortgage loan commitments or interest rate guarantee agreements to prospective borrowers.

b.   The term includes an individual acting solely as a loss mitigation specialist if the United States Department of Housing and Urban Development issues a guideline, rule, regulation, or interpretative letter that such individuals are loan originators as the term is defined by § 1503 of Title V of the Housing and Economic Recovery Act of 2008, Public Law 110-289, and only to the extent of such an issuance or determination.

c.   The term does not include:

1.   An individual engaged solely as a loan processor or underwriter;

2.   A person or entity that only performs real estate brokerage activities and is licensed or registered as such in accordance with State law, unless the person or entity is compensated by a mortgage lender, a mortgage broker, or

167

other mortgage loan originator or by any agent of a mortgage lender, mortgage broker, or other mortgage loan originator;

3.　　A person or entity solely involved in extensions of credit or sale of time share instruments relating to time share plans, as that term is defined in G.S. 93A-41(9a); or

4.　　An individual who only informs a prospective borrower of the availability of persons engaged in the mortgage business, does not take or assist in the completion of a loan application, and does not discuss specific terms or conditions of a mortgage loan. The taking of basic preapplication information for facilitating a residential mortgage loan transaction, such as the name and contact information of the prospective borrower, the prospective borrower's own assessment of creditworthiness, desired loan types, and resources to make a down payment, but not including social security number, credit score, credit or employment history, or specific rates of a desired mortgage loan, to connect prospective borrowers to persons engaged in the mortgage business does not prevent an individual from qualifying for this exclusion.

5.　　An individual who is a salesperson for a licensed manufactured housing retailer that performs the purely administrative and clerical tasks of physically handling or transmitting to a licensed mortgage loan originator on behalf of a prospective borrower an application and other forms completed by the prospective borrower. Nothing in this subpart prohibits a salesperson, upon the written request of a mortgage loan originator and after a prospective borrower completes an application, from pulling and transmitting a credit report with the application.

(22)　　"Mortgage servicer" means a person engaged in the mortgage business who directly or indirectly engages in the mortgage business as defined in sub-subdivision c. of subdivision (11) of this section.

(23)　　"Nationwide Mortgage Licensing System and Registry" means the mortgage licensing system developed and maintained by the Conference of State Bank Supervisors and the American Association of Residential Mortgage Regulators for the licensing and registration of licensed mortgage loan originators.

(24)　　"Nontraditional mortgage product" means any residential mortgage loan product other than a 30-year fixed rate mortgage.

(25)   "Person" means an individual, partnership, limited liability company, limited partnership, corporation, association, or other group engaged in joint business activities however organized.

(26)   "Principal office" means a principal place of business that shall consist of at least one enclosed room or building of stationary construction in which negotiations of mortgage loan transactions may be conducted and carried on in privacy and in which all of the books, records, and files pertaining to mortgage loan transactions relating to borrowers in this State are maintained. A principal office shall not be located at an individual's home or residence.

(27)   "Qualifying individual" means a person who meets the experience and other requirements of G.S. 53-244.050(b) and who agrees to be primarily responsible for the operations of a licensed mortgage broker or mortgage lender or mortgage servicer.

(28)   "Real estate brokerage activity" means any activity that involves offering or providing real estate brokerage services to the public, including:

a.   Acting as a real estate agent or real estate broker for a buyer, seller, lessor, or lessee of real property;

b.   Bringing together parties interested in the sale, purchase, lease, rental, or exchange of real property;

c.   Negotiating, on behalf of any party, any portion of a contract relating to the sale, purchase, lease, rental, or exchange of real property, other than in connection with providing financing with respect to any such transaction;

d.   Engaging in any activity for which a person engaged in the activity is required to be registered or licensed as a real estate agent or real estate broker under Chapter 93A of the General Statutes; and

e.   Offering to engage in any activity, or act in any capacity, described in sub-subdivision a., b., c., or d. of this subdivision.

(29)   "Registered mortgage loan originator" means any individual who meets the definition of mortgage loan originator, is registered with, and maintains a unique identifier through the Nationwide Mortgage Licensing System and Registry and is an employee of:

169

a.   A depository institution;

b.   A subsidiary that is owned and controlled by a depository institution and regulated by a federal banking agency; or

c.   An institution regulated by the Farm Credit Administration.

(30)   "Residential mortgage loan or mortgage loan" means any loan made or represented to be made to a natural person or persons primarily for personal, family, or household use that is secured by a mortgage, deed of trust, or other equivalent consensual security interest on a dwelling located within this State or residential real estate upon which is constructed or intended to be constructed a dwelling.

(31)   "Residential real estate" means any real property located in this State upon which is constructed or intended to be constructed a dwelling.

(32)   "RESPA" means the Real Estate Settlement Procedures Act, 12 U.S.C. § 2601, et seq., as it may be hereafter amended.

(33)   "Tablefunding" means a transaction in which a person closes a residential mortgage loan in its own name but with funds provided by another and in which the loan is assigned to the mortgage lender actually providing the funds within one business day of the funding of the loan.

(33a)   "Transitional mortgage loan originator" means an individual who is authorized to act as a mortgage loan originator subject to a transitional mortgage loan originator license which is limited to a term of no more than 120 days and is not subject to reapplication, renewal, or extension by the Commissioner.

(34)   "Unique identifier" means a number or other identifier assigned by protocols established by the Nationwide Mortgage Licensing System and Registry. (2009-374, s. 2; 2009-570, s. 34.1; 2013-327, s. 1.)

§ 53-244.040. License and registration requirements.

(a)   Except as provided in subsection (d) of this section, no person may engage in the mortgage business or act as a mortgage loan originator with respect to any dwelling located in this State without first obtaining and maintaining a license under this Article. It shall be unlawful for any person, other than an exempt person or a person licensed as a transitional mortgage loan originator, to act as a mortgage loan originator without a mortgage loan originator license, which authorizes an individual who is employed by a licensee holding a license as provided in subsection (b) of this section to conduct the business of a mortgage loan originator.

(a1)   In anticipation of satisfaction of all requirements necessary to obtain a license as a mortgage loan originator under this Article, a transitional mortgage loan originator license may be granted to an individual who has an active license to originate mortgage loans pursuant to the laws of any state or territory of the United States other than North Carolina, provided the individual registers, is fingerprinted, and maintains a unique identifier with the Nationwide Mortgage Licensing System and Registry at the time the individual submits a transitional mortgage loan originator application to the Commissioner. A transitional mortgage loan originator license may also be issued to a registered loan originator for the purpose of satisfying all requirements necessary to obtain a license as a mortgage loan originator under this Article if permitted by a guideline, rule, regulation, or interpretive letter which clarifies section 1503 of Title V of the Housing and Economic Recovery Act of 2008, P.L. 110-289, and only to the extent of such an issuance or determination.

(b)   Four types of licenses are granted to entities under this Article, and it shall be unlawful for any person, other than an exempt person, to engage in the mortgage business without one of the following licenses:

(1)   A mortgage broker license authorizes a person to act as a mortgage broker as defined in G.S. 53-244.030(19).

(2)   A mortgage lender license authorizes a person to act as a mortgage lender as defined in G.S. 53-244.030(20), a mortgage broker as defined under G.S. 53-244.030(19), and upon notice to the Commissioner, a mortgage servicer as defined in G.S. 53-244.030(22).

(3)   A mortgage servicer license authorizes a person to act only as a mortgage servicer as defined in G.S. 53-244.030(22).

(4)   An exclusive mortgage broker license authorizes a person to act as an exclusive mortgage broker as defined in G.S. 53-244.030(11a).

171

(c)   Each mortgage loan originator and person engaged in the mortgage business must register with and maintain a valid unique identifier issued by the Nationwide Mortgage Licensing System and Registry.

(d)   The following are exempt from all provisions of this Article except the provisions of G.S. 53-244.111:

(1)   Registered mortgage loan originators as defined in G.S. 53-244.030(29);

(2)   Any individual who offers or negotiates terms of a residential mortgage loan with or on behalf of an immediate family member of the individual when making the family member a residential mortgage loan;

(3)   Any individual seller who offers or negotiates terms and makes a residential mortgage loan secured by the dwelling that served as the selling individual's residence;

(4)   An attorney licensed pursuant to Chapter 84 of the General Statutes who negotiates the terms of a residential mortgage loan on behalf of a client in the course of and incident to the attorney's representation of the client, so long as the attorney does not hold himself out as engaged in the mortgage business and is not compensated by a mortgage lender, a mortgage broker, or other mortgage loan originator when negotiating the terms of a residential mortgage loan;

(5)   Any entity described in G.S. 53-244.030(29)a., b., or c., upon acceptance of the notice of exemption filed with the Commissioner as specified in G.S. 53-244.050(g);

(6)   Any officer or employee of an entity described in subdivision (5) of this subsection when acting within the scope of his or her employment;

(7)   A State or federally chartered credit union, upon filing of a notice of exemption with the Administrator of the Credit Union Division of the Department of Commerce as specified in G.S. 53-244.050(g); or

(8)   Any person who, as seller, receives in one calendar year no more than five residential mortgage loans as security for purchase money obligations, unless the United States Department of Housing and Urban Development has expressly and definitively determined that such persons are loan originators as the term is defined by § 1503 of Title V of the Housing and Economic Recovery

172

Act of 2008, Public Law 110-289, and such determination is in effect on July 31, 2010.

(e)   Each mortgage broker, mortgage lender, or mortgage servicer licensed under this Article shall have a qualifying individual who operates the business under that person's full charge, control, and supervision. Each mortgage broker, mortgage lender, or mortgage servicer licensed under this Article shall file through the Nationwide Mortgage Licensing System and Registry a form acceptable to the Commissioner indicating the licensee's designation of qualifying individual and each qualifying individual's acceptance of the responsibility. Each mortgage broker, mortgage lender, or mortgage servicer licensed under this Article shall notify the Commissioner within 15 days of any change in its designated qualifying individual. Any individual licensee who operates as a sole proprietorship shall qualify as and be considered the qualifying individual for the purposes of this subsection.

(f)   Mortgage lenders and mortgage brokers may not operate branch offices, except as permitted by this Article. Each principal office and each branch office of a mortgage broker or mortgage lender licensed under this Article shall have a branch manager who meets the experience requirements under G.S. 53-244.050(b). The qualifying individual for a licensee's business also may serve as the branch manager of one of the licensee's branch offices. Each mortgage broker or mortgage lender licensed under this Article shall file through the Nationwide Mortgage Licensing System and Registry a form acceptable to the Commissioner indicating the licensee's designation of branch manager for each branch. Each mortgage broker or mortgage lender licensed under this Article shall notify the Commissioner within 15 days of the change of any branch manager. (2009-374, s. 2; 2009-570, s. 48; 2013-327, s. 2.)

§ 53-244.050. License and registration application; claim of exemption.

(a)   Applicants for a license shall apply through the Nationwide Mortgage Licensing System and Registry on a form acceptable to the Commissioner, including the following information:

(1)   The applicant's name and address, including street address, mailing address, e-mail, telephone contact information, and social security number or taxpayer identification number.

(2)   The applicant's form and place of organization, if applicable.

(3)   The applicant's proposed method of and locations for doing business, if applicable.

(4)   The qualifications and business history of the applicant and, if applicable, the business history of any partner, officer, or director, any person occupying a similar status or performing similar functions, or any person directly or indirectly controlling the applicant, including:

a.   A description of any injunction or administrative order by any state or federal authority to which the person is or has been subject;

b.   Any conviction, within the past 10 years, of a misdemeanor involving moral turpitude or any fraud, false statement or omission, any theft or wrongful taking of property, bribery, perjury, forgery, counterfeiting, extortion, or conspiracy to commit any of these offenses, or involving any financial service or financial service-related business; and

c.   Any felony convictions.

(5)   With respect to an application for licensing as a mortgage lender, mortgage broker, or mortgage servicer, the applicant's financial condition, credit history, and business history, and, with respect to an application for licensing as a mortgage loan originator, the applicant's credit history and business history.

(6)   The applicant's consent to a federal and State criminal history record check and a set of the applicant's fingerprints in a form acceptable to the Commissioner. In the case of an applicant that is a person other than a natural person, each individual who has control of the applicant or who is the qualifying individual or a branch manager shall consent to a federal and State criminal history record check and submit a set of that individual's fingerprints pursuant to this subdivision.

(b)   The eligibility requirements for an application for licensure under this Article are as follows:

(1)   Each individual applicant for licensure as a mortgage loan originator or qualifying individual shall:

a.   Be at least 18 years of age;

174

b.   Have satisfactorily completed, within the three years immediately preceding the date of application, the mortgage lending prelicensing education as required under G.S. 53-244.070; and

c.   Have passed, within the five years immediately preceding the date of application, the test required under G.S. 53-244.080.

(1a)   Each individual applicant for licensure as a transitional mortgage loan originator shall:

a.   Be at least 18 years of age;

b.   Have an active license to originate mortgage loans pursuant to the laws of any state or territory of the United States other than North Carolina;

c.   Have a valid unique identifier, registration, and fingerprints on file with the Nationwide Mortgage Licensing System and Registry;

d.   Have been employed for a period of no less than two years as a mortgage loan originator; and

e.   Have provided certification of employment with a mortgage lender or mortgage broker licensed under this Article, including an attestation by the employer that the applicant is in his or her employ.

(2)   Each applicant for licensure as a mortgage broker or mortgage lender or mortgage servicer at the time of application shall comply with the following requirements:

a.   If the applicant is a sole proprietor, the applicant shall have at least three years of experience in residential mortgage lending or other experience or meet competency requirements as the Commissioner may impose.

b.   If the applicant is a corporation, limited liability company, general or limited partnership, association, or other group engaged in a joint enterprise, however organized, at least one of its principal officers, managers, or general partners shall have three years of experience in residential mortgage lending or other experience or meet competency requirements as the Commissioner may impose.

175

c.   If the applicant will be a qualifying individual or branch manager, the applicant shall have at least three years of experience in residential mortgage lending or other experience or meet competency requirements as the Commissioner may impose.

(3)   If an individual applicant to be licensed as a mortgage broker is a licensed mortgage loan originator and meets the requirements for licensure as a mortgage broker, but is not an employee as defined in G.S. 53-244.030(10) and does not meet the experience requirements of G.S. 53-244.050(b)(2)a., the individual may be licensed as an exclusive mortgage broker upon compliance with all of the following:

a.   Successfully completes the prelicensing education required under G.S. 53-244.070.

b.   Acts exclusively as a mortgage broker and shall be an agent for a single mortgage lender or mortgage broker licensee or a single exempt mortgage lender, who:

1.   Shall be responsible for supervising the broker as required by this Article and in accordance with a plan of supervision approved by the Commissioner in the Commissioner's discretion;

2.   Shall sign the license application of the applicant; and

3.   Shall be jointly and severally liable with the broker for any claims arising from the broker's mortgage brokering activities.

c.   Shall be compensated on a basis that is not dependent upon the interest rate, fees, or other terms of the loan brokered, provided that this sub-subdivision shall not prohibit compensation based on the principal balance of the loan.

d.   Shall offer only fixed-term, fixed-rate, fully amortizing mortgage loans originated by a single mortgage lender with substantially equal monthly mortgage payments and without a prepayment penalty, unless the Commissioner shall approve, in the Commissioner's discretion, the sale of other mortgage loan products for that lender.

e.   Shall not handle borrower or other third-party funds in connection with the brokering or closing of mortgage loans.

176

f.   Shall meet the surety bond requirement of a mortgage broker or otherwise be covered by a surety bond provided by the mortgage lender or broker licensee or exempt mortgage lender of the lesser of five million dollars ($5,000,000) or an amount equal to or greater than the sum of the surety bond requirements for each exclusive mortgage broker supervised by the broker or lender.

(c)   In connection with an application for licensing as a mortgage loan originator, transitional mortgage loan originator, mortgage lender, mortgage broker, or mortgage servicer, the applicant and its owners, qualifying individual, and controlling persons shall furnish to the Nationwide Mortgage Licensing System and Registry information concerning the applicant's identity, including:

(1)   Fingerprints for submission to the Federal Bureau of Investigation and any governmental agency or entity authorized to receive such information for a state, national, and international criminal history background check.

(2)   Personal history and experience in a form prescribed by the Nationwide Mortgage Licensing System and Registry and the Commissioner to obtain:

a.   Independent credit reports obtained from a consumer reporting agency described in section 603(p) of the Fair Credit Reporting Act; and

b.   Information related to any administrative, civil, or criminal findings by any governmental jurisdiction.

(3)   The personal history may be obtained by the Commissioner at any time and the fingerprint information shall be furnished upon the Commissioner's request.

(4)   An authorization for the Commissioner to obtain personal history or fingerprint information at any time.

(d)   For the purposes of this section and in order to reduce the points of contact that the Federal Bureau of Investigation may have to maintain for purposes of the criminal information required by this section, the Commissioner may use the Nationwide Mortgage Licensing System and Registry as a channeling agent for requesting information from and distributing information to the Department of Justice or any governmental agency.

(e)   For the purposes of this section and in order to reduce the points of contact that the Commissioner may have to maintain for purposes of the noncriminal information required by this section, the Commissioner may use the Nationwide Mortgage Licensing System and Registry as a channeling agent for requesting and distributing information to and from any source so directed by the Commissioner.

(f)   For purposes of this section, the Commissioner may request and the North Carolina Department of Justice may provide a criminal record check to the Commissioner for any person who has applied for or holds a mortgage lender, mortgage broker, mortgage servicer, mortgage loan originator, or transitional mortgage loan originator license as provided by this section. The Commissioner shall provide the Department of Justice, along with the request, the fingerprints of the person, any additional information required by the Department of Justice, and a form signed by the person consenting to the check of the criminal record and to the use of the fingerprints and other identifying information required by the State or national repositories. The person's fingerprints shall be forwarded to the State Bureau of Investigation for a search of the State's criminal history record file, and the State Bureau of Investigation shall forward a set of the fingerprints to the Federal Bureau of Investigation for a national criminal history check. The Department of Justice may charge a fee for each person for conducting the checks of criminal history records authorized by this section.

(g)   Except as provided by subsection (h) of this section, persons engaged in the mortgage business and exempt from licensure pursuant to G.S. 53-244.040(d)(5) shall notify the Commissioner in order to claim and confirm the exemption and to facilitate the referral of consumers that contact the Commissioner. The Commissioner shall prescribe a form for such a claim of exemption that shall contain:

(1)   The name of the exempt person;

(2)   The basis of the exempt status of the exempt person;

(3)   The principal business address and contact information for the exempt person; and

(4)   The State or federal regulatory authority responsible for the exempt person's supervision, examination, or regulation.

(h) A State or federally chartered credit union may claim and confirm an exemption from this Article by notifying the Administrator of the Credit Union Division of the Department of Commerce and providing substantially the same information required by subsection (g) of this section.

(i) The Commissioner shall keep all information pursuant to this section privileged, in accordance with applicable State law and federal guidelines, and the information shall be confidential and shall not be a public record under Chapter 132 of the General Statutes. (2009-374, s. 2; 2013-327, s. 3; 2013-412, s. 1.)

§ 53-244.060. Issuance of license.

If an applicant satisfies the requirements of G.S. 53-244.050, the Commissioner shall issue a mortgage lender, mortgage broker, mortgage servicer, mortgage loan originator, or transitional mortgage loan originator license unless the Commissioner finds any of the following:

(1) The applicant has had a mortgage loan originator or mortgage lender, mortgage broker, or mortgage servicer license revoked in any governmental jurisdiction, except that a subsequent formal vacation of the revocation shall not be deemed a revocation.

(2) The applicant or its controlling persons have been convicted of or plead guilty or nolo contendere to a felony in a domestic, foreign, or military court:

a. During the seven-year period preceding the date of the application for licensing and registration; or

b. At any time preceding the date of application, if the felony involved an act of fraud, dishonesty, a breach of trust, or money laundering.

A pardon of a conviction shall not be a conviction for purposes of this subdivision.

(3) The applicant or any of its controlling persons have been convicted of or plead guilty or nolo contendere to any charge in a domestic, foreign, or military court, within the past five years, of a misdemeanor involving moral turpitude or any fraud, false statement or omission, any theft or wrongful taking of property,

179

bribery, perjury, forgery, counterfeiting, extortion, or conspiracy to commit any of these offenses, or involving any financial service or financial service-related business.

(4)   The applicant has demonstrated a lack of financial responsibility, character, or general fitness such as to fail to command the confidence of the community and to warrant a determination that the mortgage loan originator, transitional mortgage loan originator, or other licensee will operate honestly, fairly, and efficiently within the purposes of this Article. For purposes of this subdivision, a person shows a lack of financial responsibility when the person has shown a disregard in the management of the person's own financial affairs. Evidence that a person has not shown financial responsibility may include:

a.   Current outstanding judgments, except judgments resulting solely from medical expenses;

b.   Current outstanding tax liens or other government liens and filings;

c.   Foreclosures within the past three years; or

d.   A pattern of serious delinquent accounts within the past three years.

(5)   The mortgage loan originator applicant has failed to complete the prelicensing education requirement described in G.S. 53-244.070.

(6)   The mortgage loan originator applicant has failed to pass a written test that meets the requirements described in G.S. 53-244.080.

(7)   The mortgage lender, mortgage broker, or mortgage servicer applicant has failed to meet the surety bond requirement described in G.S. 53-244.103.

(8)   The mortgage lender, mortgage broker, or mortgage servicer applicant fails to meet the minimum net worth requirement as described in G.S. 53-244.104.

(9)   The applicant's participation in the mortgage business will not be in the public interest. (2009-374, s. 2; 2013-327, s. 4.)

§ 53-244.070. Educational requirements for mortgage loan originators.

180

(a)   In order to be eligible to apply for a mortgage loan originator license, an individual must complete at least 24 hours of prelicensing education approved in accordance with subsection (b) of this section, which shall include:

(1)   Three hours of federal law and regulations;

(2)   Three hours of ethics, including instruction on fraud, consumer protection, and fair lending issues;

(3)   Two hours of training related to lending standards for nontraditional mortgage products; and

(4)   Four hours of North Carolina laws and regulations.

(b)   Prelicensing education courses and the course providers shall be reviewed and approved by the Nationwide Mortgage Licensing System and Registry using reasonable standards consistently applied, subject to the Commissioner's approval of any course of study required by subdivision (a)(4) of this section. Review and approval of a prelicensing education course shall include review and approval of the course provider.

(c)   Nothing in this section shall preclude any prelicensing education course, approved by the Nationwide Mortgage Licensing System and Registry, that is provided by the employer of the applicant or an entity that is affiliated with the applicant by an agency contract, or any subsidiary or affiliate of the employer or entity.

(d)   Except as provided in subsection (e) of this section, prelicensing education may be offered only in a classroom or classroom equivalent setting, as approved by the Nationwide Mortgage Licensing System and Registry.

(e)   An individual having successfully completed the prelicensing educational requirements in any other state, if the requirements have been approved by the Nationwide Mortgage Licensing System and Registry, shall be given credit for those hours toward the completion of the prelicensing requirements in this State, other than the hours required under subdivision (a)(4) of this section.

(f)   An individual previously licensed under this Article whose license expires and who requests a late renewal of license pursuant to G.S. 53-244.101 must prove that the individual has completed all of the continuing education requirements for the preceding year. (2009-374, s. 2.)

§ 53-244.080. Testing requirements for mortgage loan originators.

(a)   An individual must pass a qualified written test, as defined by subsection (b) of this section, developed by the Nationwide Mortgage Licensing System and Registry and administered by a test provider approved by the Nationwide Mortgage Licensing System and Registry. In addition, prior to licensure in this State, an individual must take a qualified written test that tests the individual's knowledge and comprehension of North Carolina law and regulation.

(b)   A written test shall not be treated as a qualified written test unless the test adequately measures the applicant's knowledge and comprehension in the following subject areas:

(1)   Ethics;

(2)   Federal law and regulation pertaining to mortgage origination;

(3)   North Carolina law and regulation pertaining to mortgage origination; and

(4)   Federal and North Carolina law and regulations relating to fraud, consumer protection, nontraditional mortgage products, and fair lending issues.

(c)   Nothing in this section shall prohibit a test provider approved by the Nationwide Mortgage Licensing System and Registry from providing a test at the location of the employer of the applicant or the location of any subsidiary or affiliate of the employer of the applicant, or the location of any entity which is licensed by North Carolina to engage in the mortgage lending business.

(d)   An applicant shall be considered to have passed a qualified written test provided the applicant achieves a test score of at least seventy-five percent (75%) correct answers to questions. In addition, an applicant shall not be considered to have passed a qualified written test if the individual did not achieve a test score of at least seventy-five percent (75%) correct answers to questions related to North Carolina law and regulation.

(e)   An applicant may retake a test three consecutive times with each consecutive test occurring at least 30 days after the preceding test. After failing three consecutive tests, an applicant must wait at least six months before retaking the test. A licensed mortgage loan originator who fails to maintain a valid license for a period of five years or longer must retake the test. (2009-374, s. 2; 2013-412, s. 2.)

§ 53-244.090. License application fees.

(a)   Every applicant for initial licensure shall pay a nonrefundable filing fee of one thousand two hundred fifty dollars ($1,250) for licensure as a mortgage broker, mortgage lender, or mortgage servicer, three hundred dollars ($300.00) for licensure as an exclusive mortgage broker, or one hundred twenty-five dollars ($125.00) for licensure as a mortgage loan originator or transitional mortgage loan originator. In addition, an applicant must pay the actual cost of obtaining a credit report, State and national criminal history record checks, and the processing fees required by the Nationwide Mortgage Licensing System and Registry.

(b)   Each principal and each branch office of a mortgage broker or mortgage lender licensed under the provisions of this Article shall be issued a separate license for which the Commissioner shall assess a nonrefundable filing fee of three hundred dollars ($300.00) in addition to the Nationwide Mortgage Licensing System and Registry processing fee. A licensed mortgage broker or mortgage lender shall file with the Commissioner a notice on a form prescribed by the Commissioner that identifies the address of the principal office and each branch office and its designated branch manager. Payment of the license fee under subsection (a) of this section shall be deemed to cover the location license fee for the principal office of each mortgage lender, mortgage broker, or mortgage servicer without payment of an additional three hundred dollars ($300.00) under this subsection. (2009-374, s. 2; 2010-168, s. 4; 2013-327, s. 5.)

§ 53-244.100. Active license requirements and assignability.

(a)   It is unlawful for any person to engage in the mortgage business without first obtaining a license as a mortgage loan originator, transitional mortgage loan originator, mortgage lender, mortgage broker, or mortgage servicer issued by the Commissioner under this Article. It is unlawful for any person to employ, to compensate, or to appoint as its agent a mortgage loan originator unless the person is a licensed mortgage loan originator or a transitional mortgage loan originator under this Article. Persons defined in G.S. 53-244.030(8) or G.S. 53-244.030(29) are not subject to this subsection.

(b)   The license of a mortgage loan originator or transitional mortgage loan originator is not effective during any period when that person is not employed by a mortgage lender, mortgage broker, or mortgage servicer licensed under this Article. When a mortgage loan originator or transitional mortgage loan originator ceases to be employed by a mortgage lender, mortgage broker, or mortgage servicer licensed under this Article, the mortgage loan originator or transitional mortgage loan originator and the mortgage lender, mortgage broker, or mortgage servicer licensed under this Article by whom that person is employed shall promptly notify the Commissioner in writing. The mortgage lender, mortgage broker, or mortgage servicer shall include a statement of the specific reason for the termination of the mortgage loan originator's or transitional mortgage loan originator's employment. A mortgage loan originator or transitional mortgage loan originator shall not be employed simultaneously by more than one mortgage lender, mortgage broker, or mortgage servicer licensed under this Article.

(c)   Each mortgage lender, mortgage broker, and mortgage servicer licensed under this Article shall maintain on file with the Commissioner a list of all mortgage loan originators and transitional mortgage loan originators who are employed with the mortgage lender, mortgage broker, or mortgage servicer.

(d)   No person, other than an exempt person, shall hold himself or herself out as a mortgage lender, a mortgage broker, a mortgage servicer, a mortgage loan originator, or a transitional mortgage loan originator unless the person is licensed in accordance with this Article.

(e)   Licenses issued under this Article are not assignable. Control of a licensee shall not be acquired through a stock purchase, merger, or other device without the prior written consent of the Commissioner. The Commissioner shall not give written consent if the Commissioner finds that any of the grounds for denial, revocation, or suspension of a license are applicable to the acquiring person. (2009-374, s. 2; 2013-327, s. 6.)

§ 53-244.100A. Assessments.

184

(a)　For the purpose of meeting the cost of regulation under this Article, each mortgage lender, mortgage broker, and mortgage servicer licensed under this Article shall pay into the OCOB an assessment as provided in this subsection. The annual assessment shall consist of a base amount of two thousand dollars ($2,000) for volumes of no more than one million five hundred thousand dollars ($1,500,000) plus an additional sum, calculated on the loan and servicing dollar volume reported by the licensee to the OCOB for the previous calendar year. If a licensee has both loan and servicing volume, those amounts shall be added together and the assessment shall be calculated from the table below as follows:

Loan and/or Servicing Dollar Volume		Per Thousand
$1,500,001 to	$2,500,000	$0.07
$2,500,001 to	$5,000,000	$0.06
$5,000,001 to	$10,000,000	$0.05
$10,000,001 to	$30,000,000	$0.04
$30,000,001 to	$100,000,000	$0.03
$100,000,001 to	$1,300,000,000	$0.02
More Than $1,300,000,001		$0.01

(b)　The Commissioner may collect the assessment provided for in subsection (a) of this section annually or in periodic installments as approved by the Commission. (2012-37, s. 1.)

§ 53-244.101. License renewal.

(a)　All licenses issued by the Commissioner under the provisions of this Article shall expire annually on the 31st day of December following issuance or on any other date that the Commissioner may determine. The license is invalid after that date and shall remain invalid unless renewed under subsection (b) of this section.

(b)   A license may be renewed on or after November 1 of each year by complying with the requirements of subsection (c) of this section. A mortgage loan originator shall pay a nonrefundable renewal fee of one hundred twenty-five dollars ($125.00) plus the actual cost of obtaining credit reports and State and national criminal history record checks and processing fees for the Nationwide Mortgage Licensing System and Registry as the Commissioner shall require.

(c)   Licensees may apply to renew a mortgage loan originator, mortgage lender, mortgage broker, and mortgage servicer license. The application for renewal shall demonstrate that:

(1)   The licensee continues to meet the initial minimum standards for licensure under G.S. 53-244.060;

(2)   The mortgage loan originator has satisfied the annual continuing education requirements described in G.S. 53-244.102; and

(3)   The licensee has paid all required fees and assessments.

(d)   If a mortgage lender, mortgage broker, or mortgage servicer's license is not renewed prior to the expiration date, then the licensee shall pay two hundred fifty dollars ($250.00) as a nonrefundable late fee. If a mortgage loan originator's license is not renewed prior to the expiration date, then the licensee shall pay a nonrefundable late fee of one hundred dollars ($100.00) in addition to the renewal fee set forth in subsection (b) of this section. In the event a licensee fails to obtain a reinstatement of the license prior to March 1, the Commissioner shall require the licensee to comply with the requirements for the initial issuance of a license under the provisions of this Article.

(e)   When required by the Commissioner, each person shall furnish to the Commissioner the person's consent to a criminal history record check and a set of the person's fingerprints in a form acceptable to the Commissioner or to the Nationwide Mortgage Licensing System and Registry. Refusal to consent to a criminal history record check shall constitute grounds for the Commissioner to deny renewal of the license of the person as well as the license of any other person by whom the person is employed, over which the person has control, or as to which the person is the current or proposed qualifying individual or current or proposed branch manager. (2009-374, s. 2; 2010-168, s. 5; 2011-326, s. 26; 2012-37, s. 2.)

§ 53-244.102. Continuing education for mortgage loan originators.

(a)   A licensed mortgage loan originator shall annually complete at least eight hours of continuing education approved in accordance with subsection (b) of this section, including:

(1)   Three hours of federal law and regulations;

(2)   Two hours of ethics, including instruction on fraud, consumer protection, and fair lending issues;

(3)   Two hours of training related to lending standards for nontraditional mortgage products; and

(4)   One hour of North Carolina law and regulations.

(b)   Continuing education courses shall be reviewed and approved by the Nationwide Mortgage Licensing System and Registry based upon reasonable standards. Approval of a continuing education course shall include approval of the course provider.

(c)   Nothing in this section shall preclude any continuing education course, approved by the Nationwide Mortgage Licensing System and Registry, that is provided by the employer of the mortgage loan originator or an entity affiliated with the mortgage loan originator by an agency contract, or any subsidiary or affiliate of such employer or entity. Continuing education may be offered either in a classroom, online, or by any other means approved by the Nationwide Mortgage Licensing System and Registry.

(d)   A licensed mortgage loan originator:

(1)   Except for G.S. 53-244.070(a) and subsection (e) of this section, may receive credit for a continuing education course taken prior to the end of the reinstatement period under G.S. 53-244.101(d); and

(2)   May not take the same approved course in the same or successive years to meet the annual requirements for continuing education.

(e)   A licensed mortgage loan originator who is an approved instructor of an approved continuing education course may receive credit for the licensed

187

mortgage loan originator's own annual continuing education requirement at the rate of two hours credit for every one hour taught.

(f)   A licensee having successfully completed the education requirements approved by the Nationwide Mortgage Licensing System and Registry in subdivisions (a)(1), (a)(2), and (a)(3) of this section for any state shall be accepted as credit toward completion of continuing education requirements in North Carolina. (2009-374, s. 2; 2013-412, s. 3.)

§ 53-244.103. Surety bond requirements.

(a)   Each mortgage loan originator or transitional mortgage loan originator shall be covered by a surety bond through employment with a licensee in accordance with this section. The surety bond shall provide coverage for each mortgage loan originator or transitional mortgage loan originator employed by the licensee in an amount as prescribed by subsection (b) of this section and shall be in a form prescribed by the Commissioner. The Commissioner may adopt rules with respect to the requirements for the surety bonds as needed to accomplish the purposes of the Article.

(b)   Licensees shall be required to post a surety bond with the Commissioner at application to be subsequently adjusted as follows:

(1)   A mortgage broker shall post a minimum surety bond of seventy-five thousand dollars ($75,000). Provided, however, if a mortgage broker has originated mortgage loans in North Carolina in a 12-month period ending December 31 in excess of ten million dollars ($10,000,000) but less than fifty million dollars ($50,000,000), then the mortgage broker's minimum bond amount shall be one hundred twenty-five thousand dollars ($125,000), and if a mortgage broker has originated mortgage loans in North Carolina in a 12-month period ending December 31 of fifty million dollars ($50,000,000) or more, the mortgage broker's minimum bond shall be two hundred fifty thousand dollars ($250,000).

(2)   A mortgage lender or mortgage servicer shall post a minimum surety bond of one hundred fifty thousand dollars ($150,000). Provided, however, if a mortgage lender has originated mortgage loans in North Carolina in a 12-month period ending December 31 in excess of ten million dollars ($10,000,000) but less than fifty million dollars ($50,000,000), then the mortgage lender's minimum bond amount shall be two hundred fifty thousand dollars ($250,000), and if a mortgage lender has originated mortgage loans in North Carolina in a 12-month

188

period ending December 31 of fifty million dollars ($50,000,000) or more, then the mortgage lender's minimum bond shall be five hundred thousand dollars ($500,000).

(3)   Any increased surety bond required under subdivision (1) or (2) of this subsection shall be filed with the Commissioner on or before May 31 immediately following the end of the 12-month December 31 period.

(c)   The surety bond shall be in a form satisfactory to the Commissioner and shall run to the State for the benefit of any claimants against the licensee to secure the faithful performance of the obligations of the licensee under this Article. The aggregate liability of the surety shall not exceed the principal sum of the bond. A party having a claim against the licensee may bring suit directly on the surety bond, or the Commissioner may bring suit on behalf of any claimants, either in one action or in successive actions. Consumer claims shall be given priority in recovering from the bond. When an action is commenced on a licensee's bond, the Commissioner may require the filing of a new bond. In this case, the licensee shall file a replacement bond in the required amount within 30 days. Immediately upon recovery upon any action on the bond the licensee shall file a new bond.

(d)   In the Commissioner's discretion and upon written request of the licensee, the Commissioner may waive the requirement of the bond for any licensee, if:

(1)   The licensee has been licensed by the Commissioner for at least three years;

(2)   The licensee can demonstrate a net worth, according to the most recent audited financial statement, at least four times the required bond amount, and the licensee certifies that its net worth will be maintained at or above this level at all times and agrees to notify the Commissioner and to secure an appropriate bond in the event the net worth falls below this level;

(3)   The Commissioner believes the licensee has a satisfactory history of resolving complaints from consumers and responding to findings of investigations or examinations by the Commissioner; and

(4)   The Commissioner has no reason to believe the licensee will be unable to resolve complaints, respond to examination or investigative findings, or fulfill financial obligations under this Article.

189

(e)   If the Commissioner has waived the bond requirement of a licensee based on subsection (d) of this section, the Commissioner may summarily reinstate the bond requirement on any licensee if the Commissioner has reason to believe the licensee no longer meets the standards in subsection (d) of this section. In this event, the licensee shall submit a bond, as required in subsection (b) of this section, within 30 days. Failure to submit a bond as directed by the Commissioner shall be grounds for summary suspension. (2009-374, s. 2; 2013-327, s. 7.)

§ 53-244.104. Minimum net worth requirements.

(a)   A minimum net worth shall be continuously maintained for licensees in accordance with this section. In the event that the mortgage loan originator or transitional mortgage loan originator is an employee or exclusive agent of a person subject to this Article, the net worth of the person subject to this Article can be used in lieu of the mortgage loan originator's or transitional mortgage loan originator's minimum net worth requirement. The minimum net worth to be maintained for each license is as follows:

(1)   If the licensee is a mortgage lender, it shall maintain a net worth of at least one hundred thousand dollars ($100,000), including evidence of liquidity of one million dollars ($1,000,000), which may include a warehouse line of credit of one million dollars ($1,000,000) or other evidence of funding capacity to conduct mortgage originations as documented by an unqualified audited statement of financial condition.

(2)   If the licensee is a mortgage servicer, it shall maintain a net worth of at least one hundred thousand dollars ($100,000), not including monies in any escrow accounts held for others.

(3)   If the licensee is a mortgage broker, it shall maintain a net worth of at least twenty-five thousand dollars ($25,000), including evidence of liquidity of ten thousand dollars ($10,000), as certified by the licensee in a certified statement of financial condition.

(b)   The Commissioner may adopt rules to require additional minimum net worth or otherwise amend net worth requirements as are necessary to ensure licensees maintain adequate financial responsibility and accomplish the purposes of this Article. (2009-374, s. 2; 2013-327, s. 8.)

190

§ 53-244.105. Records, addresses, escrow funds, or trust accounts.

(a)   Every licensee shall make and keep the accounts, correspondence, memoranda, papers, books, and other records as prescribed in rules adopted by the Commissioner. All records shall be preserved for three years unless the Commissioner, by rule, prescribes otherwise for particular types of records.

(b)   No person shall make any false statement or knowingly and willfully make any omission of a material fact in connection with any information or reports filed with the Commissioner, a governmental agency, or the Nationwide Mortgage Licensing System and Registry or in connection with any oral or written communication with the Commissioner or another governmental agency. If the information contained in any document filed with the Commissioner or the Nationwide Mortgage Licensing System and Registry is or becomes inaccurate or incomplete in any material respect, the licensee or exempt entity shall within 30 days file a correcting amendment to the information contained in the document.

(c)   Each mortgage broker licensee shall maintain and transact business from a principal place of business in this State. The Commissioner may, by rule, impose terms and conditions under which the records and files of a mortgage lender or mortgage servicer may be maintained outside of this State. A principal place of business shall not be located at an individual's home or residence. A mortgage lender, mortgage broker, or mortgage servicer licensee shall maintain a record of the principal place of business with the Commissioner and report any change of address of the principal place of business or any branch office within 15 days after the change.

(d)   A licensee shall maintain in a segregated escrow fund or trust account any funds which come into the licensee's possession but which are not the licensee's property and which the licensee is not entitled to retain under the circumstances. The escrow fund or trust account shall be held on deposit in a federally insured financial institution. Individual loan applicants' or borrowers' accounts may be aggregated into a common trust fund so long as (i) interests in the common fund can be individually tracked and accounted for and (ii) the common fund is kept separate from and is not commingled with the licensee's own funds. (2009-374, s. 2.)

§ 53-244.106. Display of license.

191

Each mortgage broker or mortgage lender licensed under this Article shall display, in plain public view, the certificate of licensure issued by the Commissioner in its principal office and in each branch office. Each mortgage loan originator or transitional mortgage loan originator licensed under this Article shall display, in plain public view, in each branch office in which the individual acts as a mortgage loan originator or transitional mortgage loan originator the certificate of licensure issued by the Commissioner. (2009-374, s. 2; 2013-327, s. 9.)

§ 53-244.107. Unique identifier shown.

The unique identifier of any mortgage loan originator, transitional mortgage loan originator, or other person engaged in the mortgage business as defined in G.S. 53-244.030(11) shall be clearly shown on all residential mortgage loan application forms, solicitations, advertisements, including business cards or Web sites, and any other documents as established by rule or order of the Commissioner. (2009-374, s. 2; 2013-327, s. 10.)

§ 53-244.108. Reports.

Each mortgage lender, mortgage broker, or mortgage servicer licensee shall submit to the Commissioner and to the Nationwide Mortgage Licensing System and Registry reports of condition and any other reports requested by the Commissioner pursuant to G.S. 53-244.115(d). The reports shall be in the form and shall contain any information that the Commissioner or Nationwide Mortgage Licensing System and Registry may require. (2009-374, s. 2.)

§ 53-244.109. Mortgage broker duties.

Any mortgage broker engaged in the mortgage business as defined by G.S. 53-244.030(11)a., in addition to duties imposed by other statutes or at common law, shall do all of the following:

(1)   Safeguard and account for any money handled for the borrower.

(2)   Follow reasonable and lawful instructions from the borrower.

(3)   Act with reasonable skill, care, and diligence.

192

(4)   Make reasonable efforts to secure a loan that is reasonably advantageous to the borrower considering all the circumstances, including the rates, charges, and repayment terms of the loan.

(5)   Timely and clearly disclose to the borrower material information that may be expected to influence the borrower's decision and is reasonably accessible to the mortgage broker, including the total compensation the mortgage broker expects to receive from any and all sources in connection with each loan option presented to the borrower.

(6)   Notify before closing each lender of the particulars of each of the other lender's loans if the mortgage broker knows that more than one mortgage loan will be made by different lenders contemporaneously to a borrower.

(7)   Ensure that any services offered to any applicant shall be available and offered to all similarly situated applicants on an equal basis.

(8)   In transactions where the mortgage broker has the ability to make credit decisions, use reasonable means to provide the borrower with prompt credit decisions on its loan applications and, where the credit is denied, to comply fully with the notification requirements of applicable State and federal law.

(9)   Ensure that advertising materials are designed to make customers and potential customers aware that the mortgage broker does not discriminate on any prohibited basis.

(10)   Represent the borrower's best interest in the course of brokering a mortgage loan.

(11)   Have a duty of loyalty to the borrower, which shall include a duty not to compromise a borrower's right or interest in favor of another's right or interest, including a right or interest of the mortgage broker. (2009-374, s. 2.)

§ 53-244.110. Mortgage servicer duties.

Any mortgage servicer engaged in the mortgage business as defined by G.S. 53-244.030(11)c., in addition to duties imposed by other statutes or at common law, shall do all of the following:

(1)   Safeguard and account for any money handled for the borrower.

193

(2)   Follow reasonable and lawful instructions from the borrower.

(3)   Act with reasonable skill, care, and diligence.

(4)   File with the Commissioner a complete, current schedule of the ranges of costs and fees it charges borrowers for its servicing-related activities with its application and renewal and with its supplemental filings made from time to time.

(5)   File with the Commissioner upon request a report in a form and format acceptable to the Commissioner detailing the servicer's activities in this State, including:

a.   The number of mortgage loans the servicer is servicing.

b.   The type and characteristics of the loans in this State.

c.   The number of serviced loans in default, along with a breakdown of 30-, 60-, and 90-day delinquencies.

d.   Information on loss mitigation activities, including details on workout arrangements undertaken.

e.   Information on foreclosures commenced in this State.

(6)   At the time a servicer accepts assignment of servicing rights for a mortgage loan, the servicer shall disclose to the borrower all of the following:

a.   Any notice required by RESPA or by regulations promulgated thereunder.

b.   A schedule of the ranges and categories of its costs and fees for its servicing-related activities, which shall comply with North Carolina law and which shall not exceed those reported to the Commissioner.

c.   A notice in a form and content acceptable to the Commissioner that the servicer is licensed by the Commissioner and that complaints about the servicer may be submitted to the Commissioner.

d.   Any notice required by Article 2A, 4, or 10 of Chapter 45 of the General Statutes.

194

(7)   In the event of a delinquency or other act of default on the part of the borrower, the mortgage servicer shall act in good faith to inform the borrower of the facts concerning the loan and the nature and extent of the delinquency or default and, if the borrower replies, to negotiate with the borrower, subject to the mortgage servicer's duties and obligations under the mortgage servicing contract, if any, to attempt a resolution or workout to the delinquency. (2009-374, s. 2.)

§ 53-244.111. Prohibited acts.

In addition to the activities prohibited under other provisions of this Article, it shall be unlawful for any person in the course of any residential mortgage loan transaction:

(1)   To misrepresent or conceal the material facts or make false promises likely to influence, persuade, or induce an applicant for a mortgage loan or a mortgagor to take a mortgage loan, or to pursue a course of misrepresentation through agents or otherwise.

(2)   To improperly refuse to issue a satisfaction of a mortgage.

(3)   To fail to account for or to deliver to any person any funds, documents, or other thing of value obtained in connection with a mortgage loan, including money provided by a borrower for a real estate appraisal or a credit report, which the mortgage lender, mortgage broker, mortgage servicer, mortgage loan originator, or transitional mortgage loan originator is not entitled to retain under the circumstances.

(4)   To pay, receive, or collect in whole or in part any commission, fee, or other compensation for brokering or servicing a mortgage loan in violation of this Article, including a mortgage loan brokered or serviced by any unlicensed person other than an exempt person.

(5)   To charge or collect any fee or rate of interest or to make or broker or service any mortgage loan with terms or conditions or in a manner contrary to the provisions of Chapter 24, 45, or 54 of the General Statutes.

(6)   To advertise mortgage loans, including rates, margins, discounts, points, fees, commissions, or other material information, including material limitations

on the loans, unless the person is able to make the mortgage loans available to a reasonable number of qualified applicants.

(7)   To fail to disburse funds in accordance with a written commitment or agreement to make a mortgage loan.

(8)   To engage in any transaction, practice, or course of business that is not in good faith or fair dealing or that constitutes a fraud upon any person in connection with the brokering or making or servicing of, or purchase or sale of, any mortgage loan.

(9)   To fail to pay promptly when due reasonable fees to a licensed appraiser for appraisal services that are:

a.   Requested from the appraiser in writing by the mortgage broker or mortgage lender or an employee of the mortgage broker or mortgage lender; and

b.   Performed by the appraiser in connection with the origination or closing of a mortgage loan for a customer or the mortgage broker or mortgage lender.

(10)   To broker a mortgage loan that contains a prepayment penalty if the principal amount of the loan is one hundred fifty thousand dollars ($150,000) or less or if the loan is a rate spread home loan as defined in G.S. 24-1.1F.

(11)   To improperly influence or attempt to improperly influence the development, reporting, result, or review of a real estate appraisal sought in connection with a mortgage loan. Nothing in this subdivision shall be construed to prohibit a mortgage lender, mortgage broker, or mortgage servicer from asking the appraiser to do one or more of the following:

a.   Consider additional appropriate property information.

b.   Provide further detail, substantiation, or explanation for the appraiser's value conclusion.

c.   Correct errors in the appraisal report.

(12)   To fail to comply with the mortgage loan servicing transfer, escrow account administration, or borrower inquiry response requirements imposed by sections 6 and 10 of RESPA and regulations adopted thereunder.

(13)   To broker a rate spread adjustable rate mortgage loan without disclosing to the borrower the terms and costs associated with a fixed rate loan from the same lender at the lowest annual percentage rate for which the borrower qualifies.

(14)   To fail to comply with applicable State and federal laws and regulations related to mortgage lending or mortgage servicing.

(15)   To engage in unfair, misleading, or deceptive advertising related to a solicitation for a mortgage loan.

(16)   In connection with the brokering or making of a rate spread home loan as defined under G.S. 24-1.1F, no lender shall provide nor shall any broker receive any compensation that changes based on the terms of the loan. This subdivision shall not prohibit compensation based on the principal balance of the loan.

(17)   For a mortgage servicer to fail to comply with the mortgage servicer's obligations under Article 10 of Chapter 45 of the General Statutes.

(18)   For a mortgage servicer to fail to provide written notice to a borrower upon taking action to place hazard, homeowner's, or flood insurance on the mortgaged property or to place such insurance when the mortgage servicer knows or has reason to know that the insurance is in effect.

(19)   For a mortgage servicer to place hazard, homeowner's, or flood insurance on a mortgaged property for an amount that exceeds either the value of the insurable improvements or the last known coverage amount of insurance.

(20)   For a mortgage servicer to fail to provide to the borrower a refund of unearned premiums paid by a borrower or charged to the borrower for hazard, homeowner's, or flood insurance placed by a mortgage lender or mortgage servicer if the borrower provides reasonable proof that the borrower has obtained coverage such that the forced placement is no longer necessary and the property is insured. If the borrower provides reasonable proof within 12 months of the placement that no lapse in coverage occurred such that the forced placement was not necessary, the mortgage servicer shall refund the entire premium.

(21)   For a mortgage servicer to refuse to reinstate a delinquent loan upon a tender of payment made timely under the contract which is sufficient in amount,

based upon the last written statement received by the borrower, to pay all past due amounts, outstanding or overdue charges, and restore the loan to a nondelinquent status, but this reinstatement shall be available to a borrower no more than twice in any 24-month period.

(22)   For a person acting as a mortgage servicer to fail to mail, at least 45 days before foreclosure is initiated, a notice addressed to the borrower at the borrower's last known address with the following information:

a.   An itemization of all past due amounts causing the loan to be in default.

b.   An itemization of any other charges that must be paid in order to bring the loan current.

c.   A statement that the borrower may have options available other than foreclosure and that the borrower may discuss the options with the mortgage lender, the mortgage servicer, or a counselor approved by the U.S. Department of Housing and Urban Development (HUD).

d.   The address, telephone number, and other contact information for the mortgage lender, the mortgage servicer, or the agent for either of them who is authorized to attempt to work with the borrower to avoid foreclosure.

e.   The name, address, telephone number, and other contact information for one or more HUD-approved counseling agencies operating to assist borrowers in North Carolina to avoid foreclosure.

f.   The address, telephone number, and other contact information for the consumer complaint section of the Office of the Commissioner of Banks.

(23)   To fail to make all payments from any escrow account held for the borrower for insurance, taxes, and other charges with respect to the property in a timely manner so as to ensure that no late penalties are assessed or other negative consequences result regardless of whether the loan is delinquent, unless there are not sufficient funds in the account to cover the payments and the mortgage servicer has a reasonable basis to believe that recovery of the funds will not be possible. (2009-374, s. 2; 2013-327, s. 11.)

§ 53-244.112. Criminal penalties for unlicensed activity.

Engaging in the mortgage business as defined by G.S. 53-244.030(11) or acting as a mortgage loan originator without a license as required by the provisions of G.S. 53-244.040 is a Class 3 misdemeanor. Each transaction involving unlicensed activity is a separate offense. (2009-374, s. 2.)

§ 53-244.113. Regulatory authority.

(a)   Unless otherwise provided, all actions, hearings, and procedures under this Article shall be governed by Article 3A of Chapter 150B of the General Statutes.

(b)   For purposes of this Article, the Commissioner shall be deemed to have complied with the requirements of law concerning service of process upon mailing by certified mail any notice required or permitted to a licensee under this Article, postage prepaid and addressed to the last known address of the licensee on file with the Commissioner pursuant to G.S. 53-244.105(c).

(c)   Upon the issuance of any summary order permitted under this Article, including summary suspensions and cease and desist orders, the Commissioner shall promptly notify the person subject to the order that the order has been entered and the reasons for the order. Within 20 days of receiving notice of the order, the person subject to the order may request in writing a hearing before the Commissioner. Upon receipt of such a request, the Commissioner shall calendar a hearing within 15 days. If a licensee does not request a hearing, the order will remain in effect unless it is modified or vacated by the Commissioner. (2009-374, s. 2.)

§ 53-244.114. Licensure authority.

(a)   The Commissioner may, by order, deny, suspend, revoke, or refuse to issue or renew a license of a licensee or applicant under this Article, or may restrict or limit the manner in which a licensee, applicant, or any person who owns an interest in or participates in the business of a licensee engages in the mortgage business, if the Commissioner finds both of the following:

(1)   That the order is in the public interest; and

(2)   That any of the following circumstances apply to the applicant, licensee, or any partner, member, manager, officer, director, loan originator, qualifying

199

individual, or any person occupying a similar status or performing similar functions or any person directly or indirectly controlling the applicant or licensee. The person:

a.   Has filed an application for licensure, report, or other document to the Commissioner that, as of its effective date or as of any date after filing, contained any statement that, in light of the circumstances under which it was made, is false or misleading with respect to any material fact;

b.   Has violated or failed to comply with any provision of this Article, rule adopted by the Commissioner, or order of the Commissioner;

c.   Is permanently or temporarily enjoined by any court of competent jurisdiction from engaging in or continuing any conduct or practice involving any aspect of the mortgage business;

d.   Is the subject of an order of the Commissioner denying or suspending that person's license as a mortgage loan originator, transitional mortgage loan originator, mortgage broker, mortgage lender, or mortgage servicer;

e.   Is the subject of an order entered within the past five years by the authority of any state or federal agency with jurisdiction over the mortgage brokerage, mortgage lending, or mortgage servicing industry;

f.   Fails at any time to meet the requirements of G.S. 53-244.060, 53-244.070, 53-244.080, 53-244.090, 53-244.100, 53-244.103, or 53-244.104;

g.   Controls or has controlled any mortgage broker, mortgage lender, or mortgage servicer who has been subject to an order or injunction described in sub-subdivision c., d., or e. of this subdivision;

h.   Has been the qualifying individual, branch manager, mortgage loan originator, or transitional mortgage loan originator of a licensee who had knowledge of or reasonably should have had knowledge of, or participated in, any activity that resulted in the entry of an order under this Article suspending or withdrawing the license of a licensee;

i.   Has failed to respond to inquiries from the Commissioner or the Commissioner's designee regarding any complaints filed against the licensee which allege or appear to involve violation of this Article or any law or rule affecting the mortgage lending business; or

200

j.   Has failed to respond to and cooperate fully with notices from the Commissioner or the Commissioner's designee relating to the scheduling and conducting of an examination or investigation under this Article.

(b)   In the event the Commissioner has reason to believe that a licensee, individual, or person subject to this Article may have violated or failed to comply with any provision of this Article, the Commissioner may:

(1)   Summarily order the licensee, individual, or person to cease and desist from any harmful activities or violations of this Article; or

(2)   Summarily suspend the license of the licensee under this Article.

These summary powers are in addition to the summary suspension procedures authorized by G.S. 150B-3(c). (2009-374, s. 2; 2013-327, s. 12; 2013-412, ss. 4, 4.1.)

§ 53-244.115. Investigation and examination authority.

(a)   For purposes of initial licensing, license renewal, suspension, conditioning, revocation, or termination, or general or specific inquiry, investigation, or examination to determine compliance with this Article, the Commissioner may access, receive, and use any books, accounts, records, files, documents, information, or evidence, including:

(1)   Criminal, civil, and administrative history information, including nonconviction data;

(2)   Personal history and experience information, including independent credit reports obtained from a consumer reporting agency described in section 603(p) of the Fair Credit Reporting Act; and

(3)   Any other documents, information, or evidence the Commissioner deems relevant to the inquiry, investigation, or examination regardless of the location, possession, control, or custody of the documents, information, or evidence.

(b)   For purposes of investigating violations or complaints arising under this Article, or for the purposes of examination, the Commissioner may review, investigate, or examine any licensee, individual, or person subject to this Article as often as necessary in order to carry out the purposes of this Article. The Commissioner may interview the officer, principals, person with control, qualified individual, mortgage loan originators, transitional mortgage loan originators, employees, independent contractors, agents, and customers of the licensee, individual, or person concerning their business. The Commissioner may direct, subpoena, or order the attendance of and examine under oath all persons whose testimony may be required about the loans or the business or subject matter of any examination or investigation and may direct, subpoena, or order the person to produce books, accounts, records, files, and any other documents the Commissioner deems relevant to the inquiry. The assessment set forth in G.S. 53-244.100A is for the purpose of meeting the cost of regulation under this Article. Any investigation or examination that, in the opinion of the Commissioner of Banks, requires extraordinary review, investigation, or special examination shall be subject to the actual costs of additional expenses and the hourly rate for the staff's time, to be determined annually by the Banking Commission.

(c)   Each licensee, individual, or person subject to this Article shall make available to the Commissioner upon request the books and records relating to the operations of the licensee, individual, or person. No licensee, individual, or person subject to investigation or examination under this section may knowingly withhold, abstract, remove, mutilate, destroy, or secrete any books, records, computer records, or other information. Each licensee, individual, or person subject to this Article shall also make available for interview by the Commissioner the officers, principals, persons with control, qualified individuals, mortgage loan originators, transitional mortgage loan originators, employees, independent contractors, agents, and customers of the licensee, individual, or person concerning their business.

(d)   Each licensee, individual, or person subject to this Article shall make or compile such reports or prepare other information as may be directed or requested by the Commissioner in order to carry out the purposes of this section, including:

(1)   Accounting compilations;

(2)   Information lists and data concerning loan transactions in a format prescribed by the Commissioner;

(3)   Periodic reports, including:

202

a. Annual Report Questionnaire,

b. Servicer Activity Report,

c. Servicer Schedule of the Ranges of Costs and Fees,

d. Lender/Servicer Audited Statements of Financial Condition,

e. Broker Certified Statements of Financial Condition, and

f. Quarterly Loan Origination Reports.

(4)   Any other information deemed necessary to carry out the purposes of this section.

(e)   In making any examination or investigation authorized by this Article, the Commissioner may control access to any documents and records of the licensee or person under examination or investigation. The Commissioner may take possession of the documents and records or place a person in exclusive charge of the documents and records in the place where they are usually kept. During the period of control, no individual or person shall remove or attempt to remove any of the documents and records except pursuant to a court order or with the consent of the Commissioner. Unless the Commissioner has reasonable grounds to believe the documents or records of the licensee have been or are at risk of being altered or destroyed for purposes of concealing a violation of this Article, the licensee or owner of the documents and records shall have access to the documents or records as necessary to conduct its ordinary business.

(f)   In order to carry out the purposes of this section, the Commissioner may:

(1)   Retain attorneys, accountants, or other professionals and specialists as examiners, auditors, or investigators to conduct or assist in the conduct of examinations or investigations;

(2)   Enter into agreements or relationships with other government officials or regulatory associations in order to improve efficiencies and reduce regulatory burden by sharing resources, standardized or uniform methods or procedures, documents, records, information, or evidence obtained under this section;

(3)   Use, hire, contract, or employ public or privately available analytical systems, methods, or software to examine or investigate the licensee, individual, or person subject to this Article;

(4)   Accept and rely on examination or investigation reports made by other government officials, within or without this State; or

(5)   Accept audit reports made by an independent certified public accountant for the licensee, individual, or person in the course of that part of the examination covering the same general subject matter as the audit and may incorporate the audit report in the report of the examination, report of investigation, or other writing of the Commissioner.

(g)   In addition to the authority granted by G.S. 53-244.113 and G.S. 53-244.115, the Commissioner is authorized to take action, including summary suspension of the license, if the licensee fails, within 20 days or a lesser time if specifically requested for good cause, to:

(1)   Respond to inquiries from the Commissioner or the Commissioner's designee regarding any complaints filed against the licensee that allege or appear to involve violation of this Article or any law or rule affecting the mortgage lending business;

(2)   Respond to and cooperate fully with notices from the Commissioner or the Commissioner's designee relating to the scheduling and conducting of an examination or investigation under this Article; or

(3)   Consent to a criminal history record check. The refusal shall constitute grounds for the Commissioner to deny licensure to the applicant as well as to any entity:

a.   By whom or by which the applicant is employed,

b.   Over which the applicant has control, or

c.   As to which the applicant is the current or proposed qualifying individual or a current or proposed branch manager.

(h)   The authority of this section shall remain in effect, whether a licensee, individual, or person subject to this Article acts or claims to act under any licensing law of the State, or claims to act without such authority. (2009-374, s. 2; 2012-37, s. 3; 2013-327, s. 13.)

§ 53-244.116. Disciplinary authority.

(a)   The Commissioner may, by order:

(1)   Take any action authorized under G.S. 53-244.113.

(2)   Impose a civil penalty upon a licensee, individual, or person subject to this Article, or upon any partner, officer, director, or other person occupying a similar status or performing similar functions on behalf of a licensee or other person subject to this Article for any violation of or failure to comply with this Article. The civil penalty shall not exceed twenty-five thousand dollars ($25,000) for each violation of or failure to comply with this Article. Each violation of or failure to comply with this Article shall be a separate and distinct violation.

(3)   Impose a civil penalty upon a licensee, individual, or person subject to this Article, or upon any partner, officer, director, or other person occupying a similar status or performing similar functions on behalf of a licensee or other person subject to this Article for any violation of or failure to comply with any directive or order of the Commissioner. The civil penalty shall not exceed twenty-five thousand dollars ($25,000) for each violation of or failure to comply with any directive or order of the Commissioner. Each violation of or failure to comply with any directive or order of the Commissioner shall be a separate and distinct violation.

(4)   Require a licensee, individual, or person subject to this Article to disgorge and pay to a borrower or other individual any amounts received by the licensee, individual, or person subject to the Article, including any employee of the person, to the extent that the amounts were collected in violation of Chapter 24 of the General Statutes or in excess of those allowed by law.

(5)   Prohibit licensees under this Article from engaging in acts and practices in connection with residential mortgage loans that the Commissioner finds to be unfair, deceptive, designed to evade the laws of this State, or that are not in the best interest of the borrowing public.

(b)   When a licensee is accused of any act, omission, or misconduct that would subject the licensee to disciplinary action, the licensee, with the consent and approval of the Commissioner, may surrender the license and all the rights and privileges pertaining to it. A person who surrenders a license shall not be eligible for or submit any application for licensure under this Article during any period specified by the Commissioner.

(c)   The requirements of this Article apply to any person who seeks to avoid its application by any device, subterfuge, or pretense whatsoever, including structuring a loan in a manner to avoid classification of the loan as a residential mortgage loan. (2009-374, s. 2; 2013-412, s. 5.)

§ 53-244.117: Repealed by Session Laws 2013-412, s. 6, effective August 23, 2013.

§ 53-244.118. Rule-making authority; records.

(a)   The Commissioner may adopt any rules that the Commissioner deems necessary to carry out the provisions of this Article, to provide for the protection of the borrowing public, to prohibit unfair or deceptive practices, to instruct mortgage lenders, mortgage brokers, mortgage servicers, mortgage loan originators, or transitional mortgage loan originators in interpreting this Article, and to implement and interpret the provisions of G.S. 24-1.1E, 24-1.1F, and 24-10.2 as they apply to licensees under this Article.

(b)   The Commissioner shall keep a list of all applicants for licensure under this Article or claimants of exempt status under G.S. 53-244.050(g) that includes the date of application, name, place of residence, and whether the license or claim of exempt status was granted or denied.

(c)   The Commissioner shall keep a current roster showing the names and places of business of all licensees that shows their respective mortgage loan originators and transitional mortgage loan originators and a roster of exempt persons required to file a notice under G.S. 53-244.050(g). The roster shall:

(1)   Be kept on file in the office of the Commissioner;

(2)   Contain information regarding all orders or other actions taken against the licensees and other persons; and

(3)   Be open to public inspection. (2009-374, s. 2; 2013-327, s. 14.)

§ 53-244.119. Commissioner's participation in nationwide registry.

(a)   The Commissioner shall require mortgage loan originators and transitional mortgage loan originators to be licensed and registered through the Nationwide Mortgage Licensing System and Registry. In order to carry out this requirement, the Commissioner is authorized to participate in the Nationwide Mortgage Licensing System and Registry. For this purpose, the Commissioner may establish by rule any requirements as necessary, including:

(1)   Background checks for:

a.   Criminal history through fingerprint or other databases;

b.   Civil or administrative records;

c.   Credit history; or

d.   Any other information as deemed necessary by the Nationwide Mortgage Licensing System and Registry.

(2)   The payment of fees to apply for, renew, or amend licenses through the Nationwide Mortgage Licensing System and Registry;

(3)   The setting or resetting as necessary of renewal or reporting dates; and

(4)   Requirements for amending or surrendering a license or any other activities as the Commissioner deems necessary for participation in the Nationwide Mortgage Licensing System and Registry.

(b)   The Commissioner is authorized to establish relationships or contracts with the Nationwide Mortgage Licensing System and Registry or other entities designated by the Nationwide Mortgage Licensing System and Registry to collect and maintain records and process transaction fees or other fees related to licensees or other persons subject to this Article.

(c)   For the purpose of participating in the Nationwide Mortgage Licensing System and Registry, the Commissioner is authorized to waive or modify, in whole or in part, any or all of the requirements of this Article and to establish new requirements as reasonably necessary to participate in the Nationwide Mortgage Licensing System and Registry.

(d)   The Commissioner is authorized to enter into agreements to license the use of the proprietary software owned by the Office of the Commissioner of Banks to banking, mortgage, or financial services supervisory agencies of other states.

(e)   Repealed by Session Laws 2012-37, s. 4, effective October 1, 2012. (2009-374, s. 2; 2010-168, s. 6; 2012-37, s. 4; 2013-327, s. 15.)

§ 53-244.120. Confidentiality of information.

(a)   Notwithstanding any State law to the contrary, the Commissioner shall report enforcement actions under this Article and may report other relevant information to the Nationwide Mortgage Licensing System and Registry.

(b)   The Commissioner is authorized to enter agreements or sharing arrangements with other governmental agencies, the Conference of State Bank Supervisors, the American Association of Residential Mortgage Regulators, or other associations representing governmental agencies and may share otherwise confidential information pursuant to these written agreements.

(c)   The requirements of G.S. 53C-2-7 regarding the privacy or confidentiality of any information or material provided under subsections (a) and (b) of this section, and any privilege arising under any other federal or State law with respect to such information or material, shall continue to apply to the information or material after it has been disclosed to an entity described in subsection (a) or (b) of this section. Information or material held by such an entity shall not be subject to disclosure under any State law governing the disclosure to the public of information held by an officer or agency of the State. The entities described in subsections (a) and (b) of this section may share information and material with all State and federal regulatory officials with mortgage industry oversight authority without the loss of privilege or the loss of confidentiality protections provided by State or federal law.

(d)   Any provision of Chapter 132 of the General Statutes relating to the disclosure of confidential supervisory information or of any information or material described in subsection (a) of this section that is inconsistent with this section shall be superseded by the requirements of this section.

(e)   The confidentiality provisions contained in subsection (c) of this section shall not apply with respect to the information or material relating to the employment history of and publicly adjudicated disciplinary and enforcement actions against mortgage lenders, mortgage brokers, mortgage servicers, mortgage loan originators, or transitional mortgage loan originators that are included in the Nationwide Mortgage Licensing System and Registry for access by the public. (2009-374, s. 2; 2012-56, s. 24; 2013-327, s. 16.)

§ 53-244.121. Review by Banking Commission.

The Banking Commission may review any rule, regulation, order, or act of the Commissioner made pursuant to or with respect to the provisions of this Article, and any person aggrieved by any rule, regulation, order, or act may, pursuant to G.S. 53C-2-6, appeal to the Banking Commission for review upon giving 20 days' written notice after the rule, regulation, order, or act is adopted or issued. The notice of appeal shall specifically state the grounds for appeal and, in the case of an appeal from a contested case proceeding before the Commissioner, shall set forth in numbered order the assignments of error for review by the Banking Commission. Failure to specify the assignments of error shall constitute grounds to dismiss the appeal. Failure to comply with the briefing schedule as provided by the Banking Commission shall also constitute grounds to dismiss the appeal. Notwithstanding any other provision of law, any party aggrieved by a decision of the Banking Commission shall be entitled to an appeal pursuant to G.S. 53C-2-6. (2009-374, s. 2; 2012-56, s. 25.)

Article 20.

Refund Anticipation Loan Act.

§ 53-245. Title and scope.

(a)   Title. This Article shall be known and cited as the "Refund Anticipation Loan Act".

(b)   Scope. No person may individually or in conjunction or cooperation with another person process, receive, or accept for delivery an application for a refund anticipation loan or a check in payment of refund anticipation loan proceeds or in any other manner facilitate the making of a refund anticipation loan unless the person has complied with the provisions of this Article. In addition, G.S. 143B-426.40A prohibits refund anticipation loans repaid from refunds of North Carolina tax. (1989 (Reg. Sess., 1990), c. 881, s. 2; 2006-66, s. 6.19(a); 2006-203, s. 17; 2006-221, s. 3A; 2006-259, s. 40(a).)

§ 53-246. Definitions.

The following definitions apply in this Article:

(1)   Applicant. A person who applies for registration as a facilitator of refund anticipation loans.

(2)   Commission. The State Banking Commission.

(3)   Commissioner. The Commissioner of Banks.

(4)   Creditor. A person who makes a refund anticipation loan.

(5)   Debtor. A person who receives the proceeds of a refund anticipation loan.

(6)   Facilitator. A person who individually or in conjunction or cooperation with another person processes, receives, or accepts for delivery an application for a refund anticipation loan or a check in payment of refund anticipation loan proceeds or in any other manner facilitates the making of a refund anticipation loan.

(7)   Person. An individual, a firm, a partnership, an association, a corporation, or another entity.

(8)   Refund anticipation loan. A loan that the creditor arranges to be repaid directly from the proceeds of the debtor's income tax refund.

(9)   Refund anticipation loan fee. The charges, fees, or other consideration charged or imposed by the creditor or facilitator for the making of a refund anticipation loan. This term does not include any charge, fee, or other consideration usually charged or imposed by the facilitator in the ordinary course of business for nonloan services, such as fees for tax return preparation and fees for electronic filing of tax returns.

(10)   Registrant. A person who is registered as a facilitator of refund anticipation loans under this Article. (1989 (Reg. Sess., 1990), c. 881, s. 2.)

§ 53-247. Registration requirement.

(a)   Registration Requirement. No person may individually or in conjunction or cooperation with another person process, receive, or accept for delivery an application for a refund anticipation loan or a check in payment of refund anticipation loan proceeds without first being registered with the Commissioner in accordance with the registration procedure provided in this Article.

(b)   Criminal Penalty. Violation of this section is a Class 2 misdemeanor, which may include a fine of up to two thousand dollars ($2,000).

(c)   Exemption. This section does not apply to a person doing business as a bank, savings association, or credit union, under the laws of this State or the United States. (1989 (Reg. Sess., 1990), c. 881, s. 2; 1993, c. 539, s. 427; 1994, Ex. Sess., c. 24, s. 14(c).)

§ 53-248. Registration procedure; informal hearing.

(a)   Initial Registration. An application to become registered as a facilitator shall be in writing, under oath, and in a form prescribed by the Commissioner. The application shall contain all information prescribed by the Commissioner. Each application for registration shall be accompanied by a fee, payable to the Commissioner, of two hundred fifty dollars ($250.00) for each office where the registrant intends to facilitate refund anticipation loans.

Upon the filing of an application for registration, if the Commissioner finds that the responsibility and general fitness of the applicant are such as to command the confidence of the community and to warrant belief that the business of facilitating refund anticipation loans will be operated within the purposes of this Article, the Commissioner shall register the applicant as a facilitator of refund anticipation loans and shall issue and transmit to the applicant a certificate attesting to the registration. If the Commissioner does not so find, he shall not register the applicant and shall notify the applicant of the reasons for the denial.

Upon receipt of a certificate of registration, the applicant is registered under this Article and may engage in the business of facilitating refund anticipation loans at the offices identified on the application for registration.

(b)   Renewal. Each registration as a facilitator of refund anticipation loans shall expire on December 31 following the date it was issued, unless it is renewed for the succeeding year. Before the registration expires, the registrant may renew the registration by filing with the Commissioner an application for renewal in the form and containing all information prescribed by the Commissioner. Each application for renewal of registration shall be accompanied by a fee of one hundred dollars ($100.00) for each office where the registrant intends to facilitate refund anticipation loans during the succeeding year.

Upon the filing of an application for renewal of registration under this Article, the Commissioner shall renew the registration unless the Commissioner determines that the fitness of the registrant or the operations of the registrant would not support registration of the registrant under subsection (a). If the Commissioner makes such a determination, he shall so notify the registrant, stating the reasons for the determination.

(c)   Display of Certificate. Each registrant shall prominently display a certificate issued under this Article in each place of business in the State where the registrant facilitates the making of refund anticipation loans.

(d)   Within five days of receipt of the Commissioner's notice, as required by subsections (a) and (b) of this section, the applicant may make written demand of the Commissioner for a hearing. The hearing before the Commissioner shall be an informal hearing and shall be held with reasonable promptness. (1989 (Reg. Sess., 1990), c. 881, s. 2; 1995, c. 129, s. 39.)

§ 53-249. Filing and posting of loan fees; disclosures.

(a)   Filing of Fee Schedule. On or before January 2 of each year, each registrant shall file with the Commissioner a schedule of the refund anticipation loan fees for refund anticipation loans to be facilitated by the registrant during the succeeding year. Immediately upon learning of any change in the refund anticipation loan fee for that year, the registrant shall file an amendment with the Commissioner setting out the change. Filing is effective upon receipt by the Commissioner.

(b)   Notice of Unconscionable Fee. If the Commissioner finds that a refund anticipation loan fee filed pursuant to subsection (a) is unconscionable, he shall notify the registrant that (i) in his opinion the fee is unconscionable and (ii) the consequences of charging a refund anticipation loan fee in an amount that the Commissioner has notified the registrant is unconscionable include liability to

212

the debtor for three times the amount of that fee and possible revocation of registration as a facilitator after notice and a hearing.

(c)   Posting of Fee Schedule. Every registrant shall prominently display at each office where the registrant is facilitating refund anticipation loans a schedule showing the current refund anticipation loan fees for refund anticipation loans facilitated at the office and the current electronic filing fees for the electronic filing of the taxpayer's tax return. Every registrant shall also prominently display on each fee schedule a statement to the effect that the taxpayer may have the tax return filed electronically without also obtaining a refund anticipation loan. No registrant may facilitate a refund anticipation loan unless (i) the schedule required by this subsection is displayed and (ii) the refund anticipation loan fee actually charged is the same as the fee displayed on the schedule and the fee filed with the Commissioner pursuant to subsection (a).

(d)   Disclosures. At the time a debtor applies for a refund anticipation loan, the registrant shall disclose to the debtor on a form separate from the application:

(1)   The fee for the loan.

(2)   The fee for electronic filing of a tax return.

(3)   The time within which the proceeds of the loan will be paid to the debtor if the loan is approved.

(4)   That the debtor is responsible for repayment of the loan and related fees in the event the tax refund is not paid or is not paid in full.

(5)   The availability of electronic filing of the taxpayer's tax return, along with the average time announced by the appropriate taxing authority within which a taxpayer can expect to receive a refund if the taxpayer's return is filed electronically and the taxpayer does not obtain a refund anticipation loan.

(6)   Examples of the annual percentage rates, as defined by the Truth In Lending Act, 15 U.S.C. § 1607 and 12 C.F.R. Section 226.22, for refund anticipation loans of five hundred dollars ($500.00), seven hundred fifty dollars ($750.00), one thousand dollars ($1,000), one thousand five hundred dollars ($1,500), two thousand dollars ($2,000), and three thousand dollars ($3,000). Regardless of disclosures of the annual percentage rate required by the Truth In

213

Lending Act, if the debtor is required to establish or maintain a deposit account with the creditor for receipt of the debtor's tax refund to offset the amount owed on the loan, the maturity of the loan for the purpose of determining the annual percentage rate disclosure under this section shall be assumed to be the estimated date when the tax refund will be deposited in the debtor's account. (1989 (Reg. Sess., 1990), c. 881, s. 2.)

§ 53-250. Prohibited activities.

A facilitator of a refund anticipation loan may not engage in any of the following activities:

(1)   Misrepresenting a material factor or condition of a refund anticipation loan.

(2)   Failing to arrange for a refund anticipation loan promptly after the debtor applies for the loan.

(3)   Engaging in any transaction, practice, or course of business that operates a fraud upon any person in connection with a refund anticipation loan.

(4)   Facilitating a refund anticipation loan for which the refund anticipation loan fee is (i) different from the fee posted or the fee filed with the Commissioner or (ii) in an amount that the Commissioner has notified the facilitator is unconscionable.

(5)   Directly or indirectly arranging for payment of any portion of the refund anticipation loan for check cashing, credit insurance, or any other good or service unrelated to (i) preparing and filing tax returns or (ii) facilitating refund anticipation loans.

(6)   Arranging for a creditor to take a security interest in any property of the debtor other than the proceeds of the debtor's tax refund to secure payment of the loan. (1989 (Reg. Sess., 1990), c. 881, s. 2.)

§ 53-251. Cease and desist; revocation of registration; penalties.

(a)   Cease and Desist Order. Upon the finding that any action of a registrant may be in violation of this Article or that the registrant has engaged in an unfair

214

or deceptive act or practice, the Commissioner shall give reasonable notice to the registrant of the suspected violation or unfair or deceptive act or practice, and an opportunity for the registrant to be heard. If, following the hearing, the Commissioner finds that an action of the registrant is in violation of this Article or that the registrant has engaged in an unfair or deceptive act or practice, the Commissioner shall order the registrant to cease and desist from the action.

If the registrant fails to appeal a cease and desist order of the Commissioner in accordance with G.S. 53-252 and continues to engage in an action in violation of the Commissioner's order to cease and desist from the action, the registrant shall be subject to a penalty of one thousand dollars ($1,000) for each action it takes in violation of the Commissioner's order.

The clear proceeds of penalties provided for in this subsection shall be remitted to the Civil Penalty and Forfeiture Fund in accordance with G.S. 115C-457.2.

(b)   Revocation of Registration. After notice and hearing, and upon the finding that a registrant has (i) engaged in a course of conduct that is in violation of this Article or (ii) continued to engage in an action in violation of a cease and desist order of the Commissioner that has not been stayed upon application of the registrant, the Commissioner may revoke the registration of the registrant temporarily or permanently in the discretion of the Commissioner.

(c)   Civil Penalties. Except in the case of a refund anticipation loan that is not approved by the creditor, a facilitator who fails to deliver to the debtor the proceeds of a refund anticipation loan within 48 hours after the time period promised by the facilitator when the debtor applied for the loan shall pay to the debtor an amount equal to the refund anticipation loan fee. A facilitator who engages in an activity prohibited under G.S. 53-250 in connection with a refund anticipation loan is liable to the debtor for damages of three times the amount of the refund anticipation loan fee or other unauthorized charge plus a reasonable attorney's fee. (1989 (Reg. Sess., 1990), c. 881, s. 2; 1998-215, s. 35.)

§ 53-252. Appeal of Commissioner's decision.

The Commission may review any rule, regulation, order, or act of the Commissioner done pursuant to or with respect to the provisions of this Article. Any person aggrieved by any such rule, regulation, order, or act may appeal, pursuant to G.S. 53C-2-6, to the Commission for review upon giving notice in writing within 20 days after such rule, regulation, order, or act complained of is adopted, issued, or done. Notwithstanding any other provision of law, any aggrieved party to a decision of the Banking Commission shall be entitled to petition for judicial review pursuant to G.S. 53C-2-6. (1989 (Reg. Sess., 1990), c. 881, s. 2; 1995, c. 129, s. 40; 2009-57, s. 8; 2012-56, s. 26.)

§ 53-253. Rules; enforcement.

The Banking Commission may adopt reasonable rules as necessary to effectuate the purpose of this Article, to provide for the protection of the borrowing public, and to assist registrants in interpreting this Article. In order to enforce this Article, the Commissioner may make investigations, subpoena witnesses, require audits and reports, and conduct hearings regarding possible violations of its provisions. (1989 (Reg. Sess., 1990), c. 881, s. 2; 1995, c. 129, s. 41.)

§ 53-254. Exemption.

This Article does not apply to a person who does not deal directly with debtors but who acts solely as an intermediary by processing or transmitting, electronically or otherwise, tax or credit information or by preparing for a facilitator refund anticipation loan checks to be delivered by the facilitator to the debtor. (1989 (Reg. Sess., 1990), c. 881, s. 2.)

Article 21.

Reverse Mortgages.

§ 53-255. Title.

This Article shall be known and may be cited as the Reverse Mortgage Act. (1991, c. 546, s. 1; 1995, c. 115, s. 1.)

§ 53-256. Purpose.

It is the intent of the General Assembly that reverse mortgage loans be available so that elderly homeowners may use the equity in their homes to meet their financial needs. The General Assembly recognizes that there may be restrictions and requirements governing traditional mortgage transactions that should not apply to reverse mortgages. The purpose of this Article is to authorize reverse mortgage transactions and to clarify other provisions of North Carolina law that might otherwise apply to reverse mortgage loans, and to provide protection for elderly homeowners who enter into reverse mortgage transactions. (1991, c. 546, s. 1; 1995, c. 115, s. 1.)

§ 53-257. Definitions.

The following definitions apply in this Article:

(1)   Authorized lender or lender. - The North Carolina Housing Finance Agency, any lender authorized to engage in business as a bank, savings institution, or credit union under the laws of this State or of the United States, or any other person, firm, or corporation authorized to make reverse mortgage loans by the Commissioner of Banks.

(2)   Borrower. - A natural person 62 years of age or older who occupies and owns, in fee simple individually, or with another borrower as tenants by the entireties or as joint tenants with right of survivorship, an interest in residential real property securing a reverse mortgage loan, and who borrows money under a reverse mortgage loan.

(3)   Commissioner. - The Commissioner of Banks of this State.

(4)   Counselor. - An individual who has completed a training curriculum on reverse mortgage counseling provided or approved by the North Carolina Housing Finance Agency and whose name is maintained on the Commissioner's list of approved reverse mortgage counselors.

(5)   Outstanding balance. - The current net amount of money owed by the borrower to the lender, calculated in accordance with G.S. 53-262(b), whether or not the sum is suspended under the terms of the reverse mortgage loan agreement or is immediately due and payable.

(6)   Reverse mortgage loan or loan. - A loan for a definite or indefinite term (i) secured by a first mortgage or first deed of trust on the principal residence of the mortgagor located in North Carolina, (ii) the proceeds of which are disbursed to the mortgagor in one or more lump sums, or in equal or unequal installments, either directly by the lender or the lender's agent, and (iii) that requires no

repayment until a future time, upon the earliest occurrence of one or more events specified in the reverse mortgage loan contract.

(7)   Shared appreciation. - An agreement by the lender and the borrower that, in addition to the principal and any interest accruing on the outstanding balance of a reverse mortgage loan, the lender may collect an additional amount equal to a percentage of the increase in the value of the property from the date of origination of the loan to the date of loan repayment.

(7a)   Shared value. - An agreement by the lender and the borrower that, in addition to the principal and any interest accruing on the outstanding balance of a reverse mortgage loan, the lender may collect an additional amount equal to a percentage of the value of the property at the time of loan repayment.

(8)   Total annual percentage rate. - The annual average rate of interest, which provides the total amount owed at loan maturity when this rate is applied to the loan advances, excluding closing costs not paid to third parties, over the term of the reverse mortgage loan. (1991, c. 546, s. 1; 1995, c. 115, s. 1; 1998-116, s. 3; 2004-171, s. 15.)

§ 53-258. Authority and procedures governing reverse mortgage loans.

(a)   Except as provided in subsection (b1) of this section, no person, firm, or corporation shall engage in the business of making reverse mortgage loans without first being approved as an authorized reverse mortgage lender by the Commissioner. Mortgage lenders licensed under Article 19A of this Chapter must also be authorized under this Article before making reverse mortgage loans.

(b)   An application for authorization to make reverse mortgage loans shall be in writing to the Commissioner and in the form prescribed by the Commissioner. The application shall contain the name and complete business address or addresses of the applicant. The application shall also include affirmation of financial solvency and all capitalization requirements that are required by the Commissioner. The application shall be accompanied by a nonrefundable fee, payable to the Commissioner, of five hundred dollars ($500.00).

(b1)   Each of the following lenders shall be considered authorized to engage in the business of making reverse mortgage loans without being required to

218

apply pursuant to subsection (b) of this section and may represent to the public that it is so authorized:

(1)   The North Carolina Housing Finance Agency.

(2)   A bank, savings institution, or credit union formed under the laws of this or any other state or of the United States.

(3)   A wholly owned subsidiary of an entity described in subdivision (2) of this subsection.

Each lender listed in this subsection may, upon written request to the Commissioner of Banks, obtain written confirmation of its authority to engage in the business of making reverse mortgage loans. In the case of lenders listed in subdivisions (2) and (3) of this subsection, the request shall be accompanied by the fee set forth in subsection (d) of this section.

(c)   Repealed by Session Laws 2004-171, s. 16, effective October 1, 2004, and applicable to acts occurring and transactions or agreements entered into on or after that date.

(d)   The Commissioner shall, upon determination that an applicant should be authorized to make reverse mortgage loans, issue notice of this authority to the lender. The authority to issue reverse mortgage loans is valid for the period of time specified by the Commissioner. A lender to whom a notice of authority is issued shall display the notice prominently in any and all offices of the lender that make reverse mortgage loans. Authorizations issued under this section are nontransferable. Except for lenders described in subsection (b1) of this section, each lender to which an authorization is issued shall pay an annual renewal fee of two hundred fifty dollars ($250.00). (1991, c. 546, s. 1; 1995, c. 115, s. 1; 2004-171, s. 16.)

§ 53-259. Application of rules.

In addition to the provisions of this Article, authorized lenders shall comply with rules adopted by the Commissioner that are reasonable and necessary to effectuate the purposes of this Article and to protect the public interest. Provided, however, that provisions in Chapters 24 or 45 of the General Statutes and the rules adopted under those Chapters that conflict with this Article shall not apply to reverse mortgage transactions governed by this Article. (1991, c. 546, s. 1; 1995, c. 115, s. 1.)

§ 53-260. Interest.

Notwithstanding any other provisions of law to the contrary, the parties to a reverse mortgage loan may contract for the payment of interest at a rate agreed to by the parties. Interest shall be deferred until the earliest occurrence of one or more events specified in the reverse mortgage loan contract. Payment of interest on deferred interest shall be as agreed upon by the parties to the contract. The parties may agree that the deferred interest may be added to the outstanding balance of the loan. The Commissioner may determine that the total annual percentage rate is excessive. If the Commissioner determines the total annual percentage rate to be excessive, that determination shall be included in the information provided to counselors under G.S. 53-264(a)(7), and to applicants for reverse mortgage loans under G.S. 53-264(b). (1991, c. 546, s. 1; 1995, c. 115, s. 1.)

§ 53-261. Taxes, insurance, and assessments.

A reverse mortgage loan contract may provide that it is the primary obligation of the borrower to pay all property taxes, insurance premiums, and assessments in a timely manner, and that the failure of the borrower to make these payments and to provide evidence of payment to the lender may constitute grounds for default of the loan. A reverse mortgage loan contract shall state that if a borrower fails to pay property taxes, insurance premiums, or assessments, the lender may choose, at the lender's option, to pay the amounts due, charge them to the reverse mortgage loan, and recalculate regularly scheduled payments under the loan to account for the increased outstanding loan balance. (1991, c. 546, s. 1; 1995, c. 115, s. 1.)

§ 53-262. Renegotiation of loan; calculation of outstanding balance; prepayment.

(a)   If a reverse mortgage loan contract allows for a change in the payments or payment options, the lender may charge a reasonable fee when payments are recalculated.

(b)   The outstanding loan balance shall be calculated by adding the current totals of items described in subdivisions (1) through (4) below, and subtracting the current totals of all reverse mortgage loan payments made by the borrower to the lender:

(1)   The sum of all disbursements made by the lender to the borrower, or to another party on the borrower's behalf.

(2)   All taxes, assessments, insurance premiums, and other similar charges paid to date by the lender under G.S. 53-261 and not reimbursed by the borrower within 60 days of the date payment was made by the lender.

(3)   All actual closing costs the borrower has deferred, if a deferral provision is contained in the loan agreement.

(4)   The total accrued interest to date.

(c)   Prepayment of the reverse mortgage loan, in whole or part, shall be permitted without penalty at any time during the term of the loan. (1991, c. 546, s. 1; 1995, c. 115, s. 1.)

§ 53-263. Limits on borrowers' liability.

(a)   When a reverse mortgage loan becomes due, if the borrower mortgaged one hundred percent (100%) of the full value of the house then the amount owed by the borrower shall not be greater than (i) the fair market value of the house, minus sale costs, or (ii) the outstanding balance of the loan, whichever amount is less.

(b)   If the borrower mortgaged less than one hundred percent (100%) of the full value of the house, the amount owed by the borrower shall not be greater than (i) the outstanding balance of the loan, or (ii) the percentage of the fair market value, minus sale costs, as provided in the contract, whichever amount is less.

(c)   The lender shall enforce the debt only through the sale of the property and shall not obtain a deficiency judgment against the borrower. (1991, c. 546, s. 1; 1995, c. 115, s. 1.)

§ 53-264. Disclosures of loan terms.

(a)   On forms prescribed by the Commissioner, all authorized lenders shall provide all of the following information to the Commissioner for dissemination to all counselors who provide counseling to prospective reverse mortgage borrowers:

(1)   The borrower's rights, obligations, and remedies with respect to the borrower's temporary absence from the home, late payments by the lender, and payment default by the lender.

(2)   Conditions or events that require the borrower to repay the loan obligation.

(3)   The right of the borrower to mortgage less than the full value of the home, if permitted by the reverse mortgage loan contract.

(4)   The projected total annual percentage rate applicable under various loan terms and appreciation rates and interest rates applicable at sample ages of borrowers.

(5)   Standard closing costs.

(6)   All service fees to be charged during the term of the loan.

(7)   Other information required by the Commissioner.

(8)   Information relating to contracts for shared appreciation or shared value, as required by G.S. 53-270.1.

(b)   Within 10 business days after application is made by a borrower, but not less than 20 business days before closing of the loan, lenders shall provide applicants with the same information required in subsection (a) of this section, shall inform applicants that reverse mortgage counseling is required before the loan can be closed, and shall provide the names and addresses of counselors listed with the Commissioner's office. (1991, c. 546, s. 1; 1995, c. 115, s. 1; 1998-116, s. 4.)

§ 53-265. Information required of lender.

(a)   At the closing of the reverse mortgage loan, the lender shall provide to the borrower the name of the lender's employee or agent who has been designated specifically to respond to inquiries concerning reverse mortgage loans. This information shall be provided by the lender to the borrower at least annually, and whenever the information concerning the designated employee or agent changes.

(b)   On an annual basis and when the loan becomes due, the lender shall issue to the borrower, without charge, a statement of account regarding the activity of the mortgage for the preceding calendar year, or for the period since the last statement of account was provided. The statement shall include all of the following information for the preceding year:

(1)   The outstanding balance of the loan at the beginning of the statement period.

(2)   Disbursements to the borrower.

(3)   The total amount of interest added to the outstanding balance of the loan.

(4)   Any property taxes, insurance premiums, or assessments paid by the lender.

(5)   Payments made to the lender.

(6)   The total mortgage balance owed to date.

(7)   The remaining amount available to the borrower in reverse mortgage loans wherein proceeds have been reserved to be disbursed in one or more lump sum amounts. (1991, c. 546, s. 1; 1995, c. 115, s. 1.)

§ 53-266. Effects of lender's default.

(a)   A lender's failure to make loan advances to the borrower under the reverse mortgage loan contract shall be deemed the lender's default of the contract. Upon the lender's default, the lender shall forfeit any right to collect interest or service charges under the contract. The lender's right to recovery at loan maturity shall be limited to the outstanding balance as of the date of default, minus all interest. Lenders may also be subject to other default penalties established by the Commissioner.

(b)   Subsection (a) of this section shall not apply if the lender has previously declared the borrower in default under G.S. 53-267, or if the lender makes the required loan advance within the time stated in the mortgage contract or within 30 days of receipt of notice from the borrower that the loan advance was not received. (1991, c. 546, s. 1; 1995, c. 115, s. 1.)

§ 53-267. Repayment upon borrower's default.

A reverse mortgage loan contract may provide for a borrower's default, thereby triggering early repayment of the loan, based only upon one or more of the following terms and conditions:

(1)   The borrower fails to maintain the residence as required by the contract.

(2)   The borrower sells or otherwise conveys title to the home to a third party.

(3)   The borrower dies and the home is not the principal residence of the surviving borrower.

(4)   The home is not the principal residence of at least one of the borrowers for a period of 12 consecutive months for reasons of physical or mental illness.

(5)   For reasons other than physical or mental illness, the home ceases to be the principal residence of the borrower for a period of 180 consecutive days and is not the principal residence of another borrower under the loan, without prior written permission from the lender.

(6)   The borrower fails to pay property taxes, insurance premiums, and assessments under G.S. 53-261. (1991, c. 546, s. 1; 1995, c. 115, s. 1.)

§ 53-268. Time for initiation of foreclosure.

When a borrower's obligation to repay the reverse mortgage loan is triggered under G.S. 53-267, in addition to all rights conferred upon owners and borrowers under Chapter 45 of the General Statutes, the lender must give the

224

borrower not less than 90 days' notice of its intent to initiate foreclosure proceedings. If the contract so provides, interest will continue to accrue during the 90-day period. (1991, c. 546, s. 1; 1995, c. 115, s. 1.)

§ 53-269. Counseling provisions.

(a)   The North Carolina Housing Finance Agency shall adopt rules governing the training of counselors and necessary standards for counselor training and shall establish reasonable fees for training. The North Carolina Housing Finance Agency shall forward the names of all persons satisfying counselor training requirements to the Commissioner.

(b)   The Commissioner shall maintain a list of counselors who have satisfied training requirements and shall periodically provide an up-to-date copy of the list to all authorized lenders.

(c)   The Commissioner shall provide to all counselors who have satisfied training requirements information provided to the Commissioner by authorized lenders under G.S. 53-265. (1991, c. 546, s. 1; 1995, c. 115, s. 1.)

§ 53-270. Prohibited acts.

Reverse mortgage lenders are prohibited from engaging in any of the following acts in connection with the making, servicing, or collecting of a reverse mortgage loan:

(1)   Misrepresenting material facts, making false promises, or engaging in a course of misrepresentation through agents or otherwise.

(2)   Failing to disburse funds in accordance with the terms of the reverse mortgage loan contract or other written commitment.

(3)   Improperly refusing to issue a satisfaction of a mortgage.

(4)   Engaging in any action or practice that is unfair or deceptive, or that operates a fraud on any person.

(5)   Contracting for or receiving shared appreciation or shared value, except as provided in G.S. 53-270.1.

(6)   Closing a reverse mortgage loan without receiving certification from a person who is certified as a reverse mortgage counselor by the State that the borrower has received counseling on the advisability of a reverse mortgage loan and the various types of reverse mortgage loans and the availability of other financial options and resources for the borrower, as well as potential tax consequences.

(7)   Failing to comply with this Article. (1991, c. 546, s. 1; 1995, c. 115, s. 1; 1998-116, s. 1.)

§ 53-270.1. Contracts for shared appreciation or shared value.

(a)   A lender and a borrower may agree, in writing, that in addition to the principal and any interest accruing on the outstanding balance of a reverse mortgage loan, the lender may receive:

(1)   Shared appreciation if it is in an amount not exceeding ten percent (10%) of the increase in the value of the property from the date of origination of the reverse mortgage loan to the date of loan repayment; or

(2)   Shared value if it is in an amount not exceeding ten percent (10%) of the value of the property at the time of repayment of the reverse mortgage loan; and

(3)   The shared appreciation or shared value is paid in conjunction with a loan that:

a.   Is outstanding for 24 months or longer; and

b.   Either (i) is guaranteed or insured by an agency of the federal government, or (ii) has been originated under a reverse mortgage program approved by Fannie Mae, the Government National Mortgage Association, or the Federal Home Loan Mortgage Corporation, provided the loan is sold to one of those agencies or enterprises within 90 days of loan closing, or has been originated under a reverse mortgage program of a person, firm, or corporation approved as an authorized lender by the Commissioner; and

c.   Provides that the borrower receives additional economic benefit in exchange for paying the shared appreciation or shared value, including, but not limited to, larger monthly payments or a larger line of credit. The specific nature of the economic benefit shall be provided to the Commissioner with the other

226

information about the reverse mortgage program required under G.S. 53-264 for dissemination to the reverse mortgage counselors; and

d.   At least 14 days prior to closing, the borrower receives a disclosure that explains the additional costs and benefits of shared appreciation or shared value and compares those costs and benefits with a comparable loan without shared appreciation or shared value. These costs and benefits shall also be included in the information required under G.S. 53-264.

(b)   Under subdivisions (a)(1) and (2) of this section, in determining the value of the property at the time of origination of the reverse mortgage loan and at the time of repayment, if repayment is not in conjunction with the sale of the property, the lender and the borrower shall have the right to obtain an appraisal from an appraiser licensed or certified in accordance with G.S. 93E-1-6. If the appraisals differ, and the parties cannot agree on a value, an average of the appraisals shall determine the value. If the borrower does not desire an appraisal, the lender may obtain an appraisal, which shall be controlling. Notwithstanding the foregoing, the parties may agree in writing to waive these requirements and agree upon the value of the property.

(c)   If repayment is made in conjunction with the sale of the property, the actual and reasonable costs of sale shall be deducted from the value of the property prior to the calculation of the amount of shared appreciation or shared value. (1998-116, s. 2; 2001-487, s. 14(b).)

§ 53-271. Commissioner's authority to enforce; penalties.

(a)   The Commissioner shall adopt rules necessary to implement and enforce the provisions of this Article. Upon finding probable cause to believe that an authorized lender is in violation of this Article, or of any law or any rule or regulation of this State, the United States, or an agency of the State or the United States, the Commissioner shall, after affording reasonable notice and opportunity to be heard to the lender, order the lender to cease and desist from the violation.

(b)   If a lender fails to comply with or appeal the Commissioner's cease and desist order, the lender shall be subject to a civil penalty of one thousand dollars ($1,000) for each violation that is the subject of the cease and desist order. The penalty imposed under this section shall be in addition to and not in lieu of penalties available under any other provision of law applicable to a reverse mortgage lender.

(c)   Upon a finding that a reverse mortgage lender has violated this Article, the Commissioner may revoke, temporarily or permanently, the authority of the lender to make reverse mortgage loans.

(d)   A person damaged by a lender's actions may file an action in civil court to recover actual and punitive damages. Attorneys' fees shall be awarded to a prevailing borrower. Nothing in this Article shall limit any statutory or common law right of a person to bring an action in court for any act, nor shall this Article limit the right of the State to punish a person for the violation of any law. (1991, c. 546, s. 1; 1995, c. 115, s. 1.)

§ 53-272. Appeals.

The Banking Commission may review any rule, regulation, order, or act of the Commissioner done pursuant to or with respect to the provisions of this Article. Any person aggrieved by any such rule, regulation, order, or act may appeal, pursuant to G.S. 53C-2-6, to the Commission for review upon giving notice in writing within 20 days after such rule, regulation, order, or act complained of is adopted, issued, or done. Notwithstanding any other provision of law, any aggrieved party to a decision of the Banking Commission shall be entitled to petition for judicial review pursuant to G.S. 53C-2-6. (1991, c. 546, s. 1; 1995, c. 115, s. 1; c. 129, s. 42; 2009-57, s. 9; 2012-56, s. 27.)

§ 53-273. Reserved for future codification purposes.

§ 53-274. Reserved for future codification purposes.

Article 22.

Check-Cashing Businesses.

§ 53-275. Definitions.

As used in this Article, unless the context clearly requires otherwise, the term:

228

(1)   "Cashing" means providing currency for payment instruments, but does not include the bona fide sale or exchange of travelers checks and foreign denomination payment instruments.

(2)   "Check-cashing service" means any person or entity engaged in the business of cashing checks, drafts, or money orders for a fee, service charge, or other consideration.

(3)   "Commission" means the State Banking Commission.

(4)   "Commissioner" means the Commissioner of Banks.

(5)   "Licensee" means a person or entity licensed to engage in a check-cashing business under this Article.

(6)   "Person" means an individual, partnership, association, or corporation. (1997-391, s. 1.)

§ 53-276. License required.

No person or other entity may engage in the business of cashing checks, drafts, or money orders for consideration without first obtaining a license under this Article. No person or other entity providing a check-cashing service may avoid the requirements of this Article by providing a check or other currency equivalent instead of currency when cashing payment instruments. (1997-391, s. 1.)

§ 53-277. Exemptions.

(a)   This Article shall not apply to:

(1)   A bank, savings institution, credit union, or farm credit system organized under the laws of the United States or any state; and

(2)   Any person or entity principally engaged in the bona fide retail sale of goods or services, who either as an incident to or independently of a retail sale or service and not holding itself out to be a check-cashing service, from time to time cashes checks, drafts, or money orders for a fee or other consideration, where not more than two dollars ($2.00) is charged for the service.

229

(b)   A person licensed under Article 16A of this Chapter (Money Transmitters Act) is exempt from G.S. 53-276, 53-278, 53-279, and 53-284, but is deemed a licensee for purposes of the remaining provisions of this Article. This exemption does not apply to an authorized agent of a person licensed under Article 16A of this Chapter. (1997-391, s. 1; 2001-443, s. 4.)

§ 53-278. Application for license; investigation; application fee.

(a)   An application for licensure under this Article shall be in writing, under oath, and on a form prescribed by the Commissioner. The application shall set forth all of the following:

(1)   The name and address of the applicant.

(2)   If the applicant is a firm or partnership, the name and address of each member of the firm or partnership.

(3)   If the applicant is a corporation, the name and address of each officer, director, registered agent, and principal.

(4)   The addresses of the locations of the business to be licensed.

(5)   Other information concerning the financial responsibility, background experience, and activities of the applicant and its members, officers, directors, and principals as the Commissioner requires.

(b)   The Commissioner may make such investigations as the Commissioner deems necessary to determine if the applicant has complied with all applicable provisions of this Article and State and federal law.

(c)   The application shall be accompanied by payment of a two hundred fifty dollar ($250.00) application fee and a five hundred dollar ($500.00) investigation fee. These fees are not refundable or abatable, but, if the license is granted, payment of the application fee shall satisfy the fee requirement for the first license year or remaining part thereof.

(d)   Licenses shall expire annually and may be renewed upon payment of a license fee of two hundred fifty dollars ($250.00) plus a fifty dollar ($50.00) fee for each branch location certificate issued under a license. (1997-391, s. 1.)

§ 53-279. Liquid assets required; other qualifications; denial of license; hearing.

(a)   Every licensee and applicant shall have and maintain liquid assets of at least fifty thousand dollars ($50,000) per licensee.

(b)   Upon the filing and investigation of an application, and compliance by the applicant with G.S. 53-278, and this section, the Commissioner shall issue and deliver to the applicant the license applied for to engage in business under this Article at the locations specified in the application, provided that the Commissioner finds that the financial responsibility, character, reputation, experience, and general fitness of the applicant and its members, officers, directors, and principals are such as to warrant belief that the business will be operated efficiently and fairly, in the public interest, and in accordance with law. If the Commissioner fails to make such findings, no license shall be issued, and the Commissioner shall notify the applicant of the denial and the reasons therefor. The applicant shall be entitled to an informal hearing on the denial provided the applicant requests the hearing in writing within 30 days after the Commissioner has mailed the notice required under this subsection to the applicant. In the event of a hearing, which shall be held in the offices of the Commissioner of Banks in Raleigh, the Commissioner shall reconsider the application and, after hearing, issue a written order granting or denying the application. (1997-391, s. 1.)

§ 53-280. Maximum fees for service; fees posted; endorsement of checks cashed.

(a)   Notwithstanding any other provision of law, no check-cashing business licensed under this Article shall directly or indirectly charge or collect fees or other consideration for check-cashing services in excess of the following:

(1)   Three percent (3%) of the face amount of the check or five dollars ($5.00), whichever is greater, for checks issued by the federal government, State government, or any agency of the State or federal government, or any county or municipality of this State.

(2)   Ten percent (10%) of the face amount of the check or five dollars ($5.00), whichever is greater, for personal checks.

(3)   Five percent (5%) of the face amount of the check or five dollars ($5.00), whichever is greater, for all other checks, or for money orders.

231

(b)   A licensee may not advance monies on the security of any check unless the account from which the check being presented is drawn is legitimate, open, and active. Except as provided by G.S. 53-281(a), any licensee who cashes a check for a fee shall deposit the check not later than three business days from the date the check is cashed.

(c)   A licensee shall ensure that in every location conducting business under a license issued under this Article, there is conspicuously posted and at all times displayed a notice stating the fees charged for cashing checks, drafts, and money orders. A licensee shall further ensure that notice of the fees currently charged at every location shall be filed with the Commissioner.

(d)   A licensee shall endorse every check, draft, or money order presented by the licensee for payment in the name of the licensee. (1997-391, s. 1.)

§ 53-281: Expired.

§ 53-282. Record keeping; receipt requirements.

(a)   Every person required to be licensed under this Article shall maintain in its offices such books, accounts, and records as the Commissioner may reasonably require. The books, accounts, and records shall be maintained separate from any other business in which the person is engaged, and shall be retained for a period prescribed by the Commissioner. A person required to be licensed under this Article that derives less than twenty percent (20%) of the person's annual gross revenues from check cashing shall not be required to maintain separate accounts and records.

(b)   The licensee shall ensure that each customer cashing a check shall be provided a receipt showing the name or trade name of the licensee, the transaction date, amount of the check, and the fee charged.

(c)   The Commissioner may examine the books, accounts, and records in order to determine whether the person is complying with this Article and rules adopted pursuant thereto. The cost of the examination shall be paid by the licensee and shall be determined by applying the hourly rate for special examinations adopted by the State Banking Commission by regulation. (1997-391, s. 1; 2011-325, s. 10.)

§ 53-283. Prohibited practices.

No person required to be licensed under this Article shall do any of the following:

(1)   Charge fees in excess of those authorized under this Article.

(2)   Engage in the business of making loans of money, or extensions of credit, or discounting notes, bills of exchange, items, or other evidences of debt; or accepting deposits or bailments of money or items, except as expressly provided by G.S. 53-281.

(3)   Use or cause to be published or disseminated any advertising communication which contains any false, misleading, or deceptive statement or representation.

(4)   Conduct business at premises or locations other than locations licensed by the Commissioner.

(5)   Engage in unfair, deceptive, or fraudulent practices.

(6)   Cash a check, draft, or money order made payable to a payee other than a natural person unless the licensee has previously obtained appropriate documentation from the executive entity of the payee clearly indicating the authority of the natural person or persons cashing the check, draft, or money order on behalf of the payee. (1997-391, s. 1.)

§ 53-284. Suspension and revocation of license; grounds; procedure.

(a)   The Commissioner may suspend or revoke any license or licenses issued pursuant to this Article if, after notice and opportunity for hearing, the Commissioner issues written findings that the licensee has engaged in any of the following conduct:

(1)   Violated this Article or applicable State or federal law or rules.

(2)   Made a false statement on the application for a license under this Article.

(3)   Refused to permit investigation by the Commissioner authorized under this Article.

(4)   Failed to comply with an order of the Commissioner.

(5)   Demonstrated incompetency or untrustworthiness to engage in the business of check cashing.

(6)   Been convicted of a felony or misdemeanor involving fraud, misrepresentation, or deceit.

(b)   The Commissioner may not suspend or revoke any license issued under this Article unless the licensee has been given notice and opportunity for hearing in accordance with Article 3A of Chapter 150B of the General Statutes. (1997-391, s. 1.)

§ 53-285. Cease and desist orders.

If the Commissioner determines that a person required to be licensed under this Article has violated this Article or rules adopted pursuant to it, then the Commissioner may, upon notice and opportunity for hearing in accordance with Article 3A of Chapter 150B of the General Statutes, order the person to cease and desist from the violations and to comply with this Article. The Commissioner may enforce compliance with an order issued pursuant to this section by the imposition and collection of civil penalties authorized under this Article. (1997-391, s. 1.)

§ 53-286. Civil penalties and restitution.

The Commissioner may order and impose civil penalties upon any person required to be licensed under this Article for violations of this Article or rules adopted thereunder. Civil penalties shall not exceed one thousand dollars ($1,000) per violation. All civil money penalties collected under this Article shall be paid to the county school fund. The Commissioner may also order repayment of unlawful or excessive fees charged to customers. (1997-391, s. 1.)

§ 53-287. Criminal penalties.

A violation of G.S. 53-276 by a person required to obtain a license under this Article is a Class I felony. Each transaction involving the unlawful cashing of a check, draft, or money order constitutes a separate offense. (1997-391, s. 1.)

§ 53-288. Commissioner to adopt rules.

The Commissioner may adopt rules necessary to carry out the purposes of this Article, to provide for the protection of the public, and to assist licensees in interpreting and complying with this Article. (1997-391, s. 1.)

§ 53-289. Commission may review rules, orders, or acts by Commissioner.

The Commission may review any rule, regulation, order, or act of the Commissioner done pursuant to or with respect to the provisions of this Article. Any person aggrieved by any such rule, regulation, order, or act may appeal, pursuant to G.S. 53C-2-6, to the Commission for review upon giving notice in writing within 20 days after such rule, regulation, order, or act complained of is adopted, issued, or done. Notwithstanding any other provision of law, any aggrieved party to a decision of the Banking Commission shall be entitled to petition for judicial review pursuant to G.S. 53C-2-6. (1997-391, s. 1; 2009-57, s. 10; 2012-56, s. 28.)

§§ 53-290 through 53-294. Reserved for future codification purposes.

Article 23.

Continuity of Contract Under European Monetary Union.

§ 53-295. Definitions.

The following definitions shall apply in this Article:

(1)   Euro. - The currency of participating member states of the European Union that adopt a single currency in accordance with the Treaty on European Union dated February 7, 1992.

(2)   European Currency Unit (ECU). - The currency as defined in the European Council regulation number 3320/94.

(3)   Introduction of the Euro. - The implementation of economic and monetary union of member states of the European Union in accordance with the Treaty on European Union dated February 7, 1992. (1999-312, s. 1.)

§ 53-296. Continuity of contract.

(a)   If a subject of medium of payment of a contract, security, or instrument is a currency that has been substituted or replaced by the euro, the euro shall be a commercially reasonable substitute and substantial equivalent that may either be used in determining the value of that currency, or tendered at the conversion rate specified in and otherwise calculated in accordance with the regulations adopted by the Council of the European Union.

(b)   If a subject or medium of payment of a contract, security, or instrument is the ECU, the euro will be a commercially reasonable substitute and substantial equivalent that may be either used in determining the value of that currency, or tendered at the conversion rate specified in and otherwise calculated in accordance with the regulations adopted by the Council of the European Union.

(c)   Performance of any of the obligations described in subsection (a) or (b) may be made in the currencies originally designated in the contract, security, or instrument, so long as the currencies remain legal tender, or in euro, but not in any other currency, whether or not the currency has been substituted or replaced by the euro, or is a currency that is considered a denomination of the euro and has a fixed conversion rate with respect to the euro. (1999-312, s. 1.)

§ 53-297. Effect of currency substitution on performance.

None of the following shall have the effect of discharging or excusing performance under any contract, security, or instrument, or give a party the right unilaterally to alter or terminate any contract, security, or instrument:

(1)   Introduction of the euro.

(2)   Tender of euros in connection with any obligation in compliance with G.S. 53-296.

(3)   Determination of the value of any obligation in compliance with G.S. 53-296.

(4)   Calculation or determination of the subject or medium of payment of a contract, security, or instrument with reference to an interest rate or other basis that has been substituted or replaced due to the introduction of the euro and that is a commercially reasonable substitute and substantial equivalent. (1999-312, s. 1.)

§ 53-298. References to ECU in contracts.

(a)   References to the ECU in a contract, security, or other instrument that also refers in substance to the definition of the ECU as set forth in G.S. 53-295 shall be replaced by references to the euro at a rate of one euro to one ECU.

(b)   References to the ECU in a contract, security, or instrument without a definition as set forth in G.S. 53-295 shall be presumed, rebuttable by proof of the contrary intention of the parties, to be references to the currency basket that is from time to time used as the unit of account of the European community. (1999-312, s. 1.)

§ 53-299. Application.

Notwithstanding any other law, this Article shall apply to all contracts, securities, and instruments, including contracts with respect to commercial transactions. (1999-312, s. 1.)

§ 53-300. No application to other currency alteration.

In circumstances of currency alteration other than the introduction of the euro, this Article shall not be interpreted as creating any negative inference or negative presumption regarding the validity or enforceability of contracts, securities, or instruments denominated in whole or in part in a currency affected by that alteration. (1999-312, s. 1.)

Article 24.

Trust Companies and Interstate Trust Business.

Part 1. Definitions.

§ 53-301. Definitions.

(a)   Except as otherwise provided in this Article, or when the context clearly indicates that a different meaning is intended, the following definitions shall apply throughout this Article:

(1)   "Account" means the client relationship established with a trust institution involving the transfer of real or personal property to the trust institution or the assumption of duties by the trust institution concerning real or personal property.

(2)   "Act as a fiduciary" means:

a.   To (i) act as trustee under a written instrument or by judicial appointment or order; (ii) receive money or other property as trustee for investment or reinvestment in real or personal property; (iii) act as custodian or custodial trustee under a gifts to minors act, a transfers to minors act, a custodial trust act, or similar statute; (iv) act as personal representative of the estate of a deceased person; (v) act as trustee, guardian, or conservator for the person or estate of an incompetent such as a minor or incapacitated person, or in other circumstances in which a guardian may be appointed; or (vi) act in a capacity similar to one listed in (i) through (v), however such capacity may be designated under applicable law or governing instrument; or

b.   To possess, purchase, sell, safekeep, or otherwise manage or administer property in any other fiduciary capacity.

(3)   "Affiliate" means a company that directly or indirectly controls, is controlled by, or is under common control with another company.

(3a)   "Affiliate transfer" means a transfer of an account pursuant to Part 7 of this Article by one trust institution affiliate of that trust institution.

(4)   "Authorized trust institution" means any State trust company and any trust office or representative trust office of a trust institution located in this State that is not a bank.

(5)   "Bank" has the meaning set forth in 12 U.S.C. § 1813(a)(1), except that "bank" does not include a trust company.

(6)   "Bank supervisory agency" means:

a.   Any agency of another state or a home country with primary responsibility for chartering or supervising a trust institution; and

b.   The Office of the Comptroller of the Currency, the Federal Deposit Insurance Corporation, the Board of Governors of the Federal Reserve System, a Federal Reserve Bank acting in a supervisory capacity over any bank or bank holding company, the Office of Thrift Supervision, and any successor to these agencies.

(6a)   "Board of directors" means the governing body of a company.

(7)   "Branch" has the meaning set forth in G.S. 53C-1-4(11).

(8)   "Charter" means a charter issued to a State trust company by the Commissioner or a charter, license, or other authority issued by the Commissioner or a bank supervisory agency authorizing a trust institution to act as a fiduciary in its home state or home country, and the issuance of the charter, license, or other authority.

(9)   "Client" means a person to whom a trust institution owes a duty or obligation under an account.

(10)   "Commission" means the North Carolina State Banking Commission.

(11)   "Commissioner" means the Commissioner of Banks for the State of North Carolina.

(12)   "Company" includes a bank, trust company, corporation, partnership, association, limited liability company, trust, business trust, joint venture, foundation, pool, syndicate, unincorporated organization, or other form of entity not specifically listed herein.

(13)   "Control," with respect to a State trust company, means:

a.   The ownership of or ability or power to vote directly, acting through one or more other persons, or otherwise indirectly, ten percent (10%) or more of the outstanding shares of a class of voting securities of the State trust company;

b.   The ability to control, directly or indirectly, the election of a majority of the board of the State trust company; or

c.   The power to exercise, directly or indirectly, a controlling influence over the management or policies of the State trust company.

(14)   "Debt security" means a marketable obligation evidencing indebtedness of a company in the form of a bond, note, debenture, or other debt instrument.

(15)   "Depository institution" means any company within any of the definitions of "insured depository institution" set forth in 12 U.S.C. § 1813(c).

(15a)   "Director" means a member of the board of directors.

(16)   "Equity capital" means the amount by which the total assets of a State trust company exceed its total liabilities.

(17)   "Equity security" means:

a.   Stock, other than adjustable rate preferred stock and money market (auction rate) preferred stock;

b.   A certificate of interest or participation in a profit-sharing agreement, collateral-trust certificate, preorganization certificate or subscription, transferable share, investment contract, or voting-trust certificate;

c.   A security immediately convertible at the option of the holder without payment of significant additional consideration into a security described by this subdivision;

d.   A security carrying a warrant or right to subscribe to or purchase a security described by this subdivision; and

240

e.   A certificate of interest or participation in, temporary or interim certificate for, or receipt for a security described by this subdivision that evidences an existing or contingent equity ownership interest.

(18)   "Executive officer" means an officer of a company who is named an executive officer by the company or who participates in major policy-making functions of the company.

(19)   "Federally chartered savings association" means a company described in 12 U.S.C. § 1813(b)(2).

(20)   "Fiduciary record" means a matter written, transcribed, recorded, received, or otherwise in the possession or control of a trust institution, whether in physical, electronic, magnetic, or other form, that preserves information concerning an account or a client.

(21)   "Foreign bank" means a foreign bank, as defined in 12 U.S.C. § 1813(s)(1), except for a bank organized under the laws of a territory of the United States.

(22)   "Foreign trust institution" means a trust institution, other than a foreign bank, chartered in a foreign country.

(23)   "Hazardous condition" with respect to a trust institution means:

a.   A refusal by the trust institution to permit examination of its books, papers, accounts, records, or affairs by the Commissioner or a duly appointed or authorized examiner of the Commissioner, or a refusal by the officers or directors of a trust institution to be examined under oath regarding its affairs;

b.   A material violation by a trust institution of a condition of its chartering or an agreement entered into between the trust institution and the Commissioner; or

c.   A circumstance or condition in which an unreasonable risk of loss is threatened to clients, creditors, or shareholders of a trust institution because the trust institution:

1.   Has equity capital that is, or is in substantial danger of becoming, inadequate for the safe and sound conduct of its business without regard to whether it is, or is in substantial danger of becoming, insolvent;

2.   Has concentrated an excessive or unreasonable portion of its assets in a particular type or character of investment;

3.   Violates or fails to comply with this Article, another statute or rule applicable to trust institutions, or any duly issued order of the Commissioner;

4.   Is in a condition that renders the continuation of a particular business practice hazardous to its clients, creditors, or shareholders; or

5.   Conducts business in an unsafe or unsound manner, which includes conducting business with:

I.   Materially inexperienced or inattentive management;

II.   Dangerous operating practices;

III.   Materially infrequent or inadequate audits;

IV.   Materially deficient administration of assets in relation to the volume and character of the assets it administers or the trust institution's responsibility for such assets;

V.   Materially frequent or serious failures to adhere to sound administrative practices;

VI.   Materially frequent or serious violations of applicable laws, rules, or terms of instruments governing accounts; or

VII.   Materially serious self-dealing or conflicts of interest.

(24)   "Home country" means a foreign country in which a foreign trust institution is chartered.

(25)   "Home country regulator" means the bank supervisory agency with primary responsibility for chartering and supervising a foreign trust institution.

(26)   "Home state" means:

a.   With respect to a federally chartered savings association and a national bank, the state in which the institution maintains its principal office;

b.   With respect to a foreign bank, the home state of the foreign bank as determined in accordance with the International Banking Act of 1978, 12 U.S.C. §§ 3101, et seq., and Article 18A of this Chapter or, if there is no such home state, the state in which the foreign bank maintains its principal office in the United States; and

c.   With respect to any other trust institution, the state or home country which chartered the institution.

(27)   "Home state regulator" means the bank supervisory agency with primary responsibility for chartering and supervising an out-of-state trust institution.

(28)   "Host state" means a state other than the home state of a trust institution, or a foreign country, in which the trust institution maintains or seeks to establish or acquire and maintain a trust office or representative trust office.

(29)   "Initial capital" means the amount of equity capital required for approval of a charter pursuant to G.S. 53-337.

(30)   "Insolvent," with respect to a State trust company, means a circumstance or condition in which a State trust company:

a.   Is unable or lacks the means to meet its current obligations as they come due in the regular and ordinary course of business, without regard to whether its assets exceed its liabilities;

b.   Has equity capital less than one-fourth of its initial capital, except as otherwise specified by the Commissioner; or

c.   Has purported to make a voluntary assignment of its assets for the benefit of creditors or to take any action for protection against creditors under any bankruptcy or insolvency law.

(31)   "Jeopardized" means insolvent, in a hazardous condition, or in such other condition as the Commissioner determines warrants the use of procedures set forth in this Article relating to jeopardized State trust companies.

(32)   "License", with respect to a State trust company, means the authority granted by the Commissioner pursuant to G.S. 53-160.

(33)   "National bank" means a bank chartered under 12 U.S.C. § 21.

243

(34)   "Office" with respect to a trust institution means its principal office, a trust office, or a representative trust office, but not a branch. With respect to an out-of-state trust institution or a foreign trust institution without a physical office in this State, the term "office" also means the registered office.

(35)   "Out-of-state trust institution" means a trust institution that is neither a State trust institution nor a foreign trust institution.

(36)   "Person" means an individual or a company.

(37)   "Principal office" means:

a.   With respect to a State trust company, a location, registered with the Commissioner as the State trust company's principal office, at which:

1.   The State trust company does business; and

2.   At least one executive officer of the State trust company maintains a customary place of work; and

b.   With respect to a trust institution other than a State trust company, its principal place of business.

(38)   "Principal shareholder" means a person who owns or has the ability or power to vote, directly, acting through one or more other persons, or otherwise indirectly, ten percent (10%) or more of the outstanding shares of any class of voting securities of a company.

(39)   "Private trust company" means a State trust company that is organized to engage in business with one or more family members and does not transact business with the general public, as defined in G.S. 53-363.

(39a)   "Registered office" means a registered office as described in G.S. 55D-30.

(40)   "Representative trust office" means an office at which a trust institution engages in trust marketing, but not trust business.

(41)   "Savings association" has the meaning set forth in 12 U.S.C. § 1813(b)(1).

(42)   "State" means any state of the United States, the District of Columbia, and any territory of the United States.

(43)   "State bank" means:

a.   A bank organized under the provisions of this Chapter and authorized to act as a fiduciary by this State or

b.   A foreign bank lawfully doing business in this State pursuant to Article 18A of this Chapter.

(44)   "State savings association" means a savings association organized under the laws of this State and authorized to act as a fiduciary pursuant to Chapter 54B or Chapter 54C of the General Statutes.

(45)   "State trust company" means a company organized under the provisions of this Article and a trust company previously organized under other provisions of Chapter 53 of the General Statutes to operate only as a trust company and not as a commercial bank.

(46)   "State trust company facility" has the meaning set forth in G.S. 53-340.

(47)   "State trust institution" means a trust institution organized under the laws of, or having its principal office in, this State.

(48)   "Subsidiary" means a company that is controlled by another company, and includes a subsidiary of a subsidiary.

(49)   "Territory of the United States" means any geographic area over which the United States exercises sovereignty.

(49a)   "Transferring trust institution" means a trust institution that proposes to make, or does make, an affiliate transfer.

(49b)   "Transferee trust institution" means a trust institution to which an affiliate transfer is proposed to be made, or is made.

(50)   "Trust business" means acting as a fiduciary or in other capacities permissible for a trust institution under G.S. 53-331.

(51)   "Trust company" means a trust institution that is neither a depository institution nor a foreign bank.

(52)   "Trust institution" means any company lawfully acting as a fiduciary in a state or in a foreign country.

(53)   "Trust marketing" means the holding out by a company to the public by advertising, solicitation, or other means that the company is available to act as a fiduciary.

(54)   "Trust office" means an office, other than the principal office, through which a trust institution acts as a fiduciary, including, with respect to an out-of-state trust institution or a foreign trust institution without a physical office in this State, the registered office.

(55)   "Unauthorized trust activity" means:

a.   Engaging in trust business within this State by a company other than one identified in G.S. 53-303; or

b.   Maintenance of a representative trust office by an out-of-state trust institution without approval from or in violation of an order issued by the Commissioner.

(b)   These definitions shall be liberally construed to accomplish the purposes of this Article. The Commission may adopt other definitions to accomplish the purposes of this Article.

(c)   References to statutory laws of North Carolina and of the United States of America shall be deemed to refer to recodified, amended, predecessor, or successor statutes. References to agencies of North Carolina and of the United States of America shall be deemed to refer to predecessor or successor agencies. (2001-263, s. 1; 2005-269, ss. 1, 2, 3; 2005-274, s. 1; 2011-339, s. 8; 2012-56, s. 29.)

Part 2. Multistate Trust Institutions Act.

Subpart A. General.

§ 53-302. Title and purposes.

246

(a)   This Part may be cited as the Multistate Trust Institutions Act.

(b)   It is the express intent of this Part to permit trust institutions to engage in trust business on a multistate and international basis subject to the provisions of this Part. (2001-263, s. 1.)

Subpart B. Companies Authorized to Engage in Trust Business.

§ 53-303. Companies authorized to engage in trust business.

(a)   No company shall engage in trust business in this State except:

(1)   A State trust company;

(2)   A State bank;

(3)   A State savings association;

(4)   A national bank having its principal office in this State;

(5)   A federally chartered savings association having its principal office in this State;

(6)   An out-of-state trust institution in accordance with and subject to the provisions of Subpart D of this Part;

(7)   A foreign trust institution in accordance with and subject to the provisions of Subpart E of this Part; or

(8)   A company otherwise authorized to engage in trust business or to act in a particular capacity described in G.S. 53-331(b)(2) under the laws of this State or of the United States.

(b)   No company shall engage in unauthorized trust activity, and all companies shall engage in trust business in accordance with and subject to all applicable laws of this State. (2001-263, s. 1.)

§ 53-304. Activities not requiring a charter, license, or approval.

Notwithstanding any other provision of this Article, a company does not act as a fiduciary; engage in trust business or in any other business requiring a charter, license, or approval under the provisions of this Chapter; or engage in unauthorized trust activity by:

(1)   Acting in a manner authorized by law as an agent of a trust institution with respect to any activity that is not unauthorized trust activity;

(2)   Rendering legal services in a manner authorized by the North Carolina State Bar;

(3)   Acting as trustee under a deed of trust delivered only as security for the payment of money or for the performance of another act;

(4)   Receiving and distributing rents and proceeds of sales of real property in a manner authorized by the North Carolina Real Estate Commission;

(5)   Engaging in securities transactions or providing investment advisory services in accordance with applicable securities laws;

(6)   Engaging in the issuance, sale, or administration of an insurance or annuity product in a manner authorized by the North Carolina Department of Insurance;

(7)   Engaging in the lawful sale of prepaid funeral benefits in accordance with and subject to Article 13D of Chapter 90 of the General Statutes or engaging in the lawful business of a perpetual care cemetery corporation in accordance with and subject to Chapter 65 of the General Statutes;

(8)   Acting as trustee under a voting trust;

(9)   Acting as fiduciary by an organization described in paragraphs (1) through (5) of section 170(c) or section 501(c) of the Internal Revenue Code of 1986, as amended, with respect to endowment funds or other funds owned, controlled, provided to, or otherwise made available to the organization with respect to its exempt purposes (including, without limitation, trust funds in which the organization has a beneficial interest).

(10)   Engaging in other activities expressly excluded from the application of this Article by rule, order, or declaratory ruling of the Commissioner;

(11)   Rendering services as a certified public accountant in a manner authorized by the North Carolina State Board of Certified Public Accountant Examiners;

(12)   Provided the company is a trust institution and is not barred by order of the Commissioner from engaging in trust marketing in this State pursuant to G.S. 53-321(b), (i) marketing or soliciting in this State with respect to acting as a fiduciary outside this State; (ii) delivering money or other intangible assets to, and receiving money or other intangible assets for administration outside this State from, a person in this State; or (iii) accepting an account outside this State or otherwise engaging in trust business outside this State; or

(13)   Receiving, holding, administering, or distributing real or personal property for or on behalf of another person solely incidental to a lawfully conducted activity or transaction. (2001-263, s. 1.)

§ 53-305. Trust business of State trust institution.

A State trust institution may conduct any activities outside this State that are permissible for a trust institution in the host state, subject to the laws of this State and, in the case of a State bank or a State trust company, subject to rules, orders, or declaratory rulings of the Commissioner. (2001-263, s. 1.)

§ 53-306. Trust business of out-of-state trust institution.

An out-of-state trust institution that establishes or acquires and maintains one or more trust offices or representative trust offices in this State under the provisions of this Part or that maintains one or more branches in this State may, subject to the provisions of this Part, conduct any activity through such a trust office, representative trust office, or branch that a State trust company or a State bank is authorized to conduct through a trust office, representative trust office, or branch under the laws of this State. (2001-263, s. 1; 2005-269, s. 4.)

§ 53-307. Trust business of foreign trust institution.

A foreign trust institution that establishes or acquires and maintains one or more trust offices in this State under the provisions of this Part may, subject to the provisions of this Part, also establish or acquire one or more representative trust offices and conduct any activity through the trust offices or representative trust offices that a State trust company is authorized to conduct through trust offices or representative trust offices under the laws of this State. (2001-263, s. 1; 2005-269, s. 5.)

§ 53-308. Name of trust institution.

Subject to other provisions of applicable law, a person may register or reserve any name with the Secretary of State in connection with engaging or proposing to engage in trust business or trust marketing in this State, except that the Commissioner may determine that a name registered or reserved is potentially misleading to the public and require the use of a name that is not potentially misleading. (2001-263, s. 1.)

§ 53-309. Trust deposits of authorized trust institutions.

(a)   Subsection (b) of G.S. 36A-63 shall not apply to an authorized trust institution.

(b)   In the absence of a contrary provision in an instrument governing an account, an authorized trust institution may deposit client funds with itself to satisfy its duties under G.S. 36A-63(a) provided:

(1)   It maintains, as collateral for the deposits, a separate fund of readily marketable commercial bonds having not less than a recognized "A" rating equal to one hundred and twenty-five percent (125%) of the funds so deposited;

(2)   The separate fund is designated as such; and

(3)   The separate fund either is maintained under the control of another trust institution, a bank, or a government agency, or is held by the authorized trust institution for the benefit of the accounts with deposits secured by the separate fund; provided, that the Commissioner may require such a separate fund of an authorized trust institution that is insolvent, in a hazardous condition, or jeopardized, to be held by a separate trust institution or bank approved by the Commissioner.

250

(c)   An authorized trust institution may make periodic withdrawals from or additions to the separate fund required by subsection (b) of this section as long as the required value is maintained. Income from the separate fund belongs to the authorized trust institution.

(d)   Collateral is not required for a deposit under subsection (b) of this section to the extent the deposit is insured by the Federal Deposit Insurance Corporation. (2001-263, s. 1.)

Subpart C. State Trust Company Trust Officers and Representative Trust Offices.

§ 53-310. Offices of State trust companies.

(a)   A State trust company may engage in trust business or trust marketing through its principal office and through each trust office as permitted by this Part.

(b)   A State trust company may engage in trust marketing through a representative trust office as permitted by this Part.

(c)   A State trust company may engage in trust business and trust marketing through out-of-state trust offices or representative trust offices to the same extent permitted for trust institutions located in the host state through which those out-of-state trust offices or representative trust offices are located, subject to the laws of this State and as provided by rules, orders, or declaratory rulings of the Commissioner. (2001-263, s. 1; 2005-269, s. 6.)

§ 53-311. State trust company principal office.

(a)   Each State trust company is required to maintain a principal office in this State and to register that principal office with the Commissioner by setting forth the current street address and telephone number of the principal office.

(b)   Each executive officer at a principal office is an agent of the State trust company for service of process.

(c)   Before changing the location of its principal office, a State trust company shall file a notice with the Commissioner setting forth the name of the State trust company, the current street address and telephone number of its principal office, the street address, and telephone number if known, of the proposed new principal office, and a copy of the resolution adopted by the board of directors or duly authorized committee of the board of directors of the State trust company authorizing the change. If the State trust company is unable to provide the Commissioner with the telephone number for the proposed new principal office at the time of the notice, it shall do so immediately after beginning to operate at the new principal office location.

(d)   The change of principal office shall take effect on the thirty-first day following the date the Commissioner receives the notice described in subsection (c) of this section, unless prior to the thirty-first day following receipt of the notice, the Commissioner (i) establishes an earlier or later date, or (ii) notifies the State trust company that the notice raises issues that require additional information or additional time for analysis, or (iii) disapproves the proposed trust office or representative trust office.

(e)   If the Commissioner gives a notification described in subsection (d) of this section, the State trust company may change the location of its principal office only on approval by the Commissioner. The Commissioner may disapprove the change of location if the Commissioner finds that the change will adversely affect the safe and sound operation of the State trust company. (2001-263, s. 1.)

§ 53-312. Trust offices; representative trust offices.

(a)   Before establishing or acquiring and maintaining a trust office or representative trust office in this State, a State trust company shall file a notice with the Commissioner, in the form required by the Commissioner, setting forth the name of the State trust company, the location of the proposed trust office or representative trust office, and whether the office will be a trust office or a representative trust office. The State trust company also shall furnish a copy of the resolution adopted by the board of directors or duly authorized committee of the board of directors of the State trust company authorizing the trust office or representative trust office and shall pay the filing fee, if any, set by rule.

(b)   The State trust company may commence business at the trust office or representative trust office on the thirty-first day after the date the Commissioner receives the notice, unless the Commissioner (i) establishes an earlier or later date; (ii) notifies the State trust company that the notice raises issues that require additional information or additional time for analysis; or (iii) disapproves the proposed trust office or representative trust office.

(c)   If the Commissioner gives a notification described in subsection (b) of this section, the State trust company may establish the trust office or representative trust office only on approval by the Commissioner. The Commissioner may disapprove the proposed trust office or representative trust office if the Commissioner finds that the State trust company lacks sufficient resources to undertake the proposed expansion without adversely affecting its safety or soundness. (2001-263, s. 1.)

§ 53-313. Out-of-state trust offices and representative trust offices.

(a)   Before establishing or acquiring and maintaining a trust office or representative trust office in a host state, a State trust company shall file a notice with the Commissioner, in the form required by the Commissioner, that sets forth the name of the State trust company, the location of the proposed trust office or representative trust office, whether the office will be a trust office or a representative trust office, and whether the laws of the host state permit the trust office or representative trust office to be maintained by the State trust company. The State trust company also shall furnish a copy of the resolution adopted by the board of directors or duly authorized committee of the board of directors of the State trust company authorizing the out-of-state trust office or representative trust office and shall pay the filing fee, if any, set by rule.

(b)   The State trust company may commence business at the trust office or representative trust office on the thirty-first day following the date the Commissioner receives the notice, unless the Commissioner (i) establishes an earlier or later date; (ii) notifies the State trust company that the notice raises issues that require additional information or additional time for analysis; or (iii) disapproves the proposed trust office or representative trust office.

(c)   If the Commissioner gives a notification described in subsection (b) of this section, the State trust company may establish the trust office or representative trust office only on approval by the Commissioner. The Commissioner may disapprove the proposed trust office or representative trust office if the Commissioner finds that the State trust company lacks sufficient resources to undertake the proposed expansion without adversely affecting its safety or soundness. (2001-263, s. 1.)

Subpart D. Out-of-State Trust Institution Trust Offices and Representative Trust Offices.

§ 53-314. Trust business through a branch or trust office.

An out-of-state trust institution may engage in trust business in this State only if it (i) maintains a trust office in this State as permitted by this Subpart, (ii) was allowed to maintain a trust office in this State under laws, or rules or orders of the Commissioner in effect prior to the date of enactment of this Article, but only to the extent allowed and subject to all limitations and conditions imposed under those laws, rules, or orders, or (iii) is a depository institution that maintains a branch in this State. (2001-263, s. 1; 2005-269, s. 7.)

§ 53-315. Establishing an interstate trust office.

An out-of-state trust institution that obtains approval from the Commissioner in accordance with the provisions of this Subpart may establish and maintain a trust office in this State; provided that the Commissioner shall not grant that approval unless the home state of the out-of-state trust institution permits a State trust institution to establish and maintain a trust office in that home state under restrictions not materially greater than those imposed by this Article. (2001-263, s. 1.)

§ 53-316. Acquiring an interstate trust office.

An out-of-state trust institution that obtains approval from the Commissioner in accordance with the provisions of this Subpart may acquire and maintain a trust office in this State; provided that the Commissioner shall not grant that approval unless the home state of the out-of-state trust institution permits a State trust institution to acquire and maintain a trust office in that home state under restrictions not materially greater than those imposed by this Article. (2001-263, s. 1.)

§ 53-317. Requirement of notice.

Before establishing or acquiring and maintaining a trust office in this State, an out-of-state trust institution shall provide, or cause its home state regulator to provide, notice to the Commissioner, in the form required by the Commissioner, along with copies of any applications, notices, or similar filings made with the home state regulator regarding the trust office. The notice shall be preceded or accompanied by:

(1)   Evidence satisfactory to the Commissioner of compliance by the out-of-state trust institution with all applicable requirements of Article 15 of Chapter 55 of the General Statutes;

(2)   Evidence satisfactory to the Commissioner of compliance by the out-of-state trust institution with any applicable requirements of its home state regulator for maintenance of capital, for expansion within the borders of the home state, and for acquiring or establishing and maintaining each trust office in this State;

(3)   Evidence satisfactory to the Commissioner that the out-of-state trust institution is not in a hazardous condition;

(4)   Unless waived by the Commissioner, a copy of the resolution adopted by the board of directors of the out-of-state trust institution (or similar governing body or a duly-authorized committee thereof) authorizing the trust office; and

(5)   Payment of any fee set by rule. (2001-263, s. 1; 2005-269, s. 8.)

§ 53-318. Action on notice.

(a)   The out-of-state trust institution may commence business in this State through the trust office on the sixty-first day following the date the Commissioner receives the notice described in G.S. 53-317 unless the Commissioner, within 60 days of receiving the notice:

(1)   Specifies an earlier or later date for commencing business,

(2)   Extends the period of review on a determination that the notice raises issues that require additional information or additional time for analysis; or

(3)   Disapproves the proposed trust office.

(b)   If the Commissioner gives a notification described in subdivision (2) of subsection (a) of this section, the out-of-state trust institution may establish the trust office only on approval by the Commissioner. The Commissioner may

255

disapprove the proposed trust office if the Commissioner finds that the out-of-state trust institution lacks sufficient resources to undertake the proposed expansion without adversely affecting its safety or soundness or that the requirements of G.S. 53-315 or G.S. 53-316 have not been satisfied. (2001-263, s. 1; 2005-269, s. 9.)

§ 53-319. Additional trust offices; representative trust offices.

(a)   An out-of-state trust institution that maintains a trust office in this State may establish or acquire and maintain additional trust offices or one or more representative trust offices in this State to the same extent that a State trust institution may establish or acquire and maintain trust offices or representative trust offices in this State and shall follow the procedures for establishing or acquiring and maintaining trust offices or representative trust offices set forth in G.S. 53-312.

(b)   An out-of-state trust institution that does not maintain a trust office in this State shall file a notice with the Commissioner, in the form required by the Commissioner, before establishing or acquiring a representative trust office in this State. The notice shall be preceded or accompanied by:

(1)   Evidence satisfactory to the Commissioner of compliance by the out-of-state trust institution with all applicable requirements of Article 15 of Chapter 55 of the General Statutes;

(2)   Evidence satisfactory to the Commissioner of compliance by the out-of-state trust institution with any applicable requirements of its home state regulator for maintenance of capital, for expansion within the borders of the home state, and for acquiring or establishing and maintaining each representative trust office in this State;

(3)   Evidence satisfactory to the Commissioner that the out-of-state trust institution is not in a hazardous condition;

(4)   Unless waived by the Commissioner, a copy of the resolution adopted by the board of directors of the out-of-state trust institution (or similar governing body or a duly authorized committee thereof) authorizing the representative trust office;

(5)   The proposed location of each proposed representative trust office; and

(6)   Payment of any fee set by rule.

(c)   The out-of-state trust institution may commence business at the representative trust office on the thirty-first day following the date the Commissioner receives the notice described in subsection (b) of this section, unless the Commissioner, within 30 days of receiving the notice:

(1)   Specifies an earlier or later date for commencing business;

(2)   Extends the period of review on a determination that the notice raises issues that require additional information or additional time for analysis; or

(3)   Disapproves the proposed representative trust office.

(d)   If the Commissioner gives a notification described in subdivision (2) of subsection (c) of this section, the out-of-state trust institution may commence business at the representative trust office only on approval by the Commissioner. The Commissioner may disapprove the representative trust office if the Commissioner finds that the out-of-state trust institution lacks sufficient resources to undertake the proposed expansion without adversely affecting its safety or soundness or that the requirements of G.S. 53-315 or G.S. 53-316 have not been satisfied.

(e)   An out-of-state trust institution that was allowed to maintain a representative trust office in this State under laws, or rules or orders of the Commissioner in effect prior to the effective date of this Article may continue to do so, but only to the extent allowed and subject to all limitations and conditions imposed under those laws, rules, or orders. (2001-263, s. 1; 2005-269, s. 10.)

§ 53-320. Examinations; periodic reports; cooperative agreements; assessment of fees.

(a)   The Commissioner may examine any activity conducted through a trust office or representative trust office maintained in this State by an out-of-state trust institution to determine whether these activities are being conducted in compliance with the laws of this State and in accordance with safe and sound practices. The pertinent provisions of Part 4 of this Article shall apply to these examinations.

257

(b)   The Commissioner may require periodic reports regarding any out-of-state trust institution that maintains a trust office or representative trust office in this State pursuant to this Subpart. The required reports shall be provided by the trust institution or by the home state regulator. Any reporting requirements shall be (i) consistent, to the extent practicable, with the reporting requirements applicable to State trust companies and (ii) appropriate for the purpose of enabling the Commissioner to carry out the Commissioner's responsibilities under the provisions of this Article. The pertinent provisions of Part 4 of this Article shall apply to these reports.

(c)   The Commissioner may enter into cooperative, coordinating, and information-sharing agreements with bank supervisory agencies, including agreements arranged by an organization composed of, affiliated with, or representing one or more bank supervisory agencies, with respect to the periodic supervision and examination of any trust office or representative trust office of an out-of-state trust institution in this State, or any trust office or representative trust office of a State trust institution in any host state. The Commissioner may accept and rely upon a report of examination and report of investigation of a bank supervisory agency in lieu of conducting a separate examination or investigation.

(d)   The Commissioner may enter into agreements with any bank supervisory agency supervising (i) a State trust institution engaging in trust business outside this State or (ii) an out-of-state trust institution maintaining a trust office or representative trust office in this State to engage the services of the agency's examiners at a reasonable rate of compensation or to provide the services of the Commissioner's examiners to the agency at a reasonable rate of compensation. Article 3 of Chapter 143 of the General Statutes does not apply to agreements authorized by this subsection. However, the Commissioner shall: (i) submit all proposed agreements or contracts for supplies, materials, printing, equipment, and contractual services that exceed one million dollars ($1,000,000) authorized by this subsection to the Attorney General or the Attorney General's designee for review as provided in G.S. 114-8.3; and (ii) include in all agreements or contracts to be awarded by the Commissioner under this subsection a standard clause which provides that the State Auditor and internal auditors of the Commissioner may audit the records of the contractor during and after the term of the agreement or contract to verify accounts and data affecting fees and performance. The Commissioner shall not award a cost plus percentage of cost agreement or contract for any purpose.

258

(e)   The Commissioner may enter into joint examinations or joint enforcement actions with bank supervisory agencies supervising any trust office or representative trust office maintained in this State by an out-of-state trust institution or any trust office or representative trust office maintained by a State trust institution in any host state; provided, that the Commissioner may at any time take actions independently if the Commissioner considers the actions to be necessary or appropriate to carry out the Commissioner's responsibilities under the provisions of this Article or to ensure compliance with the laws of this State.

(f)   Each out-of-state trust institution that maintains one or more trust offices or representative trust offices in this State may be assessed and, if assessed, shall pay supervisory and examination fees as provided by rules of the Commissioner. The fees may be shared with bank supervisory agencies or any organization composed of, affiliated with, or representing one or more bank supervisory agencies as agreed between those bank supervisory agencies and organizations and the Commissioner. (2001-263, s. 1; 2005-269, s. 11; 2010-194, s. 2; 2011-326, s. 15(b).)

§ 53-321. Enforcement.

(a)   Consistent with Article 3A of Chapter 150B of the General Statutes, after notice and opportunity for hearing, the Commissioner may determine:

(1)   That activities of a trust office maintained by an out-of-state trust institution in this State are being conducted in violation of the laws of this State or any rule, order, or declaratory ruling issued by the Commissioner, or in an unsafe and unsound manner, or that the out-of-state trust institution does not meet or no longer meets the requirements of this Subpart for maintaining a trust office in this State; or

(2)   That an out-of-state trust institution is engaged in unauthorized trust activity.

In either event, the Commissioner may take any enforcement actions the Commissioner would be authorized to take if the trust office or the out-of-state trust institution were a State trust company and may issue an order temporarily or permanently prohibiting the out-of-state trust institution from engaging in trust business in this State.

259

(b)   Consistent with Article 3A of Chapter 150B of the General Statutes, after notice and opportunity for hearing, the Commissioner may determine by order that an out-of-state trust institution maintaining a representative trust office in this State does not meet or no longer meets the requirements of this Subpart for maintaining a representative trust office in this State. The order shall be effective on the date of issuance or any other date the Commissioner determines.

(c)   In cases involving extraordinary circumstances requiring immediate action, the Commissioner may take any action permitted by subsection (a) or (b) of this section without notice or opportunity for hearing but shall promptly afford a subsequent hearing upon an application to rescind the action taken.

(d)   The Commissioner shall promptly give notice to the home state regulator and any other bank supervisory agency supervising the out-of-state trust institution of each enforcement action taken against an out-of-state trust institution and may consult and cooperate with other bank supervisory agencies in pursuing and resolving the enforcement action. (2001-263, s. 1; 2005-269, s. 12.)

§ 53-322. Notice of transactions that cause a change in control.

Each out-of-state trust institution that maintains a trust office or representative trust office in this State, or the home state regulator of the trust institution, shall give at least 30 days' notice or, in the case of an emergency transaction or the cessation of trust activity in this State by an out-of-state trust institution or foreign trust institution whose only office in this State is a registered office, as much notice as practicable, to the Commissioner of:

(1)   Any merger, consolidation, share exchange, or other transaction that would cause a change in control of an out-of-state trust institution (i) that would be subject to Subpart D of Part 3 of this Article if the out-of-state trust institution were a State trust company or (ii) is required to be filed with any bank supervisory agency;

(2)   Any transfer of all or substantially all of the accounts or account assets of the out-of-state trust institution to another person; or

(3)   The closing, transfer, or discontinuance of any trust office or representative trust office in this State. (2001-263, s. 1; 2005-269, s. 13.)

260

Subpart E. Foreign Trust Institution Trust Offices and Representative Trust Offices.

§ 53-323. Foreign trust institution application for trust office or representative trust office.

Before establishing or acquiring and maintaining a trust office in this State, a foreign trust institution shall make application to the Commissioner for permission to do so in the English language and in the form required by the Commissioner. The application shall be preceded or accompanied by:

(1)   Evidence satisfactory to the Commissioner of compliance with all applicable requirements of Article 15 of Chapter 55 of the General Statutes;

(2)   Evidence satisfactory to the Commissioner of compliance by the foreign trust institution with any applicable requirements of its home country regulator for maintenance of capital, for expansion within the borders of its home country or within a political subdivision of its home country, and for acquiring or establishing and maintaining the trust office in this State;

(3)   Evidence satisfactory to the Commissioner that the foreign trust institution is not in a hazardous condition;

(4)   Unless waived by the Commissioner, a copy of the resolution adopted by the board of directors of the foreign trust institution, or similar governing body or a duly-authorized committee thereof, authorizing the trust office; and

(5)   Payment of any fee set by rule.

The Commissioner may require any materials not written in the English language to be translated, and the translation certified in a manner satisfactory to the Commissioner, at the expense of the foreign trust institution. (2001-263, s. 1; 2005-269, s. 14.)

§ 53-324. Conditions for approval.

(a)   A foreign trust institution may engage in trust business in this State only on approval by the Commissioner of an application described in G.S. 53-323, which may be given upon conditions required by the Commissioner for prudential reasons consistent with any applicable international agreements to which the United States is a party.

(b)   The Commissioner may deny approval of the application if the Commissioner finds that the foreign trust institution lacks sufficient resources to undertake the proposed expansion without adversely affecting its safety or soundness or that the management, integrity, or reputation of the foreign trust institution does not justify approval. The Commissioner also may deny approval if the Commissioner is unable to determine from the application materials whether the foreign trust institution possesses sufficient resources to undertake the proposed expansion without adversely affecting its safety or soundness or whether the management, integrity, or reputation of the foreign trust institution justifies approval. (2001-263, s. 1; 2005-269, s. 15.)

§ 53-325. Additional trust offices and representative trust offices.

A foreign trust institution that maintains a trust office in this State under the provisions of this Subpart may establish or acquire and maintain additional trust offices or representative trust offices in this State in the manner provided by G.S. 53-319 for out-of-state trust institutions, except that the Commissioner may require any additional information and impose any additional conditions as the Commissioner deems necessary for prudential reasons consistent with any applicable international agreements to which the United States is a party. (2001-263, s. 1.)

§ 53-326. Examinations; periodic reports; cooperative agreements; assessment of fees.

(a)   The Commissioner may examine any activity conducted through a trust office or representative trust office maintained in this State by a foreign trust institution to determine whether these activities are being conducted in compliance with the laws of this State and in accordance with safe and sound practices. The pertinent provisions of Part 4 of this Article shall apply to these examinations.

(b)   The Commissioner may require periodic reports regarding any foreign trust institution that maintains a trust office or representative trust office in this State. The required reports shall be provided in the English language by the trust institution or by its home country regulator. The reporting requirements shall be those the Commissioner considers appropriate for the purpose of enabling the Commissioner to carry out the Commissioner's responsibilities under the provisions of this Article for prudential reasons consistent with any applicable international agreements to which the United States is a party. The pertinent provisions of Part 4 of this Article shall apply to these reports.

(c)   The Commissioner may enter into cooperative, coordinating, and information-sharing agreements with bank supervisory agencies supervising foreign trust institutions, including agreements arranged by an organization composed of, affiliated with, or representing one or more bank supervisory agencies, with respect to the periodic supervision and examination of any trust office or representative trust office of a foreign trust institution in this State, or any trust office or representative trust office of a State trust institution engaged in trust business or trust marketing in a foreign country. The Commissioner may accept and rely upon a report of examination and report of investigation of a bank supervisory agency in lieu of conducting a separate examination or investigation of a foreign trust institution.

(d)   The Commissioner may enter into agreements with bank supervisory agencies supervising (i) a State trust institution engaging in trust business in a foreign country or (ii) a foreign trust institution maintaining a trust office or representative trust office in this State to engage the services of the bank supervisory agency's examiners at a reasonable rate of compensation or to provide the services of the Commissioner's examiners to the bank supervisory agency at a reasonable rate of compensation. Article 3 of Chapter 143 of the General Statutes does not apply to agreements authorized by this section. However, the Commissioner shall: (i) submit all proposed agreements or contracts for supplies, materials, printing, equipment, and contractual services that exceed one million dollars ($1,000,000) authorized by this subsection to the Attorney General or the Attorney General's designee for review as provided in G.S. 114-8.3; and (ii) include in all agreements or contracts to be awarded by the Commissioner under this subsection a standard clause which provides that the State Auditor and internal auditors of the Commissioner may audit the records of the contractor during and after the term of the agreement or contract to verify accounts and data affecting fees and performance. The Commissioner shall not award a cost plus percentage of cost agreement or contract for any purpose.

(e)   The Commissioner may enter into joint examinations or joint enforcement actions with bank supervisory agencies supervising any trust office or representative trust office maintained in this State by a foreign trust institution or any trust office or representative trust office maintained by a State trust institution in any foreign country; provided, that the Commissioner may at any time take actions independently if the Commissioner considers the actions to be necessary or appropriate to carry out the Commissioner's responsibilities under the provisions of this Article or to ensure compliance with the laws of this State.

(f)   Each foreign trust institution that maintains one or more trust offices or representative trust offices in this State may be assessed and, if assessed, shall pay supervisory and examination fees as provided by rules of the Commissioner. The fees may be shared with bank supervisory agencies or with any organization composed of, affiliated with, or representing one or more bank supervisory agencies, as agreed between the bank supervisory agencies and organizations and the Commissioner. (2001-263, s. 1; 2005-269, s. 16; 2010-194, s. 3; 2011-326, s. 15(c).)

§ 53-327. Enforcement.

(a)   Consistent with Article 3A of Chapter 150B of the General Statutes, after notice and opportunity for hearing, the Commissioner may determine:

(1)   That activities of a trust office or representative trust office maintained by a foreign trust institution in this State are being conducted in violation of the laws of this State or any rule, order, or declaratory ruling issued by the Commissioner, or in an unsafe and unsound manner, or that the foreign trust institution does not meet or no longer meets the requirements of this Subpart for maintaining a trust office or representative trust office in this State; or

(2)   That a foreign trust institution is engaged in unauthorized trust activity.

In either event, the Commissioner may take any enforcement actions the Commissioner would be authorized to take if the foreign trust institution were a State trust company and may issue an order temporarily or permanently prohibiting the foreign trust institution from engaging in trust business or trust marketing in this State.

(b)   Consistent with Article 3A of Chapter 150B of the General Statutes, after notice and opportunity for hearing, the Commissioner may determine by order that a foreign trust institution maintaining a representative trust office in this State does not meet or no longer meets the requirements of this Subpart for maintaining a representative trust office in this State. The order shall be effective on the date of issuance or any other date the Commissioner determines.

(c)   In cases involving extraordinary circumstances requiring immediate action, the Commissioner may take any action permitted by subsection (a) or (b) of this section without notice or opportunity for hearing but shall promptly afford a subsequent hearing upon request to rescind the action taken.

(d)   The Commissioner shall promptly give notice to the home country regulator and any other bank supervisory agency supervising the foreign trust institution of each enforcement action taken against a foreign trust institution and may consult and cooperate with bank supervisory agencies in pursuing and resolving the enforcement action. (2001-263, s. 1; 2005-269, s. 17.)

§ 53-328. Notice of transactions that cause a change in control.

Each foreign trust institution that maintains a trust office or representative trust office in this State, or the home country regulator of the foreign trust institution, shall give at least 30 days' notice (or, in the case of an emergency transaction or the cessation of trust activity in this State by an out-of-state trust institution or foreign trust institution whose only office in this State is a registered office, as much notice as practicable) to the Commissioner, in the form required by the Commissioner, of:

(1)   Any merger, consolidation, share exchange, or other transaction that would cause a change of control of a foreign trust institution:

a.   That would be subject to Subpart D of Part 3 of this Article if the foreign trust institution were a State trust company; or

b.   Is required to be filed with any bank supervisory agency;

(2)   Any transfer of all or substantially all of the accounts or account assets of the foreign trust institution to another person; or

(3)   The closing, transfer, or discontinuance of any trust office or representative trust office in this State. (2001-263, s. 1; 2005-269, s. 18.)

§ 53-329. International agreements.

If any provision of this Article concerning foreign trust institutions, or the application of that provision, is found by any competent adjudicatory body to violate any international agreement to which the United States is a party, the provision shall be deemed modified only to the extent and only in the particular circumstances necessary to make the provision as modified comply with the international agreement, and the remaining provisions of this Article shall not be affected and shall continue to apply to foreign trust institutions. (2001-263, s. 1.)

Part 3. State Trust Company Charter Act.

Subpart A. General.

§ 53-330. Title and purposes.

(a)   This Part may be cited as the State Trust Company Charter Act.

(b)   It is the express intent of this Part to provide for the chartering of trust companies apart from the provisions of Article 2 of this Chapter and to permit trust companies to engage in trust business subject to the provisions of this Article. (2001-263, s. 1.)

Subpart B. Organization and Powers of State Trust Company.

§ 53-331. Organization and powers of State trust company.

(a)   Subject to the other provisions of this Part, one or more persons may organize and charter a State trust company, which may be established in the manner described in this Part and in no other way.

(b)   Subject to G.S. 53-313 and G.S. 53-336(b) and other applicable provisions of State and federal law, a State trust company may:

(1)   Act as a fiduciary within or outside this State;

(2)   Act within or outside this State as agent, advisory agent, assignee, assignee for the benefit of creditors, attorney-in-fact, authenticating agent, bailee, bond or indenture trustee, conservator, conversion agent, curator,

266

custodian, escrow agent, exchange agent, fiscal or paying agent, financial adviser, investment adviser, investment manager, managing agent, purchase agent, receiver, registrar, safekeeping agent, subscription agent, transfer agent, warrant agent, or in similar capacities generally performed by corporate trustees, and in so acting to possess, purchase, sell, invest, reinvest, safekeep, or otherwise manage or administer real or personal property of other persons;

(3)   Engage in trust marketing within this State; and

(4)   Exercise the powers of a business corporation organized under North Carolina law and any incidental powers that are reasonably necessary to enable it to fully exercise, in accordance with commonly accepted fiduciary customs and usages, a power conferred in this Article. (2001-263, s. 1; 2011-339, s. 9.)

§ 53-332. Articles of incorporation of State trust company.

(a)   The articles of incorporation of a State trust company shall be signed and acknowledged by or on behalf of each organizer and shall contain:

(1)   The information required to be set forth in G.S. 55-2-02(a) and, except for telephone information, G.S. 53-311(c); and

(2)   Any provision consistent with G.S. 55-2-02(b) and other applicable law that the organizers elect to set forth in the articles of incorporation for the regulation of the internal affairs of the State trust company.

(b)   The Commissioner may allow a State trust company to be organized as a company other than a corporation, and, in such case, references in this Article to provisions of Chapter 55 of the General Statutes shall refer to analogous provisions of law governing the formation and operation of that State trust company. (2001-263, s. 1; 2011-339, s. 10.)

§ 53-333. Application for State trust company charter and permission to incorporate State trust company.

(a)   An application for a State trust company charter and permission to incorporate the State trust company shall be made to the Commissioner in the form required by the Commissioner and shall be supported by information, data, and records that the Commissioner requires. The application shall be accompanied by the fee set by the Commissioner by rule.

(b)   Upon receipt of the application, the Commissioner shall at once conduct an examination of all relevant facts connected with the formation of the proposed State trust company. The Commissioner may consider the following factors:

(1)   The proposed market or markets to be served;

(2)   Whether the proposed organizational and capital structure and the amount of initial capital appear adequate in relation to the proposed business and market or markets;

(3)   Whether the anticipated volume and nature of business indicate a reasonable probability of success and profitability based on the market or markets proposed to be served;

(4)   Whether the proposed officers and directors, as a group, have sufficient experience, ability, standing, competence, trustworthiness, and integrity to justify a belief that the proposed State trust company will be free from improper or unlawful influence and otherwise will operate in compliance with law, and that success of the proposed State trust company is reasonably probable; and

(5)   Whether the proposed name of the proposed State trust company is likely to mislead the public as to its character or purpose or is the same as a name already adopted by an existing bank, savings association, or trust institution in this State, or so similar thereto as to be likely to mislead the public.

(c)   The failure of an applicant to furnish required information, data, other material, or the required fee within 30 days after a request may be considered an abandonment of the application. (2001-263, s. 1.)

§ 53-334. Notice and investigation of charter application.

(a)   The Commissioner shall notify the organizers when the application is complete and accepted for filing and all required fees have been paid.

(b)   The Commissioner shall investigate the application and inquire into the identity and character of each proposed director, officer, and principal

268

shareholder. Notwithstanding any laws to the contrary, information in the application bearing on the character, or information about the personal finances, of an existing or proposed organizer, officer, director, or shareholder is confidential and not subject to public disclosure. (2001-263, s. 1.)

§ 53-335. Decision on charter application and hearing.

(a)   The Commissioner, based on the application and investigation described in this Subpart, shall enter an order approving or denying approval of the application.

(b)   If the Commissioner orders that the proposed State trust company may be formed, the Commissioner shall issue a State trust company charter and a certification to the Secretary of State permitting the establishment of the State trust company. The Commissioner may make approval of any application conditional and shall include any conditions in the order granting the charter.

(c)   Any order entered by the Commissioner with respect to a charter application shall be subject to review by the Commission for entry of final agency decision. (2001-263, s. 1; 2011-339, s. 11.)

§ 53-336. Issuance of charter.

(a)   A proposed State trust company shall not be incorporated or engage in trust business or trust marketing until it receives a charter issued by the Commissioner. The Commissioner shall not issue the charter until the State trust company certifies that it has:

(1)   Received cash or United States government securities having a market value on the date of capitalization in at least the full amount of required initial capital from subscriptions for the issuance of shares;

(2)   Elected the initial officers and directors named in the application for charter or other officers and directors approved by the Commissioner; and

(3)   Complied with all other requirements of this Subpart relative to the organization of a State trust company.

(b)   The charter issued by the Commissioner shall set forth the trust powers of the State trust company, which may be stated as:

(1)   All powers granted to a State trust company in this State; or

(2)   Specific powers that the State trust company chooses and is authorized by the Commissioner to exercise.

(c)   If a State trust company does not open and engage in trust business within six months after the date it receives its charter, or within such further period as may be extended by the Commissioner, the Commissioner may cancel the charter. (2001-263, s. 1.)

§ 53-337. Required initial capital.

(a)   The Commissioner shall not issue a charter to a proposed State trust company having initial capital of less than two million dollars ($2,000,000), except as provided in subsection (b) of this section.

(b)   The Commissioner may require additional initial capital for a proposed State trust company if the Commissioner finds the proposed scope or type of operation of a proposed State trust company requires additional initial capital for the safe and sound operation of the State trust company. The Commissioner may reduce the amount of minimum initial capital required for a proposed State trust company if the Commissioner finds the proposed scope or type of operation of a proposed State trust company may be formed with reduced initial capital consistent with the safe and sound operation of the State trust company. The safety and soundness factors to be considered by the Commissioner in the exercise of the Commissioner's discretion include:

(1)   The nature and type of business proposed to be conducted;

(2)   The nature and liquidity of assets proposed to be held in a corporate capacity;

(3)   The amount of fiduciary assets projected to be under management;

(4)   The type of fiduciary assets proposed to be held and the proposed depository of the assets;

(5)   The complexity of fiduciary duties and degree of discretion proposed to be undertaken;

(6)   The competence and experience of proposed management;

(7)   The extent and adequacy of proposed internal controls;

(8)   The proposed presence or absence of annual unqualified audits by an independent certified public accountant;

(9)   The reasonableness of business plans for retaining or acquiring additional equity capital; and

(10)   The existence and adequacy of insurance proposed to be obtained by the trust company for the purpose of protecting its clients, beneficiaries, and grantors. (2001-263, s. 1.)

§ 53-338. Subordinated notes or debentures.

The amount of any outstanding notes or debentures that are subordinated to creditors or classes of creditors of the State trust company may be treated as equity capital of the State trust company for purposes of determining equity capital adequacy, hazardous condition, or insolvency, and for other purposes, as provided by rules, orders, or declaratory rulings of the Commissioner. (2001-263, s. 1.)

§ 53-339. Application of laws relating to general business corporations.

Chapter 55 of the General Statutes applies to a State trust company to the extent not inconsistent with this Article. Except for the filing of annual reports and statement of change of registered agent or registered office, unless expressly authorized by this Article or a rule adopted by the Commission, a State trust company shall not take an action authorized by Chapter 55 of the General Statutes that requires a filing with the Secretary of State without first obtaining the approval of the Commissioner. (2001-263, s. 1.)

Subpart C. Investments and Activities.

271

§ 53-340. Investment in State trust company facilities.

(a)   A State trust company may invest in one or more State trust company facilities consistent with the safe and sound operation of a State trust company.

(b)   For the purposes of this Part, "State trust company facility" means real estate owned, or leased to the extent the lease or the leasehold improvements are capitalized, by a State trust company for the purposes of:

(1)   Providing space for State trust company employees, officers, and directors to perform their duties and space for appropriate parking;

(2)   Conducting trust business, including meeting the reasonable needs and convenience of the State trust company's customers, employees, officers, and directors, and providing for necessary computer operations, data processing, maintenance, and record retention and storage;

(3)   Future expansion of the State trust company's facilities; or

(4)   Conducting another activity authorized by law or by rules, orders, or declaratory rulings of the Commissioner.

(c)   Without the approval of the Commissioner, a State trust company shall not, within the first three years following issuance of its charter, directly or indirectly, invest an amount in excess of one-half of its initial capital in State trust company facilities, furniture, fixtures, and equipment. Except as otherwise provided by rules, orders, or declaratory rulings of the Commissioner, in computing this limitation, a State trust company shall include:

(1)   Its direct investment in State trust company facilities;

(2)   Any investment in a company with an interest in a State trust company facility;

(3)   Any indebtedness incurred on State trust company facilities by an affiliate of the State trust company.

Except as otherwise provided by rules, orders, or declaratory rulings of the Commissioner, in computing this limitation, a State trust company may exclude an amount included under subdivisions (1) through (3) of this subsection to the

272

extent any lease of a facility from the company holding title to the facility is capitalized by the State trust company.

(d)   Real estate acquired under subdivision (3) of subsection (b) of this section ceases to be a State trust company facility if it is not used for a purpose listed in subdivision (1), (2), or (4) of subsection (b) of this section on the third anniversary of the date of its acquisition unless the Commissioner grants approval to hold the real estate for a longer period. (2001-263, s. 1.)

§ 53-341. Other real estate.

(a)   A State trust company shall not acquire real estate other than a State trust company facility for its own account except:

(1)   Securitized interests in real estate and obligations secured by real estate;

(2)   As necessary to avoid or minimize a loss on an investment previously made in good faith; or

(3)   As provided by rules, orders, or declaratory rulings of the Commissioner.

(b)   To the extent reasonably necessary to avoid or minimize loss on real estate acquired as permitted by subsection (a) of this section or under G.S. 53-340, a State trust company may exchange real estate for other real estate or personal property, invest additional funds in or improve such real estate, or acquire additional real estate.

(c)   Except as provided in subsection (d) of this section, a State trust company shall dispose of any real estate acquired as permitted by subdivision (2) of subsection (a) of this section or under G.S. 53-340:

(1)   In the case of real estate acquired under subdivision (2) of subsection (a) of this section, on or before the fifth anniversary of:

a.   The date it was acquired; or

b.   The date it ceases to be used as a State trust company facility if it began to be so used after its acquisition.

273

(2)   In the case of real estate acquired under G.S. 53-340, on or before the third anniversary of the date it ceases to be a State trust company facility as provided by G.S. 53-340.

(d)   The Commissioner may grant one or more extensions of time for disposing of real estate if the Commissioner determines that:

(1)   The State trust company has made a good faith effort to dispose of the real estate and has been unable to do so on reasonably advantageous terms; or

(2)   Disposal of the real estate otherwise would be detrimental to the State trust company. (2001-263, s. 1.)

§ 53-342. Securities and other investments.

(a)   A State trust company may invest its corporate funds in any type or character of equity securities or debt securities subject to the limitations provided by this section.

(b)   Unless the Commissioner approves maintenance of a lesser amount, a State trust company shall invest and maintain an amount equal to at least forty percent (40%) of its equity capital in unencumbered cash, cash equivalents, and readily marketable securities.

(c)   Subject to subsections (d) and (e) of this section, the total investment in equity and investment securities of any one issuer, obligor, or maker held by a State trust company for its own account shall not exceed an amount equal to fifteen percent (15%) of the State trust company's equity capital. The Commissioner may authorize investments in excess of this limitation if the Commissioner concludes that the safe and sound operation of a State trust company would not be adversely affected by a proposed investment exceeding this limitation.

(d)   In calculating compliance with the investment limits set forth in subsection (c) of this section, a State trust company shall not be required to combine:

(1)   The State trust company's pro rata share of the securities of an issuer in the portfolio of a collective investment vehicle with the State trust company's pro

274

rata share of the securities of that issuer held by another collective investment vehicle in which the State trust company has invested; or

(2)   The State trust company's own direct investment in the securities of an issuer with the State trust company's pro rata share of the securities of that issuer held by collective investment vehicles in which the State trust company has invested under the provisions of this section.

(e)   Notwithstanding subsection (c) of this section, a State trust company may purchase for its own account, without limitation and subject only to the exercise of prudent judgment:

(1)   Bonds and other general obligations of a state, an agency, or political subdivision of a state, the United States, or an agency or instrumentality of the United States;

(2)   A debt security that this State, an agency or political subdivision of this State, the United States, or an agency or instrumentality of the United States has unconditionally agreed to purchase, insure, or guarantee;

(3)   Securities that are offered and sold under 15 U.S.C. § 77d(5);

(4)   Mortgage-related securities as defined in 15 U.S.C. § 78c(a);

(5)   Investment securities issued or guaranteed by the Federal Home Loan Mortgage Corporation, Fannie Mae, the Government National Mortgage Association, the Federal Agricultural Mortgage Association, or the Federal Farm Credit Banks Funding Corporation; and

(6)   Investment securities issued or guaranteed by the North American Development Bank.

(f)   The Commissioner may allow State trust companies to make other investments of its corporate funds not specified in this Subpart by rules, orders, or declaratory rulings. (2001-263, s. 1.)

§ 53-343. Prohibited distributions, acquisitions, liens, or pledges.

A State trust company shall not make any distribution to its shareholders, acquire its own shares, acquire a lien upon its own shares, or pledge its own

275

assets while an order of the Commissioner prohibiting such distributions, acquisitions, liens, or pledges is in effect. (2001-263, s. 1.)

§ 53-344. Subsidiaries.

(a)   Before acquiring, establishing, or performing activities through a subsidiary, a State trust company shall file a notice with the Commissioner, in the form required by the Commissioner, describing in detail the proposed activities of the subsidiary, the amount of the State trust company's proposed investment in the subsidiary, and the State trust company's proposed ownership interest in the subsidiary.

(b)   The State trust company may acquire or establish a subsidiary or begin performing activities in an existing subsidiary 30 days following the date the Commissioner receives the notice, unless the Commissioner:

(1)   Establishes an earlier or later date;

(2)   Notifies the State trust company that the notice raises issues that require additional information or additional time for analysis; or

(3)   Disapproves the acquisition, establishment, or performance of activities through the subsidiary.

(c)   If the Commissioner gives a notification described in subdivision (2) of subsection (b) of this section, the State trust company may acquire, establish or conduct activities through the subsidiary only on approval by the Commissioner. The Commissioner may disapprove the subsidiary if the Commissioner finds that the State trust company lacks sufficient resources to undertake the proposed expansion or perform the activity without adversely affecting its safety or soundness.

(d)   The Commissioner may make the establishment, acquisition, or performance of new activities through a subsidiary conditional and shall include any such conditions in an order.

(e)   The provisions of this section, rather than G.S. 53-342, shall apply to the establishment of a subsidiary by a State trust company.

(f)   Changes in ownership or control of a subsidiary of a State trust company shall be made only upon the approval of the Commissioner obtained in accordance with the procedures set forth in this section. (2001-263, s. 1.)

§ 53-345. Engaging in commerce prohibited.

Except as otherwise provided by this Part, or by rules, orders, or declaratory rulings of the Commissioner, a State trust company shall not engage in trade or commerce by buying, selling, or otherwise dealing in goods, or by conducting business other than trust business and trust marketing, except as necessary to fulfill a fiduciary obligation to a client. (2001-263, s. 1.)

§ 53-346. Lending and lease financing; conversion to State bank.

(a)   Except as may be appropriate for extensions of credit in connection with trust or other account relationships, and as provided in and subject to the provisions of Article 5 of Chapter 36A of the General Statutes and other provisions of applicable law, a State trust company shall not engage in a loan business or in lease financing transactions as the party extending credit.

(b)   Notwithstanding any other provision of this Chapter, a State trust company may, with the approval of the Commissioner, convert to a State bank by following the procedures and requirements set forth in Article 2 of this Chapter, subject to any modifications to those procedures and requirements that are necessary and appropriate for the conversion of a State trust company. The Commissioner may make modifications to procedures or requirements of Article 2 of this Chapter by rule, order or declaratory ruling. (2001-263, s. 1.)

Subpart D. Ownership; Governance; Mergers.

§ 53-347. Acquisition of control.

(a)   Except as this section otherwise expressly permits, a person shall not, without the approval of the Commissioner, directly or indirectly acquire control of a State trust company.

(b)   This Subpart does not prohibit a person from contracting to acquire control of a State trust company subject to required approvals.

277

(c)   This Subpart does not require the approval of the Commissioner for the acquisition of securities in the following circumstances:

(1)   The acquisition of securities in connection with securing, collecting, or satisfying a debt previously contracted for in good faith if the acquiring person files notice of acquisition of control with the Commissioner, in the form required by the Commissioner, at least 10 days before the person votes the securities acquired;

(2)   The acquisition of additional voting securities in any class or series by a controlling person who previously has complied with and received approval under the provisions of this Article or who was identified as a controlling person in a prior application filed with and approved by the Commissioner if the acquiring person files notice of acquisition of those securities with the Commissioner, in the form required by the Commissioner, at least 10 days before the person votes the securities acquired;

(3)   An acquisition or transfer of securities by operation of law, will, or intestate succession if the acquiring person files notice of acquisition of control with the Commissioner, in the form required by the Commissioner, at least 10 days before the person votes the securities acquired;

(4)   An acquisition of securities by gift, unless the gift is made for the purpose of circumventing this section, if the acquiring person files notice of acquisition of control with the Commissioner, in the form required by the Commissioner, at least 10 days before the person votes the securities acquired; or

(5)   A transaction exempted by the Commissioner by rules, orders, or declaratory rulings because (i) the transaction is not within the purposes of this Article, or (ii) regulation of the transaction is not necessary or appropriate to achieve the objectives of this Article.

(d)   Information provided under the provisions of subsection (c) of this section shall be subject to G.S. 53-348(c), and persons providing that information shall be subject to G.S. 53-348(d).

(e)   Upon receiving a notice described in subsection (c) of this section, the Commissioner may, on or before the tenth day after the acquiring person files the notice, notify the acquiring person of objection to the voting of securities by the acquiring person or of a request for further information concerning the

278

acquisition of control. If the Commissioner notifies the acquiring person of the objection or request for further information, the acquiring person may vote the shares only on approval by the Commissioner and:

(1)   The acquiring person shall follow the procedures prescribed in this Subpart for an application to acquire control of a State trust company;

(2)   The Commissioner may request any information that may be requested under the procedures prescribed in this Subpart in connection with an application to acquire control of a State trust company; and

(3)   For purposes of determining a quorum of shareholders of a State trust company, the shares shall be treated as authorized but unissued shares unless (i) the Commissioner approves the application to vote the securities or (ii) the acquiring person no longer has the power to vote the shares, either directly or indirectly. (2001-263, s. 1.)

§ 53-348. Application regarding acquisition of control.

(a)   A person seeking approval to acquire control of a State trust company shall file with the Commissioner:

(1)   An application in the form required by the Commissioner;

(2)   Any filing fee required by rule; and

(3)   All information required by rule or that the Commissioner requires in connection with a particular application in order to make an informed decision to approve or reject the proposed acquisition of control.

(b)   If any group of individuals or entities acting in concert seek approval to acquire control, the information the Commissioner may require under the provisions of this Subpart may be required of each member of the group.

(c)   Notwithstanding any laws to the contrary, information bearing on the character or information about the personal finances of an existing or proposed shareholder of a State trust company or other individual is confidential and not subject to public disclosure.

(d)   If a person seeking approval to acquire control is not a North Carolina resident, a North Carolina corporation, or an out-of-state corporation qualified to do business in this State, the Commissioner may require the person to appoint a resident agent for service of process. (2001-263, s. 1.)

§ 53-349. Decision on acquisition of control.

(a)   Not later than the sixtieth day following receipt of the application, the Commissioner shall either approve or deny the proposed acquisition of control.

(b)   The Commissioner may deny an acquisition of control if:

(1)   The financial condition of the person seeking approval to acquire control, or any member of a group seeking approval to acquire control, might jeopardize the financial stability of the State trust company or the interests of its clients;

(2)   Investigation of the character, competence, general fitness, experience, or integrity of the person seeking approval to acquire control, or any member of a group seeking approval to acquire control, shows that the proposed acquisition of control would not be in the best interests of the clients of the State trust company;

(3)   Plans or proposals to operate, liquidate, or sell the State trust company or its assets following the acquisition of control are not in the best interests of the State trust company's clients;

(4)   The State trust company would not be solvent, have adequate equity capital, or be in compliance with the laws of this State after the acquisition of control; or

(5)   The person seeking approval to acquire control has failed to furnish all information required by the Commissioner.

(c)   If an application filed under the provisions of this section is approved by the Commissioner, the transaction may be consummated. Any written commitment from the person seeking approval to acquire control made as a condition for approval of the application is enforceable against the State trust company and the person acquiring control. (2001-263, s. 1.)

280

§ 53-350. Appeal.

Any order entered by the Commissioner with respect to an application for acquisition or control of a State trust company shall be subject to review by the Commission for entry of a final agency decision. (2001-263, s. 1.)

§ 53-351. Report of changes in chief executive officer or directors.

Each State trust company shall report to the Commissioner within 48 hours, on the forms and with the information required by the Commissioner, any changes in the chief executive officer or the directors of the State trust company, including in its report a statement of the past and current business and professional affiliations of each new chief executive officer or director. (2001-263, s. 1.)

§ 53-352. Board of directors.

(a)   All corporate powers of a State trust company shall be exercised under the authority of, and the business and affairs of a State trust company shall be managed under the direction of, a board of directors. Without the approval of the Commissioner, the board shall consist of not less than five directors. Except as specifically provided otherwise in this section, the number, election, term, and classification of the directors of a State trust company shall be governed by the provisions of Chapter 55 of the General Statutes.

(b)   Before each term to which a person is elected to serve as a director of a State trust company, the person shall submit an affidavit for filing in the minutes of the State trust company stating that the person:

(1)   Accepts the position;

(2)   Will not knowingly violate, or knowingly permit an officer, director, or employee of the State trust company to violate, any law applicable to the conduct of business of the State trust company; and

(3)   Will diligently perform the duties of a director.

(c)   A person designated with a title such as advisory director is not considered a director if that person:

281

(1)   Is not elected by the shareholders of the State trust company; and

(2)   Does not vote on matters before the board of directors or any committee of the board and is not counted for purposes of determining a quorum of the board or any committee of the board. (2001-263, s. 1; 2011-339, s. 12.)

§ 53-353. Required board meetings.

The board of directors of a State trust company shall hold at least one regular meeting each quarter. At each regular meeting, the board shall review and approve, or disapprove and correct, the minutes of the prior meeting and review the operations, activities, and financial condition of the State trust company. The board may designate committees from among its members to perform these duties and approve or disapprove the committees' reports at each regular meeting. All material actions of the board shall be recorded in its minutes. (2001-263, s. 1.)

§ 53-354. Officers.

The board of directors shall annually appoint the officers of the State trust company who shall serve at the pleasure of the board. The contract rights of officers, if any, shall be governed by applicable provisions of Chapter 55 of the General Statutes and general law. The State trust company shall have a chief executive officer primarily responsible for the execution of board policies and operation of the State trust company. The State trust company also shall have an officer responsible for the maintenance and storage of all corporate books and records of the State trust company and for required attestation of signatures. These positions shall not be held by the same person. The board may appoint any other officers of the State trust company, including assistants to the officers required by this section, the board considers necessary or appropriate. (2001-263, s. 1.)

§ 53-355. Certain criminal offenses.

(a)   An officer, director, employee, or shareholder of a State trust company commits an offense if the person knowingly:

(1)   Conceals information or a fact, or removes, destroys, or conceals a book or record of the State trust company for the purpose of concealing information or a fact, from the Commissioner or an agent of the Commissioner; or

(2)   For the purpose of concealing information or a fact, removes or destroys any book or record of the State trust company that is material to a pending or anticipated legal or administrative proceeding.

(b)   An officer, director, or employee of a State trust company commits an offense if the person knowingly makes a false entry in the books or records or in any report or statement of the State trust company.

(c)   An offense under the provisions of this section shall be a Class H felony. (2001-263, s. 1.)

§ 53-356. Responsibility of directors.

(a)   The standard of conduct for directors shall be as set forth in G.S. 55-8-30.

(b)   Any director of a State trust company who shall knowingly violate, or who shall knowingly permit to be violated by any officers, agents, or employees of such State trust company, any of the provisions of this Article shall be held personally and individually liable for all damages which the State trust company, its shareholders, or any other person has sustained in consequence of the violation. Any aggrieved shareholder of any State trust company in liquidation may prosecute an action for the enforcement of the provisions of this section. Only one such action may be brought. The procedure shall follow, as much as possible, that prescribed by Article 3 of Chapter 44A of the General Statutes, relative to suits on bonds of contractors with municipal corporations. (2001-263, s. 1.)

§ 53-357. Record keeping.

A State trust company shall keep its fiduciary records separate and distinct from its other records. The fiduciary records shall contain all material information relative to each account as appropriate under the circumstances. (2001-263, s. 1.)

§ 53-358. Bonding requirements; reports of apparent crime.

(a)   The board of directors of a State trust company shall require protection and indemnity for the State trust company and its clients in amounts established by rules, orders, or declaratory rulings of the Commissioner, or otherwise in reasonable amounts, against dishonesty, fraud, defalcation, forgery, theft, and other similar insurable losses, with corporate insurance or surety companies:

(1)   Authorized to do business in this State; or

(2)   Acceptable to the Commissioner and otherwise lawfully permitted to issue coverage against those losses in this State.

(b)   Except as otherwise provided by rules, orders, or declaratory rulings of the Commissioner, coverage required under subsection (a) of this section shall include each director, officer, and employee of the State trust company without regard to whether the person receives salary or other compensation.

(c)   A State trust company that is the victim of a robbery, has a shortage of corporate or account assets in excess of five thousand dollars ($5,000), or is the victim of an apparent or suspected misapplication of its corporate property or account assets in any amount shall report the robbery, shortage, or apparent or suspected misapplication to the Commissioner within 48 hours after the time it is discovered. The initial report may be oral if a written report is made promptly following the oral report. Neither the State trust company nor any director, officer, employee, or agent of the State trust company is subject to any liability for providing any information in any such report in good faith. (2001-263, s. 1.)

§ 53-359. Merger, share exchange, or asset transfer authority.

(a)   With the approval of the Commissioner, a State trust company may merge or exchange its shares with, or acquire or be acquired through a merger or share exchange with, another company, or may transfer to another company all or substantially all of its assets and liabilities, or may acquire from another company all or substantially all of its assets and liabilities.

(b)   A merger or share exchange authorized by subsection (a) of this section, shall be governed by Article 11 of Chapter 55 of the General Statutes and G.S. 53C-7-205. An acquisition or transfer of assets authorized by

284

subsection (a) of this section shall be governed by Article 12 of Chapter 55 of the General Statutes and G.S. 53C-7-205. (2001-263, s. 1; 2012-56, s. 30.)

§ 53-360. Merger, share exchange, or asset transfer application.

(a)   A copy of the proposed articles of merger or share exchange, or asset transfer agreement, and an application in the form required by the Commissioner, shall be filed with the Commissioner. The Commissioner shall investigate the condition of the parties proposing to engage in the merger, share exchange, or asset transfer and may require the submission of additional information.

(b)   The Commissioner may approve the merger or share exchange if:

(1)   Each resulting trust institution will be solvent and have adequate capitalization;

(2)   Each resulting trust institution appears able and ready to comply substantially with the statutes and rules relative to its organization;

(3)   Each resulting State trust company will be a "domestic corporation" as that term is defined in G.S. 55-1-40(4);

(4)   All fiduciary obligations and liabilities of each trust institution that is a party to the merger, share exchange, or asset transfer have been discharged properly or otherwise have been or will be assumed or retained properly by a person;

(5)   Each surviving, new, acquiring, or transferring party that is not authorized to engage in trust business will not engage in trust business and appears able and ready to comply substantially with applicable laws and rules; and

(6)   All conditions imposed by the Commissioner have been satisfied or otherwise resolved. (2001-263, s. 1.)

§ 53-361. Notice and investigation of merger, share exchange, or asset transfer; decision, hearing, and appeal.

285

(a)   The Commissioner shall notify the parties to the proposed merger, share exchange, or asset transfer when the application is complete and all required fees have been paid. Promptly following this notification, the parties shall provide notice to clients who may be affected by the proposed merger, share exchange, or asset transfer in the form and manner specified by the Commissioner.

(b)   At the expense of the parties to the proposed merger, share exchange, or asset transfer, the Commissioner may investigate the proposed transaction, including the character of the proposed directors, officers, and principal shareholders of each resulting trust institution and of any other person proposed to succeed to the accounts of the applying institutions. Notwithstanding any laws to the contrary, information bearing on the character or information about the personal finances of an existing or proposed organizer, officer, director, or shareholder is confidential and not subject to public disclosure.

(c)   Based on the application and investigation, the Commissioner shall enter an order approving or denying approval of the proposed merger, share exchange, or asset transfer not later than the sixtieth day following the date the Commissioner notifies the parties that the application is complete, unless extraordinary circumstances require a longer period of review.

(d)   Any written commitment made by a person proposing to engage in the merger, share exchange, or asset transfer as a condition for approval of the application is enforceable against that person.

(e)   Any order entered by the Commissioner under the provisions of this section shall be subject to review by the Commission for entry of a final agency decision. (2001-263, s. 1.)

§ 53-362. Appraisal rights of shareholders in mergers, share exchanges, or asset transfers.

A shareholder of a State trust company may exercise appraisal rights in connection with the proposed merger, share exchange, or asset transfer to the extent allowed under, and by following the procedures prescribed by, Article 13 of Chapter 55 of the General Statutes. (2001-263, s. 1; 2011-347, s. 2.)

Subpart E. Private Trust Companies.

§ 53-363. Private trust companies.

(a)   The following definitions apply in this Subpart:

(1)   "Designated relative" means the individual required to be named in the application under G.S. 53-364(a)(5) requesting an exemption from certain provisions of this Act pursuant to G.S. 53-364.

(2)   "Family member" means the designated relative and

a.   Any individual within the fifth degree of lineal kinship to the designated relative computed in accordance with G.S. 104A-1;

b.   Any individual within the ninth degree of collateral kinship to the designated relative computed in accordance with G.S. 104A-1;

c.   The spouse of the designated relative and of any individual qualifying as a family member under sub-subdivision a. and b. of this subdivision;

d.   A company controlled by one or more family members;

e.   A trust established by (i) a family member or (ii) an individual who is not a family member if income or principal of the trust could be distributed currently to or for the benefit of a family member;

f.   The estate of a family member; or

g.   A charitable foundation or other charitable entity created by a family member.

For purposes of this subdivision, a legally adopted individual shall be treated as a natural child of the adoptive parents.

(3)   "Transact business with the general public" means to engage in any sales, solicitations, arrangements, agreements, or transactions to provide trust business services, whether or not for a fee, commission, or other type of remuneration, to more than 35 persons who are not family members, except that rules, orders, or declaratory rulings of the Commissioner may provide for other circumstances in which a State trust company either does or does not

transact business with the general public. For the purposes of this subdivision, an estate, a trust, or any other legal entity having multiple beneficiaries or owners shall be deemed to constitute one person.

(b)   A private trust company engaging in trust business in this State shall comply with all provisions of this Article applicable to a State trust company unless expressly exempted from a provision of this Article by the Commissioner pursuant to this section or prior to the enactment of this Article. However, notwithstanding G.S. 53-352(a), the holders of the equity securities of a private trust company may by unanimous agreement limit the authority of its board of directors; restrict, enlarge, or modify the rights or duties of particular directors; or allocate to an individual or group other than the board of directors some or all of the duties of a board of directors. A private trust company shall notify the Commissioner of the adoption of any agreement affecting the authority of the board of directors within 48 hours and shall provide such information as the Commissioner requests about the agreement. To the extent that an individual or group other than the board of directors is vested with the authority of the board of directors under this section, that individual or group shall be deemed to be acting as the board of directors in the exercise of that authority for all purposes of this Chapter.

(c)   A private trust company or proposed private trust company may request in writing that it be exempted from specified provisions of G.S. 53-333(b), 53-337(a), 53-339, 53-340, 53-341, 53-342, 53-345, 53-346, and 53-394(b). The Commissioner may grant the exemption request in whole or in part. The Commissioner also may issue rules, orders, or declaratory rulings granting exemptions to all private trust companies, or to private trust companies that meet specified conditions.

(d)   The Commissioner may examine or investigate the private trust company or proposed private trust company in connection with the application for exemption. Unless the application presents novel or unusual questions, the Commissioner shall approve or deny the application for exemption no later than the sixty-first day after the date the Commissioner considers the application complete and accepted for filing. The Commissioner may require the submission of additional information in order to make an informed decision to approve or reject the proposed exemption.

(e)   Any exemption granted under the provisions of this section may be made subject to conditions or limitations imposed by the Commissioner

288

consistent with this Subpart, and those conditions or limitations shall be included in an order.

(f)   Rules, orders, or declaratory rulings of the Commissioner may provide for other circumstances that justify exemption from specific provisions of this Article, specifying the provisions of this Act that are subject to the exemption request, and establishing procedures and requirements for obtaining, maintaining, or revoking exemptions. (2001-263, s. 1; 2011-339, ss. 13, 14.)

§ 53-364. Requirements to apply for and maintain status as a private trust company.

(a)   A private trust company or a proposed private trust company requesting an exemption from the provisions of this Article pursuant to G.S. 53-363 shall file an application with the Commissioner, in the form required by the Commissioner, containing, preceded, or accompanied by:

(1)   An application fee as set by rules of the Commissioner;

(2)   A statement under oath of the reasons for requesting the exemption;

(3)   A statement under oath showing that the private trust company is not currently transacting business with the general public and that the company will not transact business with the general public without the approval of the Commissioner;

(4)   A listing of the specific provisions of the Act from which exemption is requested; and

(5)   The name of the designated relative whose relationship to other individuals determines whether the individuals are family members under G.S. 53-363(a)(2). The designated relative must be living and 18 years of age or older at the time the application is made.

(b)   The Commissioner may make further inquiry and investigation as the Commissioner deems appropriate. Notwithstanding any other law to the contrary, information bearing on actual or proposed accounts of the private trust company or proposed private trust company applying for the exemption is confidential and not subject to public disclosure.

(c)   To maintain its status as a private trust company and to maintain any exemptions from the provisions of this Article granted by the Commissioner, a private trust company shall file with the Commissioner an annual certification that it is in compliance with the provisions of this Subpart and the conditions and limitations of all exemptions granted. This annual certification shall be filed in the form required by the Commissioner and accompanied by any fee required by the Commissioner by rule. The annual certification shall be filed on or before December 31 of each year. The Commissioner may examine or investigate the private trust company periodically as necessary to verify the certification.

(d)   In any transaction involving a private trust company for which an application is required under G.S. 53-360, any exemption from the provisions of this Article granted to the private trust company shall automatically terminate upon the consummation of the transaction unless the Commissioner approves the continuation of the exemption.

(e)   The Commissioner may revoke any exemption from the provisions of this Article granted to a private trust company in the following circumstances:

(1)   An officer or director of the private trust company makes a false statement under oath on any document required to be filed by this Article or by any rules or orders of the Commissioner;

(2)   The private trust company fails to submit to an examination as required by G.S. 53-367;

(3)   An officer or director of the private trust company withholds requested information from the Commissioner; or

(4)   The private trust company violates any provision of this Subpart or fails to meet any condition on which the exemption is based.

(f)   If the Commissioner determines from examination or other credible evidence that a private trust company has violated any of the requirements of this Subpart or fails to meet any condition or limitation on which an exemption from the provisions of this Article is based, the Commissioner may by personal delivery or registered or certified mail, return receipt requested, notify the private trust company that the private trust company's exemptions from the provisions of this Article will be revoked unless the private trust company corrects the violation or failure or shows cause why any exemptions should not be revoked. The notification shall state grounds for the revocation with reasonable certainty and shall advise of an opportunity for a hearing. The notice shall state the date upon which the revocation shall become effective absent a correction or showing of cause why the exemption should not be revoked, which shall not be before the thirtieth day after the date the notification is mailed or delivered, except as provided in subsection (g) of this section. The revocation shall take effect for the private trust company on the date stated in the notice if the private trust company does not request a hearing in writing before the effective date. After the revocation takes effect, the private trust company shall be subject to all of the requirements and provisions of this Article applicable to a State trust company.

(g)   If the Commissioner determines from examination or other credible evidence that a private trust company appears to be engaging or attempting to engage in acts intended, designed, or likely to deceive or defraud the public, the Commissioner may shorten or eliminate the 30-day notice period specified in subsection (f) of this section, but shall promptly afford a subsequent hearing upon request to rescind the action taken.

(h)   If the private trust company does not comply with all of the provisions of this Article or correct any failure to meet any condition or limitation on which an exemption is based within the notice period specified in subsection (f) of this section, the Commissioner may institute any action or remedy prescribed by this Article or any applicable rule. (2001-263, s. 1.)

§ 53-365. Conversion to public trust company.

(a)   Before transacting business with the general public, a private trust company shall file a notice on a form prescribed by the Commissioner, which shall set forth the name of the private trust company and an acknowledgment that any exemption granted or otherwise applicable to the private trust company pursuant to G.S. 53-363 shall cease to apply once the Commissioner terminates private trust company status. The private trust company shall furnish a copy of the resolution adopted by its board of directors authorizing the private trust company to commence transacting business with the general public, and shall pay the filing fee, if any, prescribed by rule of the Commissioner.

(b)   The private trust company may commence transacting business with the general public on the thirty-first day after the date the Commissioner receives the notice, unless the Commissioner:

(1)   Establishes an earlier or later date;

(2)   Notifies the private trust company that the notice raises issues that require additional information or additional time for analysis; or

(3)   Disapproves the termination of private trust company status.

(c)   If the Commissioner gives a notification described in subdivision (2) of subsection (b) of this section, the private trust company status may be terminated only on approval by the Commissioner.

(d)   The Commissioner may deny approval of the proposed termination of private trust company status if the Commissioner finds that the private trust company lacks sufficient resources to undertake the proposed conversion without adversely affecting its safety or soundness or if the Commissioner determines that the private trust company could not within a reasonable period be in compliance with any provision of this Article from which it previously had been exempted pursuant to G.S. 53-363. (2001-263, s. 1.)

Part 4. Applicable Law; Enforcement Actions.

Subpart A. Supervision and Examination.

§ 53-366. Applicability of other laws to authorized trust institutions; status of State trust company.

(a)   Except as otherwise provided in this Article, the following provisions of this Chapter and Chapter 53C of the General Statutes shall apply to authorized trust institutions:

(1),   (2) Repealed by Session Laws 2012-56, s. 31, effective October 1, 2012.

(3)   G.S. 53C-7-205.

(4)   through (6) Repealed by Session Laws 2012-56, s. 31, effective October 1, 2012.

(7)   Article 8 of Chapter 53C of the General Statutes, except where it clearly appears from the context that a particular provision is not applicable to trust

business or trust marketing, and except that the provisions of this Article shall apply in lieu of:

a.   G.S. 53C-8-2.

b.   G.S. 53C-8-3.

c.   G.S. 53C-8-17.

(8),   (9) Repealed by Session Laws 2012-56, s. 31, effective October 1, 2012.

(10)   Article 14 of this Chapter.

(11)   G.S. 53C-2-7(b).

(b)   Rules adopted by the Commissioner to implement those provisions of this Chapter made applicable to authorized trust institutions by subsection (a) of this section also shall apply to authorized trust institutions unless the rules are inconsistent with this Article or it clearly appears from the context that a particular provision is inapplicable to trust business or trust marketing.

(c)   Activities of authorized trust institutions for clients shall not be considered the sale or issuance of checks under Article 16 of Chapter 53 of the General Statutes.

(d)   Until the Commissioner has issued new rules governing State trust companies, State trust companies shall be governed by rules issued by the Commissioner for banks acting in a fiduciary capacity, except to the extent the rules are inconsistent with this Article or it clearly appears from the context that a particular provision is inapplicable to the business of a State trust company.

(e)   Notwithstanding any other provision of this Chapter, a State trust company:

(1)   Repealed by Session Laws 2012-56, s. 31, effective October 1, 2012.

(2)   Is a "bank" for purposes of laws made applicable to authorized trust institutions in this section and for purposes of G.S. 53-277.

(3)   Is a trust company organized and doing business under the laws of the State of North Carolina, a substantial part of the business of which is exercising fiduciary powers similar to those permitted national banks under authority of the Comptroller of the Currency, and which is subject by law to supervision and examination by the Commissioner as a banking institution; and

(4)   Is a financial institution similar to a bank.

(f)   In the case of a State trust company controlled by a company that has declared itself to be a "financial holding company" under 12 U.S.C. § 1843(l)(1)(C)(i), deposits held for an account shall be deemed to be "trust funds" within the meaning of 12 U.S.C. § 1813(p) unless all fiduciary duties with respect to the account are explicitly disclaimed. This subsection does not prescribe the nature or extend the scope of any fiduciary duties; the nature and extent of any fiduciary duties with respect to deposits held for accounts shall be as provided by the instruments and laws applicable to those accounts.

(g)   Subject to any limitations contained in this Article, an authorized trust institution is a "trust company", a "corporate trustee", a "corporate fiduciary", and a "corporation acting in a fiduciary capacity", as such and similar terms are used in the General Statutes, except where it clearly appears from the context in which those terms are used that a different meaning is intended. (2001-263, s. 1; 2012-56, s. 31; 2013-29, s. 22.)

§ 53-367. Commissioner shall have supervision over authorized trust institutions and shall examine.

Every authorized trust institution shall be under the supervision of the Commissioner. The Commissioner may periodically examine and require reports from authorized trust institutions, and shall execute and enforce, through examiners and any other agents as are now or may hereafter be created or appointed, all laws and all rules, orders, and declaratory rulings relating to authorized trust institutions. All authorized trust institutions shall conduct their business in a manner consistent with all laws and all rules, orders, and declaratory rulings that may be adopted or issued by the Commissioner relating to authorized trust institutions. (2001-263, s. 1.)

§ 53-368. Assessment of State trust companies.

(of operating and maintaining the office of the Commissioner, each State trust company shall pay into the office of the Commissioner, within 10 days after notice, an annual assessment of ten thousand dollars ($10,000) plus one dollar ($1.00) per one hundred thousand dollars ($100,000) of assets held for its accounts, exclusive of nonsecuritized real estate interests. For purposes of this assessment, the amount of assets held for accounts shall be determined as of the close of business on December 31 of each year.

(b)   If an application for merger, share exchange, sale of assets, change of control, conversion, or a similar transaction occasions an examination or if the Commissioner determines that the financial condition or manner of operation of a State trust company warrants further examination or an increased level of supervision, a State trust company may be subject to an additional assessment not to exceed the amount required of all State trust companies by subsection (a) of this section.

(c)   Repealed by Session Laws 2012-56, s. 32, effective October 1, 2012. (2001-263, s. 1; 2007-55, s. 2; 2012-56, s. 32.)

Subpart B. Enforcement Orders; Trust Company Management.

§ 53-369. Administrative orders; penalties for violation; increase of equity capital.

(a)   In addition to any other powers conferred by this Chapter, the Commissioner may:

(1)   Order any authorized trust institution, or affiliate thereof, or any director, officer, or employee of an authorized trust institution, to cease and desist violating any provision of this Article or any rule issued thereunder.

(2)   Order any authorized trust institution, or affiliate thereof, or any director, officer, or employee of an authorized trust institution, to cease and desist from a course of conduct that is unsafe or unsound and which is likely to cause insolvency or dissipation of the assets of an authorized trust institution, or is likely to jeopardize or otherwise seriously prejudice the interests of the clients, creditors, shareholders, or the public in their relationships with the authorized trust institution.

(3)   Order any company to cease engaging in unauthorized trust activity.

(4)   Enter orders described in G.S. 53-321, 53-327, and 53-343.

(b)   The Commissioner may impose a civil money penalty of not more than one thousand dollars ($1,000) for each violation of an order issued under subdivision (1) of subsection (a) of this section. The Commissioner may impose a civil money penalty of not more than five hundred dollars ($500.00) per day for each violation of a cease and desist order issued under subdivision (2) or (3) of subsection (a) or this section. The clear proceeds of civil money penalties imposed pursuant to this section shall be remitted to the Civil Penalty and Forfeiture Fund in accordance with G.S. 115C-457.2.

(c)   The Commissioner may order that a State trust company in a hazardous condition increase its equity capital to a level that is adequate for the safe and sound conduct of its business. The order shall specify the period of time for meeting the requirement to increase equity capital, which period of time may be extended by further order of the Commissioner. (2001-263, s. 1.)

§ 53-370. Notice and opportunity for hearing.

Consistent with Chapter 150B of the General Statutes, notice and opportunity for hearing shall be provided before the Commissioner may act under the provisions of this Subpart. In cases involving extraordinary circumstances requiring immediate action, however, the Commissioner may take action without a hearing, but shall promptly afford a subsequent hearing upon request to rescind the action taken. (2001-263, s. 1.)

§ 53-371. Removal of directors, officers, and employees.

The Commissioner may require the immediate removal from office of any officer, director, or employee of any State trust company, who shall be found to be dishonest, incompetent, or reckless in the management of the affairs of the State trust company, or who persistently violates the laws of this State or the rules, orders, and declaratory rulings issued by the Commissioner. (2001-263, s. 1.)

Part 5. Dissolution and Receivership; Conservatorship; Jeopardized State Trust Companies.

Subpart A. Voluntary Dissolution and Liquidation.

§ 53-372. Required vote of shareholders.

With the approval of the Commissioner, a State trust company may go into voluntary liquidation, be closed, and surrender its charter and franchise as a corporation of this State by the affirmative vote of its shareholders owning two-thirds of its stock. (2001-263, s. 1.)

§ 53-373. Corporate procedure.

Shareholder action to liquidate a State trust company shall be taken at a meeting of the shareholders duly called by resolution of the board of directors. Notice of the meeting, stating the purpose of the meeting, shall be mailed to each shareholder, addressed to the shareholder's last known residence at least 10 days prior to the date of the meeting. If the shareholders, by the required vote, elect to liquidate a trust company, a certified copy of all proceedings of the meeting at which the action was taken, verified by the oath of the president and secretary, shall be transmitted to the Commissioner for approval. (2001-263, s. 1.)

§ 53-374. Authority to liquidate; publication.

If the Commissioner approves the liquidation, the Commissioner shall issue to the State trust company, under the Commissioner's seal, a permit for liquidation. No permit shall be issued by the Commissioner until the Commissioner is satisfied that provision has been made by the State trust company to satisfy and pay off all creditors and to transfer all client accounts and fiduciary records to successor fiduciaries in the manner provided by G.S. 53-383(c). If not so satisfied, the Commissioner shall refuse to issue a permit, and shall be authorized to take possession of the State trust company and its assets and business and to hold and liquidate the State trust company in the manner provided in this Part. When the Commissioner approves the voluntary liquidation of a State trust company, the directors of the State trust company shall notify clients of the State trust company in the manner prescribed by the Commissioner and shall cause to be published in a newspaper in the county in which the principal office of the trust company is located, or if no newspaper is published in that county, then in a newspaper having a general circulation in that county, a notice that the State trust company is closing down its affairs and going into liquidation and that creditors of the State trust company shall present their claims for payment. The notice shall be published once a week for four consecutive weeks. (2001-263, s. 1.)

§ 53-375. Examination and reports.

When any State trust company is in the process of voluntary liquidation, it shall be subject to examination by the Commissioner and shall furnish any reports required by the Commissioner. (2001-263, s. 1.)

§ 53-376. Unclaimed property.

All unclaimed property remaining with a State trust company voluntarily liquidated under the provisions of this Subpart shall be subject to the provisions of Chapter 116B of the General Statutes. (2001-263, s. 1.)

Subpart B. Seizure by Commissioner; Involuntary Dissolution and Liquidation.

§ 53-377. When Commissioner may take charge.

The Commissioner may take possession of the business and property of any State trust company whenever it appears that the trust company:

(1)   Is in a hazardous condition;

(2)   Has become insolvent or is in substantial danger of becoming insolvent;

(3)   Has sold or attempted to sell substantially all of its assets or has merged or attempted to merge its business with another entity without meeting the requirements of this Article;

(4)   Has dissolved or liquidated or attempted to dissolve or liquidate without meeting the requirements of this Article; or

(5)   Has suspended operations. (2001-263, s. 1.)

§ 53-378. Directors may act.

A State trust company may place its assets and business under the control of the Commissioner by a resolution of a majority of its directors upon notice to the Commissioner, and, upon taking possession of the State trust company, the Commissioner shall retain possession thereof until the State trust company is authorized by the Commissioner to resume business or until the affairs of the State trust company are fully liquidated as provided in this Subpart. No State trust company shall make any general assignment for the benefit of its creditors except by surrendering possession of its assets to the Commissioner as provided in this Subpart; and any other purported general assignment for the benefit of creditors by a State trust company shall be void. (2001-263, s. 1.)

§ 53-379. Notice of seizure; bar to attachment of liens.

When the Commissioner takes possession of any State trust company under G.S. 53-377 or G.S. 53-378, the Commissioner shall, within 48 hours, file with the clerk of the superior court in the county where the principal office of the State trust company is located a notice of the action which shall state the reason for the action, and which shall be deemed the equivalent of a summons and complaint against the State trust company in an action in the superior court except that it shall not be necessary to serve the notice. The taking possession of any State trust company shall be effective on the date when the authority is first exercised and from and after that time all assets and property of the State trust company, of whatever nature, shall be deemed to be in possession of the Commissioner, and the exercise of the authority shall operate as a bar to any attachment or other legal proceeding against the State trust company or its assets. After the Commissioner's exercise of authority, no lien shall attach in any manner binding or affecting any of the assets of the State trust company, and every purported transfer or assignment made thereafter by the State trust company, or by its authority, of the whole or any part of its assets, shall be null and void; and the Commissioner shall be substituted in place of the State trust company in any civil actions or proceedings pending at the time of the exercise of the authority. (2001-263, s. 1.)

§ 53-380. Notice to trust institutions, corporations, and others holding assets; existing liens.

Upon taking possession of the assets and business of any State trust company, the Commissioner shall forthwith give notice, by mail or otherwise, of the action to all banks, clearing corporations, brokers, trust institutions, or other persons or corporations holding, or having in possession, any assets of the State trust company. No lien against any assets of the State trust company shall be enforced in any manner other than as provided in this Article after the Commissioner has taken possession of the State trust company. (2001-263, s. 1.)

§ 53-381. Permission to resume business.

(a)   After the Commissioner has taken possession of a State trust company under the provisions of this Subpart, the State trust company may resume business only upon approval and subject to terms and conditions specified by the Commissioner.

(b)   When possession of a State trust company has been taken pursuant to either G.S. 53-377 or G.S. 53-378, the terms and conditions under which it may resume business shall be fully stated in writing, and a copy thereof shall be filed with the clerk of superior court of the county in which the action is pending.

(c)   Notwithstanding subsections (a) and (b) of this section, no State trust company possessed by the Commissioner under the provisions of this Article shall resume trust business unless and until the State trust company has been completely restored to solvency and it clearly appears to the Commissioner that the State trust company may be reopened with safety to the clients, creditors, and shareholders of the State trust company and to the public.

(d)   If the Commissioner determines that the State trust company shall not resume business, the State trust company shall be liquidated in accordance with the provisions of this Part and shall cancel the charter and revoke the license of the State trust company as provided in G.S. 53-414. (2001-263, s. 1.)

§ 53-382. Remedy for seizure; answer to notice; injunction; appeal; and motions.

(a)   Whenever any State trust company of which the Commissioner has taken possession under G.S. 53-377 shall deem itself aggrieved thereby, it may file an answer to the notice as in other civil actions and may also, upon notice to the Commissioner, apply to the resident or presiding judge of the superior court for an injunction to enjoin further proceedings by the Commissioner. The judge of the superior court may cite the Commissioner to show cause why further proceedings should not be enjoined and, after hearing the allegations and proof of the parties with respect to the condition of the State trust company, may dismiss an application for injunction or may enjoin further proceedings under the provisions of this section by the Commissioner. If the judge enjoins further action of the Commissioner and permits the reopening of the State trust company, the judge may require of the State trust company a surety bond as the judge deems necessary, payable to the Commissioner for the sole benefit of the creditors and clients of the State trust company and upon any terms the judge deems proper. Either party has the right to appeal a decision as in other civil actions.

(b)   The State trust company or any person interested may be heard by motion as to actions taken or proposed to be taken by the Commissioner, but the judge hearing the motion shall enter an order as in the judge's discretion will best serve the parties interested. (2001-263, s. 1.)

§ 53-383. Collection of debts and claims; Commissioner succeeds to all property of the State trust company.

(a)   Upon taking possession of the assets and business of any State trust company, the Commissioner is authorized to collect all money due the State trust company and to do any other acts necessary to conserve its assets and property. The Commissioner shall collect all debts due and claims belonging to the State trust company, and by order of the court may sell, compromise, or compound any bad or doubtful debt or claim or sell the real and personal property of the State trust company on any terms provided by the order. Where the sale is made under power contained in any mortgage or lien bond or other paper wherein the title is retained for sale and the terms of sale set out, sale may be made under that authority.

(b)   Upon taking possession of any State trust company under the provisions of this section, the Commissioner shall have the possession and the right to the possession of all the property, assets, choses in action, rights, and privileges of the State trust company. The property rights and privileges shall vest in the Commissioner absolutely for the purpose of liquidating, selling, or conveying the property rights and privileges, together with all other incidental rights, privileges, and powers necessary for the right of conveyance and sale.

(c)   Upon taking possession of any State trust company under the provisions of this section, the Commissioner shall administer each account of the State trust company on a temporary basis until either (i) a successor to the State trust company is appointed or the account is terminated in the manner provided by the terms of its governing instrument consistent with applicable law, or by applicable law in the absence of a provision in the governing instrument, or (ii) the Commissioner has granted the State trust company permission to resume business under the provisions of G.S. 53-381. The Commissioner may take appropriate steps for the appointment of successors or termination of accounts as the Commissioner deems necessary as to some or all of the accounts of the State trust company. If the governing instrument or other applicable law do not prescribe methods for appointing successors, or if the methods prescribed are unfeasible, the applicable law for appointment of a successor shall be as set forth in G.S. 53-399.

(d)   The officers and directors of any State trust company that is in the possession of the Commissioner under this Part shall not exercise any powers declared by this Subpart to be vested in the Commissioner. (2001-263, s. 1.)

§ 53-384. Bond of the Commissioner; surety; condition; minimum penalty.

Upon taking possession of any State trust company, the Commissioner shall execute and file a bond payable to this State for the benefit of creditors, clients, and shareholders of the State trust company, with some surety company as surety thereon, with the clerk of the superior court of the county in which the action is pending, conditioned upon the faithful performance of all duties imposed upon the Commissioner under the provisions of this Subpart with respect to the State trust company, the penal sum of the bond to be fixed by order of the Commissioner, which in no case shall be less than two hundred fifty thousand dollars ($250,000). Any person interested, by motion in the pending action, shall be heard by the resident or presiding judge of the superior court as to the sufficiency of the bond. The judge hearing the motion may fix the bond. (2001-263, s. 1.)

§ 53-385. Inventory.

302

Within 90 days after the filing of a notice described in G.S. 53-379, the Commissioner shall file an inventory of the assets and liabilities, not including assets and liabilities held in accounts of the State trust company, of the State trust company. A copy of the inventory shall be filed with the clerk of the superior court of the county in which the action is pending, and a copy shall be kept on file with the State trust company. The inventory shall be open for inspection during usual business hours, provided that nothing herein shall require the State trust company to remain open unnecessarily. (2001-263, s. 1; 2012-56, s. 33.)

§ 53-386. Notice and time for filing claims.

Notice shall be given by advertisement once a week for four consecutive weeks in a newspaper published in the county where the principal office of the State trust company is located, or if no newspaper is published in the county, then in some newspaper having a general circulation in the county, calling on all persons who may have claims against the State trust company to present them to the Commissioner at the principal office of the State trust company, and within the time to be specified in the notice which time shall not be less than 90 days from the date of the first publication. A copy of this notice shall be mailed to all persons whose names appear as creditors upon the books of the State trust company. Affidavit by the Commissioner to the effect that the notice was mailed shall be conclusive evidence thereof. For purposes of this section, clients and accounts of the State trust company shall not be considered creditors of the State trust company as to the assets held by the State trust company for the benefit of its accounts. (2001-263, s. 1.)

§ 53-387. Power to reject claims; notice; affidavit of service; action on claims.

If the Commissioner doubts the validity of any claim, the Commissioner may reject the claim, in whole or in part, and serve notice of the rejection upon the claimant, either personally or by certified mail, and an affidavit of the service of the notice shall be filed in the office of the clerk of the superior court of the county in which the action is pending and shall be conclusive evidence of the notice. Any action or suit upon a rejected claim shall be brought by the claimant against the Commissioner in the superior court of the county in which the action is pending within 90 days after service, or the action or suit shall be barred. Objections to any claim not rejected by the Commissioner may be made by any person interested by filing the objection in the pending action and by serving a

303

copy thereof on the Commissioner. The Commissioner, after investigation, shall either allow the objection and reject the claim, or disallow the objection. If the objection is not allowed and the claim is not rejected, the Commissioner shall file a notice in the pending action and serve the notice upon the person making the claim and the person objecting to the claim. Within 10 days after the notice is filed, the person filing objection by motion in the pending action may question the validity of the claim, and the questions of law and issues of fact shall thereupon be determined as in other civil actions. (2001-263, s. 1.)

§ 53-388. List of claims presented, copies, and proviso.

Upon the expiration of the time fixed for presentation of claims, the Commissioner shall make a full and complete list of the claims presented, including and specifying any claims that have been rejected. One copy shall be filed in the office of the clerk of the superior court of the county in which the action is pending, and one copy shall be kept on file with the inventory in the principal office of the State trust company for examination. Any indebtedness against any State trust company which has been established or recognized as a valid liability of the State trust company before it went into liquidation, for which no claimant has filed claim, or any liability for which a claim has been filed and rejected, shall be listed by the Commissioner in the office of the clerk of the superior court of the county in which the action is pending. Any claim that may be presented after the expiration of the time fixed for the presentation of claims in the notice provided in G.S. 53-386 shall, if allowed, share pro rata in the distribution but only as to those assets of the State trust company in the hands of the Commissioner that are undistributed at the time the claim is presented. (2001-263, s. 1.)

§ 53-389. Declaration of dividends; order of preference in distribution.

(a)   At any time after the expiration of the date fixed by the Commissioner for the presentation of claims against the State trust company, and from time to time thereafter, the Commissioner may declare and pay dividends to the creditors and shareholders of the State trust company. In paying and calculating dividends, all disputed claims shall be taken into account, but no dividend shall be paid upon the disputed claims until the claims have been finally determined. The following shall be the order of preference in the distribution of the assets of any State trust company liquidated hereunder:

(1)   State, county, and federal taxes owed and fees due the Commissioner other than those due under the provisions of this Subpart;

(2)   Wages and salaries due officers and employees of the State trust company for a period of not more than four months;

(3)   Expenses of liquidation, including those described in G.S. 53-391 and G.S. 53-395;

(4)   Amounts due creditors, honoring the priorities of valid security interests and subject to orders of the court concerning disputes among creditors;

(5)   Amounts due shareholders.

(b)   A statement of all dividends paid shall be filed in the office of the clerk of the superior court of the county in which the action is pending, and the statements shall show the expenses deducted and the disputed claims in determining dividends. (2001-263, s. 1.)

§ 53-390. Deposit of funds collected.

All funds collected by the Commissioner, in liquidating any State trust company, shall be deposited from time to time in a bank as may be selected by the Commissioner and shall be subject to withdrawal by check of the Commissioner. (2001-263, s. 1.)

§ 53-391. Employment of counsel, accountants, and other experts; compensation.

The Commissioner, for the purpose of exercising any power under the provisions of this Subpart, may (i) employ any liquidating agents, attorneys, accountants, consultants, and clerks necessary to properly conduct the business of or liquidate and distribute the assets of a State trust company; (ii) fix the compensation for the agents, attorneys, accountants, consultants, and clerks; and (iii) pay the compensation of those persons out of the assets of the State trust company. Provided, that all expenditures described in this section shall be approved by the resident or presiding judge in the county in which the action is pending. Payments made by the Commissioner pursuant to this section shall not be subject to the requirements of Article 3 of Chapter 143 of the

305

General Statutes. As used in this Subpart, the term "Commissioner" includes the Commissioner's duly appointed agents. The Commissioner shall: (i) submit all proposed agreements or contracts for supplies, materials, printing, equipment, and contractual services that exceed one million dollars ($1,000,000) authorized by this section to the Attorney General or the Attorney General's designee for review as provided in G.S. 114-8.3; and (ii) include in all agreements or contracts to be awarded by the Commissioner under this section a standard clause which provides that the State Auditor and internal auditors of the Commissioner may audit the records of the contractor during and after the term of the agreement or contract to verify accounts and data affecting fees and performance. The Commissioner shall not award a cost plus percentage of cost agreement or contract for any purpose. (2001-263, s. 1; 2010-194, s. 4; 2011-326, s. 15(d).)

§ 53-392. Unclaimed dividends held in trust.

Unclaimed dividends for claims described in subdivisions (a)(1) through (a)(4) of G.S. 53-389 shall be held by the Commissioner in trust for the claimants to whom the dividends are owed; and the dividends so held by the Commissioner shall be paid over to the persons entitled to the dividends when they furnish satisfactory evidence of their right to the dividends. In case of doubtful or conflicting claims, the Commissioner may apply to the superior court, by motion in the pending action, for an order from the resident or presiding judge of the superior court directing the payment of the dividends so claimed. Issues of fact raised by motion may, upon request of any claimant, be determined as in other civil actions. Interest earned on any unclaimed dividends so held shall be applied toward defraying the expenses incurred in the distribution of the unclaimed dividends. The balance of interest, if any, shall be deposited and held as other funds to the credit of the Commissioner. After the Commissioner has held any unclaimed dividends in trust under the provisions of this statute for the creditors of the liquidated State trust company for a period of three years following the resumption of business by or cancellation of the charter of the State trust company, the unclaimed dividends shall be subject to the provisions of Chapter 116B of the General Statutes. Upon payment of unclaimed dividends to the State Treasurer, the Commissioner shall be fully discharged from all further liability therefor. (2001-263, s. 1.)

§ 53-393. Action by the Commissioner following full settlement.

306

Whenever the Commissioner has paid all duly proven and allowed claims described in subdivisions (a)(1) through (a)(4) of G.S. 53-389, has made proper provision for unclaimed and unpaid and disputed claims, and has other assets of the State trust company, the Commissioner shall, unless the State trust company is granted permission to resume business in accordance with G.S. 53-381, call a meeting of the shareholders of the State trust company by giving notice thereof by publication once a week for four consecutive weeks in a newspaper published in the county, or if no newspaper is published in the county, then in a newspaper having general circulation in the county, and by mailing a copy of the notice to each shareholder's address as it appears on the books of the State trust company. Affidavit of the mailing of the notice herein required and of the newspaper as to the publication shall be conclusive evidence of notice hereunder. At the meeting, any shareholders may be represented by proxy and the shareholders shall elect, by a majority vote of the shares present, an agent or agents who shall be authorized to receive from the Commissioner all the remaining assets of the State trust company. The shareholders also may specify the means of resolving disputes between multiple agents and appointing successors to the agent or agents. The Commissioner shall cause to be transferred and delivered to the agent, or agents, all the remaining assets of the State trust company. The Commissioner shall thereupon cause to be filed in the office of the clerk of the superior court of the county in which the action is pending a full and complete report of all transactions showing the assets of the State trust company so transferred together with the name of the agent or agents giving receipt for the assets; and the filing of the report shall act as a full and complete discharge of the Commissioner from all further liabilities to the shareholders of the State trust company by reason of the liquidation of the State trust company. The agent shall convert the assets coming into the agent's hands into cash, except as otherwise provided by the court upon motion in the cause made by a shareholder of the State trust company, and shall make distribution to the shareholders of the State trust company as herein provided. The agent shall file semiannually a report of all transactions with the superior court of the county in which the State trust company is located, and with the Commissioner, and shall be allowed for the services such fees, not in excess of five percent (5%) of receipts and disbursements, as may be fixed by the court. In case of death, removal, or refusal to act of any agent or agents elected by the shareholders, the Commissioner or any interested person may seek an order from the resident or presiding judge in the county in which the action is pending appointing a successor to the agent or agents as determined by the shareholders or, if no method was set forth by the shareholders, as determined by the court to be in the best interests of the shareholders. The court in its discretion may either appoint a successor or order the call of a further meeting of shareholders for the election of a successor and make any orders that are appropriate. (2001-263, s. 1.)

§ 53-394. Annual report of the Commissioner; items included; reports of condition of State trust companies.

(a)   The Commissioner shall file, as a part of an annual report to the Governor, a list of the names of any State trust companies of which possession was taken and liquidated in the preceding year, the sum of unclaimed assets with respect to each State trust company, and all depositories of all sums coming into the hands of the Commissioner under the provisions of this Part.

(b)   The Commissioner shall, from time to time, compile and make available for public inspection reports showing the condition of State trust companies. (2001-263, s. 1.)

§ 53-395. Compensation of the Commissioner's office.

The office of the Commissioner, for services rendered in connection with the duties described in this Subpart, shall be entitled to actual expenses incurred in connection with the liquidation of each State trust company, including a reasonable sum for the time of the examiners and other agents of the Commissioner. The Commissioner may adopt rules or orders for fixing these expenses. (2001-263, s. 1.)

§ 53-396. Exclusive method of liquidation.

No State trust company shall be liquidated other than as provided in this Part. (2001-263, s. 1.)

§ 53-397. Disposition of books and records.

All fiduciary records relating to the administration of particular accounts shall be turned over to the successors in charge of administration of the accounts. All other books, papers, and records of a State trust company that has been finally liquidated shall be deposited by the receiver in the office of the clerk of the superior court of the county in which the action is pending, or in any other place as in the clerk's judgment, after consultation with the Commissioner, will provide for the proper safekeeping and protection of those books, papers, and records. Such books, papers, and records shall be held subject to the orders of the clerk of the superior court of the county in which the action is pending, including orders necessary for preserving the confidentiality of any information relating to accounts contained in those books, papers, and records. (2001-263, s. 1.)

§ 53-398. Destruction of books and records.

(a)   After the expiration of five years from the date of filing, in the office of the clerk of the superior court of the county in which the action is pending, of a final order approving the liquidation of a State trust company and the delivery to the clerk or into the clerk's custody of books, papers, records of the State trust company, the books, papers, and records may be destroyed by the clerk of the superior court of the county in which the action is pending.

(b)   After five years from the filing by the Commissioner of a final report of liquidation of any insolvent State trust company, the Commissioner, by and with the consent of the Commission, may destroy the records of any State trust company held in the office of the Commissioner in connection with the liquidation of the State trust company. However, in connection with any unpaid dividends, the Commissioner shall preserve the records or other evidence of indebtedness of the State trust company with reference to the unpaid dividends until the dividends have been paid.

(c)   Nothing in this section shall be construed to authorize the destruction by the clerk of superior court of any county or by the Commissioner of any of the formal records of liquidation or the records made in the office of the Commissioner with reference to the liquidation. (2001-263, s. 1.)

§ 53-399. Petition for new trustee.

Any person interested in any account, either as trustee, beneficiary, client, or otherwise, may petition the clerk of superior court of the county in which court accountings are filed or, if there is no such county, the county in which the account is being administered, for a new trustee or other successor to a State trust company in all cases in which use of the procedures set forth in this Part are employed. The petition and the order appointing a new trustee or other successor may relate to any number of accounts administered by the State trust company. Except as specified in this section, the procedure shall be as provided in Chapter 36A of the General Statutes for the appointment of successor trustees. (2001-263, s. 1.)

§ 53-400. Report to the Secretary of State.

The Commissioner shall, on or before the first day of each year, file with the Secretary of State a report showing any State trust companies under liquidation in this State and the names of any auditors or attorneys employed in connection with the liquidation of these State trust companies, together with the amounts paid or contracted to be paid to each of the auditors or attorneys. If any attorney has been employed on a fee contingent upon recovery, the report shall set forth the material terms of the fee arrangements. (2001-263, s. 1.)

=cx=ctC=sph Conservatorship.

Subpart C. Conservatorship.

§ 53-401. Provisions for conservator; duties and powers.

Whenever the Commissioner deems it necessary in order to conserve the assets of a State trust company for the benefit of clients or creditors, the Commissioner may appoint a conservator for the State trust company and require of the conservator a bond with any surety the Commissioner deems necessary and proper in an amount deemed sufficient by the Commissioner. The conservator, under the direction of the Commissioner, shall take possession of the fiduciary records and other books, records, and assets of every description of the State trust company placed under conservatorship and take actions necessary to conserve those assets pending further disposition of its business as provided by law. Except as provided in G.S. 53-405, the conservator shall have all rights, powers, and privileges, subject to the approval of the Commissioner, now possessed by or given to the Commissioner under the provisions of Subpart B and Subpart D of this Part. All expenses of the conservator shall be paid out of the assets of the State trust company under conservatorship and shall be a lien thereon which shall be prior to any other lien provided by law. The compensation of the conservator shall be determined by the Commissioner and shall be based on the time and experience of the conservator and the complexity of the conservatorship. Compensation of the conservator shall not be subject to the requirements of Article 3 of Chapter 143 of the General Statutes. However, the Commissioner shall: (i) submit all proposed agreements or contracts for supplies, materials, printing, equipment, and contractual services that exceed one million dollars ($1,000,000) authorized by this section to the Attorney General or the Attorney General's designee for review as provided in G.S. 114-8.3; and (ii) include in all agreements or contracts to be awarded by the Commissioner under this section a standard clause which provides that the State Auditor and internal auditors of the Commissioner may audit the records of the conservator during and after the term of the agreement or contract to verify accounts and data affecting fees and performance. The Commissioner shall not award a cost plus percentage of cost agreement or contract for any purpose. (2001-263, s. 1; 2010-194, s. 5; 2011-326, s. 15(e).)

§ 53-402. Examination.

The Commissioner shall examine the affairs of a State trust company placed under conservatorship in the manner deemed necessary by the Commissioner to oversee the conservatorship. (2001-263, s. 1.)

§ 53-403. Termination of conservatorship.

If the Commissioner is satisfied that the conservatorship may be terminated with safety to the clients, creditors, and shareholders of the State trust company, and to the public, the Commissioner may terminate the conservatorship of a State trust company and permit the company to resume the transaction of its business, subject to such terms, conditions, restrictions, and limitations as the Commissioner prescribes. (2001-263, s. 1.)

§ 53-404. Rights and liabilities of conservator.

A conservator appointed pursuant to the provisions of this Subpart is subject to the provisions of G.S. 53-331 and to the penalties prescribed by G.S. 53-129 and G.S. 53-355. (2001-263, s. 1.)

§ 53-405. Naming of conservator not liquidation.

No power conferred in this Subpart upon the Commissioner, when exercised, shall be deemed as an act of possession for the purposes of liquidation; and whenever the Commissioner shall, with reference to any State trust company for which a conservator is appointed, deem that liquidation is necessary, the Commissioner shall exercise the powers for the purposes of liquidation as provided in Subpart B of Part 5 of this Article. (2001-263, s. 1.)

Subpart D. Sale of Assets; Issuance of Preferred Stock by Jeopardized State Trust Company.

§ 53-406. Sale of assets by board of jeopardized State trust company.

(a)   With the Commissioner's approval, the board of directors of a jeopardized State trust company, acting without shareholder approval and notwithstanding any other provision of this Article or any other law, or any of the provisions of the articles of incorporation or bylaws of the State trust company, may cause the State trust company to sell to one or more buyers all or substantially all of its assets, including the right to control and act as fiduciary for accounts established with the trust company, if the Commissioner finds:

(1)   The interests of the State trust company's clients, creditors, and shareholders are jeopardized by the continued operation of the State trust company; and

(2)   The sale is in the best interests of the State trust company's clients and creditors.

(b)   Sales under the provisions of this section shall include assumptions and promises by one or more buyers to pay or otherwise discharge, except as provided in G.S. 53-407:

(1)   All of the State trust company's liabilities to clients and creditors;

(2)   All of the State trust company's liabilities for salaries of the State trust company's employees incurred before the date of the sale;

(3)   Expenses incurred by the Commissioner arising out of the supervision or sale of the State trust company; and

(4)   Taxes owed and fees and assessments due the Commissioner's office.

(c)   This section does not limit the power of a State trust company to buy and sell assets in the ordinary course of business.

(d)   This section does not affect the Commissioner's right to take action under another law or sale under other provisions of this Article. (2001-263, s. 1.)

§ 53-407. Authority to act as disbursing agent.

If a purchasing trust institution acts under a written agency contract that (i) is approved by the Commissioner; (ii) specifically names each creditor and the amount to be paid each; and (iii) limits the agency to the purely ministerial act of paying creditors the amounts due them as determined by the selling institution and does not involve discretionary duties or authority other than the identification of the creditors named, then the purchasing trust institution:

(1)   May rely on the contract of agency and the instructions included in it; and

(2)   Is not responsible for:

a.   Any error made by the selling institution in determining its liabilities, the creditors to whom the liabilities are due, or the amounts due the creditors; or

b.   Any preference that results from the payments made under the contract of agency and the instructions included in it. (2001-263, s. 1.)

§ 53-408. Payment to creditors.

Payment to a creditor of the selling institution of the amount to be paid under the terms of a contract of agency described in G.S. 53-407 may be made by the purchasing trust company by (i) opening an agency account in the name of the creditor; (ii) crediting the account with the amount to be paid the creditor under the terms of the agency contract; and (iii) mailing or personally delivering a duplicate ticket evidencing the credit to the creditor at the creditor's address shown in the records of the selling institution. (2001-263, s. 1.)

§ 53-409. Issuance of preferred shares by jeopardized trust company.

Notwithstanding any other provisions of this Article or any other laws, and notwithstanding any of the provisions of its articles of incorporation or bylaws, any jeopardized State trust company may, with the approval of the Commissioner, and by vote of shareholders owning a majority of the shares of such State trust company, upon not less than two days' notice given by registered mail pursuant to action taken at a meeting of its board of directors (which may be held upon not less than one day's notice) issue shares of preferred stock in such amount, with such voting rights, with such preferences, at such dividend rate, and with such other rights and limitations as shall be approved by the Commissioner. A copy of the minutes of such directors' and shareholders' meetings, certified by the proper officer and under the corporate seal of the State trust company, and accompanied by the written approval of the Commissioner, shall be immediately filed in the office of the Secretary of State, and when so filed, shall be deemed and treated as an amendment to the articles of incorporation of such State trust company. For purposes of this section, a State trust company shall be considered jeopardized when it is critical that the State trust company obtain additional equity capital to avoid, or to cease to be in, a hazardous condition, and other means of raising additional equity capital do not appear to be feasible. No issue of preferred shares shall be valid until the amount of all shares so issued shall have been paid for in full in cash, except as may otherwise be specifically approved by the Commissioner. The provisions of this section do not limit the authority of a State trust company to issue shares as provided under other applicable law. (2001-263, s. 1.)

Part 6. Authority, Hearings, Enforcement, and Severability.

§ 53-410. Commissioner to act under authority of the Commission.

All the powers, duties, and functions granted to or imposed upon the Commissioner by law shall be exercised under the direction and supervision of the Commission. Wherever provision is made in this Article authorizing and permitting the Commissioner to make rules, the words "the Commissioner" shall be construed to mean the Commission. (2001-263, s. 1.)

§ 53-411. Rules.

314

The Commission may adopt rules in accordance with Chapter 150B of the General Statutes to carry out the provisions of this Article relating to authorized trust institutions and to ensure safe and conservative management of authorized trust institutions under its supervision, taking into consideration the appropriate interests of the clients, creditors, shareholders, and the public in their relations with the authorized trust institutions. (2001-263, s. 1.)

§ 53-412. Commissioner hearings; appeals.

(a)   This section does not grant a right to a hearing to a person that is not otherwise granted by governing law.

(b)   The Commissioner may convene a hearing to receive evidence and argument regarding any matter before the Commissioner for decision or review under the provisions of this Article. The hearing shall be conducted in accordance with Article 3A of Chapter 150B of the General Statutes.

(c)   Disputes over decisions and actions of the Commissioner under the provisions of this Article shall be "contested cases" as defined in G.S. 150B-2(2).

(d)   Except as expressly provided otherwise by this Chapter, an order of the Commissioner may be appealed, in writing, to the Commission for review, pursuant to G.S. 53C-2-6. The Commission may affirm, modify, or reverse a decision of the Commissioner.

(e)   Petitions for judicial review from the Commission shall be made to the Wake County Superior Court and shall proceed as provided in G.S. 53C-2-6. (2001-263, s. 1; 2009-57, s. 11; 2012-56, s. 34.)

§ 53-413. Civil enforcement.

The Commissioner may bring any appropriate civil action against any person the Commissioner believes has committed or is about to commit a violation of this Article or a rule, order, or declaratory ruling of the Commissioner pertaining to this Article. (2001-263, s. 1.)

§ 53-414. Cancellation of charter.

Whenever a merger, share exchange, sale of assets, liquidation, or other transaction occurs by which a State trust company ceases to exist or ceases to be eligible for a charter, the Commissioner shall cancel the State trust company's charter, revoke its license, and provide notice of the revocation in the manner provided in G.S. 53-163. The filing, in the office of the Secretary of State, of a certified copy of the cancellation under seal of the Commissioner shall authorize the cancellation of the charter of the State trust company, subject, however, to its continued existence, as provided by this Article and the general law relative to corporations, for the purpose of winding up and liquidating its business and affairs. (2001-263, s. 1.)

§ 53-415. Severability.

If any provision of this Article, or its application, is found by any court of competent jurisdiction in the United States to be invalid as to any trust institution or other person or circumstance, or to be superseded by federal law, the provision shall be deemed modified only to the extent and only in the particular circumstances necessary to render the provision valid, and the remaining provisions of this Article shall not be affected and shall continue to apply to any trust institution or other person or circumstance. (2001-263, s. 1.)

§ 53-416. Reserved for future codification purposes.

§ 53-417. Reserved for future codification purposes.

§ 53-418. Reserved for future codification purposes.

§ 53-419. Reserved for future codification purposes.

Part 7. Affiliate Transfers; Agent Appointments.

§ 53-420. Affiliate transfers authorized; procedure.

(a)   A trust institution may make an affiliate transfer of one or more accounts subject to the provisions of this Part unless the provisions governing the account explicitly provide that an affiliate transfer shall not be made.

(b)   The affiliate transfer shall be made pursuant to a written agreement between the transferring trust institution and the transferee trust institution.

(c)   Between 90 and 30 days prior to the proposed date of the affiliate transfer, the transferring trust institution shall give written notice of the proposed affiliate transfer to all clients and other persons to whom the transferring trust institution last sent reports or statements for the account or to whom the next regular report or statement would be sent. The notice shall include the following information:

(1)   A brief description of the proposed affiliate transfer.

(2)   The client's right to object in writing to the affiliate transfer, and the physical and mailing addresses to which the written objection may be sent; the transferring trust institution also may provide electronic mail or facsimile addresses, or both, as additional methods for giving written notice of objection.

(3)   The date upon which the affiliate transfer is proposed to be effective.

(4)   The identity, mailing address, and telephone number of one or more employees of the transferee trust institution who can respond to inquiries if the affiliate transfer is complete.

(5)   The identity, mailing address, and telephone number of one or more employees of the transferring trust institution who can respond to inquiries about the proposed affiliate transfer.

(d)   Notices shall be sent to the addresses for clients or their representatives on record with the transferring trust institution and shall be effective upon receipt. Notices shall be deemed received three days after they have been posted for mailing with the United States Postal Service or deposited for delivery with a reputable courier service, with all postage or delivery charges prepaid. (2005-274, s. 2.)

§ 53-421. Objection to affiliate transfer.

If a client, or a person acting on behalf of the client, delivers a written objection to the affiliate transfer to the transferring trust institution at anytime prior to the date of the affiliate transfer, the transferring trust institution shall exclude that account from the affiliate transfer unless the objection is withdrawn. An objection

317

to an affiliate transfer shall not affect the right of the transferring trust institution to continue to administer the account or to seek to transfer the account pursuant to the documents and law governing the account. (2005-274, s. 2.)

§ 53-422. Effect of affiliate transfer.

(a)   Following an affiliate transfer, the transferee trust institution shall have all of the rights, powers, privileges, appointments, accounts, and designations of the transferring trust institution and shall be deemed successor to the transferring trust institution in any deed, trust, agreement, filing, instrument, notice, certificate, pleading, or other document related to the account.

(b)   Following an affiliate transfer, the transferee trust institution is responsible for the performance of all duties, responsibilities, and obligations related to an account subject to the affiliate transfer.

(c)   The affiliate transfer does not limit the transferring trust institution's liability for any of its acts as fiduciary.

(d)   Unless the affiliate transfer is authorized by the documents governing the account, the transferring trust institution remains liable and responsible, while affiliated with the transferee trust institution, for the transferee trust institution's administration of accounts subject to an affiliate transfer. For purposes of this subsection, an affiliate transfer of an account made in reliance on subsection (e) of this section shall not be deemed to be authorized by the documents governing the account.

(e)   Except as explicitly provided in provisions or laws governing accounts:

(1)   Qualifications for administration such as capital, assets, assets under management, or similar standards set forth in documents or laws governing the account may be satisfied by the combined financial resources of the transferring trust institution and the transferee trust institution.

(2)   Standards relating to the location or charter of the trust institution administering the account may be satisfied by the transferring trust institution or the transferee trust institution.

(f)   Nothing in this Part shall be construed to impair any right of a trust institution to resign from administration of an account, or the right of a trust institution or a person interested in the account to seek the appointment of a replacement.

(g)   Neither the rights of creditors to nor any liens upon the property held in an account shall be impaired by an affiliate transfer.

(h)   Any claim or proceeding by or against the transferring trust institution pending at the time of the affiliate transfer may proceed as if the affiliate transfer had not taken place. (2005-274, s. 2.)

§ 53-423. Trust institution as agent.

A trust institution may appoint another trust institution that is its affiliate as its agent for the performance of acts, obligations, and responsibilities with respect to any account. In that event, the trust institution shall remain fully responsible and liable with respect to all actions of the affiliated trust institution as if those actions were performed by the trust institution. Except as explicitly provided in documents or laws governing an account, appointment of an affiliate agent is not:

(1)   An impermissible delegation of responsibility or duty by the appointing trust institution.

(2)   A transfer or relinquishment of account powers by the appointing institution.

(3)   A resignation or disqualification from the account by the appointing trust institution. (2005-274, s. 2.)

§ 53-424. Construction.

(a)   Except as expressly provided in this Part, nothing in this Part shall be construed to amend or modify the laws of this State governing the establishment or administration of accounts or the actions of trust institutions.

(b)   An affiliate transfer is not, in itself, a transfer of substantially all of the transferring trust institution's assets and liabilities.

(c)   Except as explicitly provided by the documents governing the account, neither an affiliate transfer nor an agency appointment under G.S. 53-423 shall be subject to any provision of law requiring court approval for removal of fiduciary funds from this State.

(d)   Except as explicitly provided by the documents governing the account, an affiliate transfer, but not an agency appointment, shall be subject to any provision of law requiring notice of a transfer of the principal place of administration of the account. The manner or timing of a notice required under G.S. 53-420(c) may be altered to comport with any provision of law requiring notice of a transfer of the principal place of administration of the account. (2005-274, ss. 2, 3.)

Article 25.

Asset-Backed Securities Facilitation.

§ 53-425. Definitions.

The following definitions apply in this Article:

(1)   Beneficial interest. - Debt or equity interests or obligations of any type that are issued by a special purpose entity and entitle the holder of the interest or obligation to receive payments that depend primarily on the cash flow from financial assets owned by the special purpose entity.

(2)   Financial asset. - Cash or a contract or instrument that conveys to an entity a contractual right to receive cash or another financial instrument from another entity.

(3)   Securitization. - The issuance by a special purpose entity of evidences of beneficial interest that meets one of the following criteria:

a.   Its most senior class at the time of issuance is rated in one of the four highest categories assigned to long-term debt or in an equivalent short-term category (within either of which there may be sub-categories or graduations indicating relative standing) by one or more nationally recognized rating organizations.

b.   It is sold in transactions by an issuer not involving any public offering under section 4 of the Securities Act of 1933 (15 U.S.C. 77d), as amended, or in transactions exempt from registration under the Securities Act of 1933 pursuant to Regulation S issued in accordance with the Act, or any successor regulations issued under the Act.

(4)   Special purpose entity. - A trust, corporation, limited liability company, or other entity demonstrably distinct from the transferor that is primarily engaged in acquiring and holding (or transferring to another special purpose entity) financial assets, and in activities related or incidental thereto, in connection with the issuance by the special purpose entity (or by another special purpose entity that acquires financial assets directly or indirectly from the special purpose entity) of evidences of beneficial interests.

(5)   Transferor. - A financial institution insured by the Federal Deposit Insurance Corporation. (2002-88, s. 1; 2002-159, s. 33.)

§ 53-426. Waiver of equity of redemption.

(a)   Notwithstanding any other provision of law, except to the extent otherwise set forth in the transaction documents relating to a securitization, all of the following apply:

(1)   Any property, assets, or rights purported to be transferred, in whole or in part, in a securitization or in connection with a securitization are considered no longer the property, assets, or rights of the transferor, to the extent purported to be transferred.

(2)   A transferor in the securitization, its creditors, and, in any insolvency proceeding with respect to the transferor or the transferor's property, a bankruptcy trustee, receiver, debtor, debtor in possession, or similar person, to the extent the transfer is governed by State law, has no rights, legal or equitable, to reacquire, reclaim, recover, repudiate, disaffirm, redeem, or recharacterize as property of the transferor any property, assets, or rights purported to be transferred to the special purpose entity, in whole or in part, by the transferor.

(3)   In the event of a bankruptcy, receivership, or other insolvency proceeding with respect to the transferor or the transferor's property, to the extent the transfer of property, assets, and rights are governed by State law, the

property, assets, and rights are not considered part of the transferor's property, assets, rights, or estate.

(b)   Nothing in this Article:

(1)   Requires any securitization to be treated as a sale for federal or state tax purposes;

(2)   Precludes the treatment of any securitization as debt for federal or state tax purposes; or

(3)   Changes any applicable laws relating to the perfection and priority of security or ownership interests of persons other than the transferor, any hypothetical lien creditor of the transferor, or, in the event of a bankruptcy, receivership, or other insolvency proceeding with respect to the transferor or its property, a bankruptcy trustee, receiver, debtor, debtor in possession, or other similar person. (2002-88, s. 1; 2002-159, s. 33.)

Vision Books Order Form

Fax Orders:	1-980-299-5965
Phone Orders:	1-704-898-0770
E-mail Orders:	www.visionbooks.org
Mail Orders:	Vision Books, LLC P.O. Box 42406 Charlotte, NC 28215

Shipp To:
Name_____
Address_____
City_____State_____Zip_____
Phone_____Fax_____
Email_____@_____

Bill To: We can bill a third party on your behalf.
Name_____
Address_____
City_____State_____Zip_____
Phone____(_____)_____Fax_____
Email_____@_____

Pamphlet Number ($15.00 Each)	Qty	Total Cost
_____	_____	_____
_____	_____	_____
_____	_____	_____
_____	_____	_____
_____	_____	_____
_____	_____	_____
_____	_____	_____
Full Volume Set 1-92	92 Pamphlets	1,380.00

Free Shipping Shipping & Handling on Full Volume Orders
Add $1.00 Shipping & Handling per pamphlet $_____

Total Cost $_____

Thank you for your support. Management!

DID YOU ENJOY THIS BOOK?

Vision Books, LLC would like to hear from you! If you or someone you know has been fasely imprisoned, we would like to hear your story. If the 'North Carolina Criminal Law and Procedure' has had an effect in your life or if you have suggestions, we would like to hear from you. Send your letters to:

Vision Books, LLC
Attn: Staff Writers
P.O. Box 42406
Charlotte, NC 28215
Email: staff@visionbooks.org

Order Additional Copies:

Fax Orders: 1-980-299-5965

Phone Orders: 1-704-898-0770

E-mail Orders: www.visionbooks.org

Mail Orders: Vision Books, LLC
                     P.O. Box 42406
                     Charlotte, NC 28215

www.ingramcontent.com/pod-product-compliance
Lightning Source LLC
Chambersburg PA
CBHW051626170526
45167CB00001B/75